GCSE OCR 21st Century Additional
Applied Science
The Study Guide

This book is for anyone doing **GCSE OCR 21st Century Additional Applied Science** at foundation level.

Applied Science is all about **experiencing science**.
But more than that — it means **understanding** the role of scientists in the real world by actually **doing the science yourself**.

And you can't do that without a fair chunk of **background knowledge**. Hmm, tricky.

Happily this CGP book includes all the **science facts** you need to learn, and shows you how they work in the **real world**. Not only that, we've given you loads of **handy advice** for doing **practicals** and getting stuck into those **reports**. And in true CGP style, we've explained it all as **clearly and concisely** as possible.

It's also got some daft bits in to try and make the whole experience at least vaguely entertaining for you.

What CGP is all about

Our sole aim here at CGP is to produce the highest quality books — carefully written, immaculately presented and dangerously close to being funny.

Then we work our socks off to get them out to you — at the cheapest possible prices.

Contents

MODULE 1 — LIFE CARE

Organisations Involved in Life Care 1
People Involved in Life Care 2
Medical History 3
Basic Tests 4
Extra Tests 5
Interpreting Test Results 6
Treatment 8
Prioritising Treatment and Resources 11
Health and Fitness Practitioners 12
The Blood and Blood Vessels 13
The Heart 14
The Breathing System 15
The Skeletal System 16
Pregnancy 17
Controlling Body Temperature 18
The Kidneys 19
Revision Summary for Module 1 21

MODULE 2 — AGRICULTURE AND FOOD

Products from Organisms 22
Agriculture in the UK 23
Regulating Agriculture and Food 25
Products from Plants 26
The Plant Life-Cycle 27
Plant Growth 28
Crop Yield 29
Growing Plants 30
Cuttings and Tissue Culture 31
Products from Animals 32
Intensive and Organic Farming 33
Sexual Reproduction in Animals 34
Selective Breeding and Embryo Transplants 35
Products from Microorganisms 36
Growth of Microorganisms 38
Testing Food 39
The Food Market 40
Sustainable Agriculture 41
Revision Summary for Module 2 42

MODULE 3 — SCIENTIFIC DETECTION

The Work of Scientific Detection 43
Good Laboratory Practice 44
Visual Examination 45
Light Microscopes 46
Electron Microscopes 48
Chromatography 49
Electrophoresis 50
Colour Matching 51
Colorimetry 52
Scientific Evidence 53
Revision Summary for Module 3 55

Module 4 — Harnessing Chemicals

Chemistry and Symbols 56
Laboratory Equipment 57
Acids and Alkalis 59
Reactions of Acids 60
Solutions 61
Making Insoluble Salts 62
Titrations 64
Organic and Inorganic Chemicals 65
Making Esters 66
Mixtures 67
Rates of Reaction 68
Sustainable Chemical Production 70
Chemical Purity 71
Industrial Production of Chemicals 72
Scaling Up 73
Planning Chemical Synthesis 74
Testing Formulations 75
Regulating the Chemical Industry 76
Revision Summary for Module 4 77

Module 5 — Communications

Communicating Information 78
The Communications Industry 79
Designing Communication Systems 80
Jobs in the Communication Industry 82
Health and Safety 83
Flowcharts and Datasheets 84
Block Diagrams 85
Circuit Diagrams 87
Series and Parallel Circuits 89
Electric Current and Power 90
Wireless Communication 91
Analogue and Digital Signals 94
Converting Analogue to Digital 95
Communication Links 96
Pictures and Video 97
Revision Summary for Module 5 98

Module 6 — Materials and Performance

Selecting Materials 99
Health and Safety 100
Mechanical Properties 101
Measuring Properties 102
Interpreting Data 103
Elastic and Plastic Behaviour 104
Metals, Ceramics and Polymers 105
Alloys and Composites 106
Materials and Forces 107
Electrical and Thermal Properties 109
Acoustic Properties 111
Optical Properties 113
Lenses 114
Lenses and Images 115
Camera Lenses 116
Matching Properties and Uses 117
Revision Summary for Module 6 118

Module 7 — Coursework Advice

Standard Procedures 119
Suitability Tests 120
Work-Related Report 124
Report Writing Advice 128

Index 129
Answers 132

Published by Coordination Group Publications Ltd.

Editors:
Ellen Bowness, Tom Cain, Katherine Craig, Gemma Hallam, Sarah Hilton,
Kate Houghton, Paul Jordin, Andy Park, Rose Parkin, Ami Snelling,
Laurence Stamford, Jane Towle, Julie Wakeling, Sarah Williams.

Contributors:
Neil Atkin, Mike Bossart, Mark A. Edwards, James Foster, Richard Parsons, Andy Rankin,
Philip Rushworth, Adrian Schmit, Claire Stebbing, Sophie Watkins, Chris Workman.

ISBN: 978 1 84146 771 9

With thanks to Barrie Crowther, Ian Francis, Sue Hocking and Glenn Rogers for the proofreading.
With thanks to Laura Phillips for the copyright research.
With thanks to Science Photo Library for permission to reproduce the photographs used on pages 7, 48 and 53.
With thanks to Defra for permission to reproduce the crop data on page 23.
With thanks to the Soil Association for permission to reproduce their logo on page 40.
With thanks to BSI for permission to reproduce the Kitemark symbol on page 83. Kitemark and the Kitemark symbol are registered trademarks of BSI.

Groovy website: www.cgpbooks.co.uk

Printed by Elanders Hindson Ltd, Newcastle upon Tyne.
Jolly bits of clipart from CorelDRAW®

Text, design, layout and original illustrations © Coordination Group Publications Ltd. 2007
All rights reserved.

Module 1 — Life Care

Organisations Involved in Life Care

Hello, good evening and welcome to Additional Applied Science. Now, if you want to be any good at this applied lark you'll need to be on top form — mentally and physically. So what better way to start than with a whole section on everyone and everything involved in keeping you fit and healthy.

Local Organisations Provide Services for the Community

You need to know two examples of local organisations and the range of services they provide.

There are some organisations that provide HEALTH CARE — e.g. hospitals

For most illnesses like an upset tummy or a funny, itchy rash, your general practitioner (GP) will be able to diagnose and prescribe medicines. But for some illnesses patients have to be referred to the local general hospital. They have doctors who specialise in certain areas of treatment, for example:

1) Routine surgery — e.g. having your tonsils removed.
2) Paediatrics — children's medicine.
3) Ophthalmology — if you've got an eye problem.
4) Cardiology — for people with heart problems.
5) Gastroenterology — if your bowels are causing the problem.

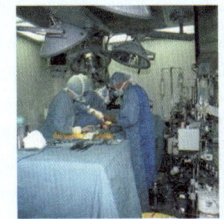 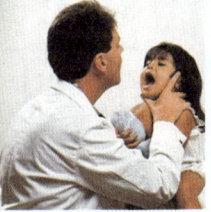

Some hospitals also have an accident and emergency (or casualty) department — these provide emergency treatment for people who have, e.g. broken bones, head injuries, serious wounds etc.

There are some organisations that provide FITNESS FACILITIES — e.g. leisure clubs

Regular exercise has lots of health benefits. It can also be important in rehabilitation after illness or injury — e.g. patients who are recovering from surgery. Some leisure centres are provided by local authorities (paid for by taxes) but others are privately run (everything is paid for by the members). Leisure clubs offer a range of different services, for example:

1) Fitness equipment — e.g. weights and cardiovascular machines.
2) Personal trainers — devise a fitness plan for clients to follow and help motivate them.
3) Fitness classes — e.g. aerobics or yoga provide different ways of working out.

The National Health Service Provides Free Health Care

In the UK, the National Health Service (NHS) is the organisation that's responsible for running hospitals and other health care services, e.g. pharmacy services, general practitioners, health centres, midwives and health visitors. The NHS has some important features:

1) The NHS provides everyone with free health care (unlike in some other countries where you have to pay for it).
2) It provides specialist care that isn't available locally — local hospitals can't treat every medical condition so there are specialist hospitals that provide care nationally, one example is the London Hospital for Tropical Diseases, which treats all sorts of weird infections.
3) It monitors national trends, for example the spread of infectious diseases.
4) The NHS also plans how resources should be distributed — e.g. where to build new hospitals or clinics, how many new staff are needed in an area, what machinery and equipment needs replacing, etc.

Gastroenterology — getting to the bottom of the matter...

If you've ever been to hospital (or watched Casualty) then you'll already be an expert on all the stuff at the top of the page. Don't worry if all the big words like ophthalmology and gastroenterology are a bit scary — you don't need to learn them, they're just there to show the range of services offered. Phew.

People Involved in Life Care

It's all very well having all these organisations but they're not going to run themselves — there's a whole army of skilled people out there responding to emergencies, providing treatment and keeping us all fit.

There are Lots of Careers in Health Care and Fitness

For anyone who decides they fancy a career as a heath or fitness practitioner there are loads of different careers to choose from. For example:

DOCTOR	FITNESS TRAINER	MIDWIFE
		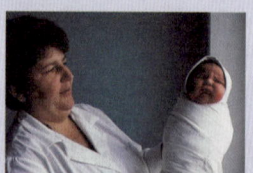
Doctors may become general practitioners or they may specialise in a particular area of medicine. Doctors diagnose people and decide on the best course of treatment.	Fitness trainers supervise exercise programmes in gyms and leisure clubs and provide personal training.	Midwives look after pregnant women — they don't just deliver children. They also provide information and advice so that the mother can make the right choices for herself and her baby.

There are plenty of others as well, e.g. paramedics (who treat people at the scene of an accident before they're taken to hospital), physiotherapists (who specialise in the treatment of muscle and joint injuries), speech therapists, dieticians and technicians to name just a few.

It's Good for Practitioners to Meet Their Patients Regularly

There are a number of advantages to regular contact between a health practitioner and their patients.

1) Regular appointments allow the practitioner looking after a patient to make sure that a treatment is going well and that the patient is getting better.
2) It also means that the health practitioner and the patient get to know and trust each other. This is important because it makes the patient more relaxed.

The same is also true for a fitness trainer and their client.

Health Education and Information are Important

Many organisations work to encourage people to follow a healthy lifestyle and they also provide information about how to prevent diseases.

EXAMPLE: the Health Protection Agency has run campaigns to raise awareness of the dangers of smoking and the sexually transmitted infection chlamydia.

1) If you go to your GP or hospital you're likely to see leaflets and posters giving information on preventing diseases and how to live a healthy lifestyle.
2) There are now many campaigns on TV to encourage people to eat healthily and stay fit, and the Government is in the process of banning commercials advertising unhealthy snack foods.
3) Schools sometimes get a speaker to come in and give information and advice to children — this is usually a representative from a health organisation, such as the British Heart Foundation.

Leaflets — always useful for making paper planes with...

When you're out and about (on your revision breaks, of course...), keep your eyes peeled for health promotion campaigns, posters and leaflets. They're a really important way for the many health organisations to get information and advice about health, fitness and disease to the public.

Module 1 — Life Care

Medical History

If you change doctors or join a new gym you'll more than likely be hit with a barrage of questions. Doctors might even go over these questions again when you go in feeling under the weather or before starting a course of treatment. All of the information they collect makes up your medical history.

A Medical History Needs to be Very Thorough

A medical history provides a health care practitioner or fitness trainer with a good picture of your general health and lifestyle. Here are some of the questions you'll be asked:

1) "Do you have any symptoms?"

Symptoms are things that a patient feels, such as pain or tiredness. Knowing the symptoms that a patient is suffering from will help a doctor to diagnose any condition they might have.

Some of these questions are more relevant to doctors than fitness practitioners, for example "Do you have any symptoms?"

2) "Are you taking any medication?"

This includes over-the-counter medicines like cold-relief powders as well as prescription drugs. Doctors need to know what medication you're already taking before they can prescribe any other drugs. This is because when some drugs are taken together they can cause nasty side-effects.

3) "How much alcohol do you drink?"

They'll usually want to know how much you drink in a typical week because any symptoms you're suffering from could be related to alcohol intake.

4) "How much tobacco do you smoke?"

They'll usually want to know if you smoke and, if you do, how many cigarettes you smoke a day. Any symptoms you're suffering could be related to smoking. Fitness practitioners will also take how much you smoke into account when designing fitness plans.

5) "How much exercise do you do?"

This might be how many hours you spend in the gym or it might be how far you walk or cycle in a typical day. Exercise has an impact on general health and fitness. Also, if a fitness trainer is planning an exercise programme for you, they need to know the level of exercise you're used to doing.

6) "Is there any history of illness in the family?"

If there's a history of certain diseases in your family, this might mean you have a greater chance of developing that disease. Diabetes and heart disease are conditions that 'run in families'.

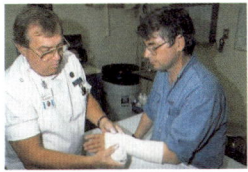

7) "Have you had any previous illnesses or injuries?"

Some symptoms could be related to a previous illness or injury. So knowing what the previous illness or injury was could help with the diagnosis.

Me? — I run at least 10 miles a day...

Remember, the person who takes your medical history isn't spying on you — they need to know this information to plan the best treatment or fitness programme for you. It doesn't help anyone if you don't tell the truth — like saying you run 10 miles a day if you couldn't even walk it...

Module 1 — Life Care

Basic Tests

After you've been interrogated, the next part of an initial health screen or fitness assessment involves taking a number of basic measurements such as pulse rate, body temperature, blood pressure, height, body mass and aerobic fitness.

A Health Assessment Will Involve...

Recording Simple Statistics Like Age, Gender and Height

These might seem like pretty irrelevant facts for a doctor to need to know, but they're actually quite important. For example, pulse rate (a measure of your heart rate) and blood pressure can be affected by age. Height is important when calculating things like body mass index (see below).

Taking Your Pulse Rate

The first and second fingers are placed on the artery on the underside of the wrist. Using a stopwatch, the number of pulses in sixty seconds are counted.

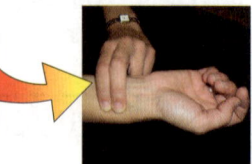

Measuring Body Temperature Using a Thermometer

There are various types of thermometer that can be used to record body temperature:

1) A clinical thermometer — a bog standard thermometer that you stick under your armpit or tongue.
2) An electronic digital thermometer — a fancy thermometer that you put in your ear — it gives a digital reading.
3) A liquid crystal thermometer — a plastic strip that's placed on the skin (usually on the forehead) and changes colour to show the temperature.

Measuring Blood Pressure With a Sphygmomanometer

A sphygmomanometer is made up of an inflatable cuff that goes around your arm, and a pressure monitor. Blood pressure is determined using a stethoscope. You can also get ones with electronic sensors that do it all automatically.

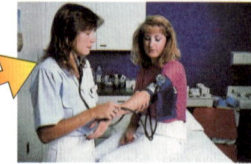

Calculating Body Mass Index From Body Mass and Height

Body mass index (BMI) tells you whether a person's body weight is below, above or within the normal range. A person's height is measured using a tape measure and their weight on some weighing scales. Their BMI is calculated using the formula on the right, and the doctor can compare the result to values in a table (see p.7 for more).

$$\text{Body mass index} = \frac{\text{Body mass in kg}}{(\text{Height in m})^2}$$

Measuring Aerobic Fitness

Aerobic fitness is another important health indicator. One way to measure aerobic fitness is to carry out a step test. This basically involves stepping up and down on a step for five minutes and measuring the pulse rate at one, two and three minutes after stopping. A formula can then be used to calculate the step test score. There are many other ways to measure aerobic fitness, for example the dreaded bleep test, which I'm sure everyone is familiar with.

All results must be recorded in a patient's medical records — see page 10 for why this has to be done.

I can spell sphygmomanometer — what's my prize...

Ah... the good old bleep test — hated by children up and down the country (apart from a few really weird ones). Bleep....... bleep...... bleep..... bleep.... bleep... bleep.. — aghh, too fast...

Module 1 — Life Care

Extra Tests

Doctors may need more detailed information about a patient's condition, which means even more tests...

Blood and Urine Samples Can Be Taken for Analysis

Blood and urine are a bit yucky but they can be pretty useful for making a diagnosis.

Blood Samples

1) Blood samples are normally taken from a vein on the inside of your elbow using a needle and syringe.
2) They're usually sent off to a pathology lab where the levels of certain chemicals are measured (e.g. blood cholesterol, sugar levels and enzyme activities) and they're examined under a microscope (e.g. to count the number and type of blood cells present and to check for infections).

Urine Samples

1) Urine testing is often done with test sticks that are dipped into the urine sample and change colour depending on the concentration of a substance in the urine.
2) After a certain time, the colour on the stick is compared to standard colours on a chart.
3) These can test for the amount of nitrite (which indicates bacteria), protein, blood or glucose present. You can also tell if a woman is pregnant by the presence of a certain hormone.

Advantages of test sticks:	Disadvantages of test sticks:
1) They can be used in a surgery/clinic. 2) They're cheap to buy. 3) The results are available instantly. 4) Many tests can be done at once.	They're not as accurate as carrying out a lab test — this means that positive samples have to be sent off to a lab to confirm the outcome. (This can save time and money though as not every sample has to be sent away.)

Heart Function Can Be Studied Using Electrocardiographs

1) An electrocardiograph is a machine that measures electrical events during a heartbeat.
2) Electrodes are placed on the chest and limbs to record the electrical changes in the heart as it beats.
3) The machine produces a graph called an electrocardiogram (ECG), which can show if the heart isn't functioning properly.

Medical Imaging Techniques Allow Us to See Inside the Body

In order to get a better idea of what's going on inside the body, doctors often use imaging techniques — these are non-invasive (they don't involve breaking the skin or sticking things in holes) and can provide both structural and functional (how things work) information about the body. The two common ones are X-rays and ultrasound:

X-Rays
1) X-rays are usually used to check whether bones are broken.
2) X-rays pass straight through most body tissues but are absorbed by bone.
3) A fetus can easily be damaged by X-rays so pregnant women aren't X-rayed unless absolutely necessary — ultrasound scans are much safer. Read on...

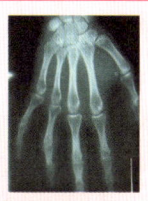

Ultrasound
1) Ultrasound scanners use sound waves to make an image of the internal organs.
2) They can be used for all sorts of things, e.g. studying heart function and checking that a fetus is developing properly.

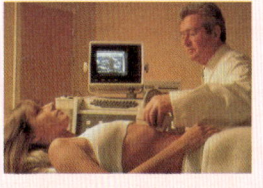

Module 1 — Life Care

Interpreting Test Results

It's time to don your white coat and stethoscope as we play an exciting game of doctors and nurses... well... more like medical detectives. Health practitioners need to be able to interpret the results of all the tests covered on the last few pages so they can diagnose illnesses — and so do you for your exam...

A Healthy Adult Pulse Rate is 60-100 Beats Per Minute

When a doctor takes your pulse they check that the rate isn't too high or the pulse isn't too weak.

A person's pulse rate might be HIGH because...
1) They've been exercising. Heart rate increases during exercise so that the blood can transport more oxygen to the muscles.
2) They're anxious. This can cause problems for doctors because some people get really anxious around them, especially when they're having tests carried out. This makes the patient's pulse rate higher than it usually is.
3) They're having a panic attack.
4) They suffer from a heart disorder (some cause a person's pulse rate to increase).

A person's pulse might be WEAK because...
1) They have low blood pressure.
2) They're in cardiovascular shock — when there isn't enough blood being pumped around the body. This can be caused by losing a lot of blood or by heart problems.
3) They have a heart disorder.

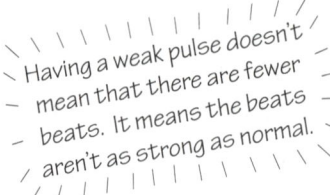
Having a weak pulse doesn't mean that there are fewer beats. It means the beats aren't as strong as normal.

Normal Core Body Temperature is 36.5-37 °C

A person's core body temperature might be HIGH because...
1) They've got an infection. The body may increase its core temperature when it's infected — this is known as a fever.
2) They've got heat stroke. This is when the body is unable to regulate its temperature (for example in really hot conditions) and the core temperature rises.

A person's core body temperature might be LOW because...
They've got hypothermia. Hypothermia is caused by exposure to low temperatures and can be fatal.

Normal Blood Pressure is About 120/80 mmHg

1) Blood pressure is measured in millimetres of mercury (mmHg).
2) The first figure is the blood pressure when the heart is contracting — systolic blood pressure.
3) The second figure is the blood pressure when the heart is relaxing — diastolic blood pressure.
4) Blood pressure changes with age, fitness level and stress.

Pulse rate — number of lentils eaten per second...

You could be asked to suggest a possible cause for any of the symptoms on this page. So make sure that you have some examples ready. Unfortunately, although it's true, I don't think that the examiners will accept an answer of 'taking exams causes a high pulse rate and high blood pressure'...

Module 1 — Life Care

Interpreting Test Results

Pulse rate, temperature and blood pressure down, only BMI, blood, urine, X-rays and ultrasound to go.

A Normal Body Mass Index is 18.5-24.9

Once a person's BMI has been calculated the results are interpreted using a table like this one.

In the exam you might be asked to calculate BMI then interpret the results. It's pretty easy — e.g. say the BMI is calculated as 27.5. This falls between 25-29 so the person's condition is overweight and the advice would be to lose weight.

BMI	Condition	Advice
<18.5	underweight	gain weight
18.5-24.9	healthy weight	-
25-29.9	overweight	weight loss advisable
>30	obese	need to lose weight

See p.4 for how BMI is calculated.

Blood and Urine Can Help Diagnose Many Disorders

BLOOD TESTS (for chemicals)

These can help diagnose:
1) High cholesterol levels.
2) Diabetes — by looking at glucose levels.
3) Liver disease — by looking at enzyme levels.

URINE TESTS

These can help diagnose:
1) Diabetes — if there are high levels of glucose in the urine.
2) Kidney damage — if there's blood or protein in the urine.
3) Bacterial infection — if there's nitrites in the urine.

BLOOD TESTS (using a microscope)

These can help diagnose diseases such as:
1) Deficiency anaemia — where there are low numbers of red blood cells.
2) Infections — a higher white blood cell count or bacteria in the blood are both indicators of infection.

See p.13 for more about blood cells.

X-rays and Ultrasound Show What is Going On Inside the Body

Doctors look at X-rays and ultrasound scans to see if everything is normal inside the body. You might be asked to interpret one or the other in the exam — feast your eyes on these beauties:

This X-ray shows a broken leg.

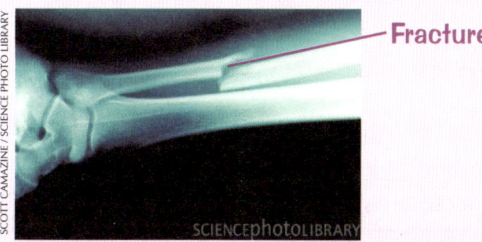

Fracture

Look for things like breaks in the bone or bones out of their sockets (dislocations).

This ultrasound image shows a fetus in the womb.

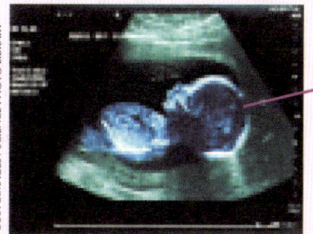

Head

Look for obvious features like the head or limbs. Remember there might be twins.

Interpreting test results — I thought that was just examiners...

Yet again it's those good old examples that are really important here. It's all good and well knowing that blood and urine tests are great at diagnosing illnesses, but what'll get you the big marks is being able to come up with some examples of diagnoses that can be made from the samples.

Module 1 — Life Care

Treatment

After making a diagnosis, a health or fitness practitioner will decide on what treatment or programme is needed. The treatment will proceed if the patient or client is happy with the plan and gives their consent.

Treatments Can Have Side Effects...

Treatments are designed to increase the rate of healing and to reduce the chances of further damage. But some treatments can also have damaging side effects. The benefits and side effects are weighed against each other and, as long as the benefits outweigh the side effects then the treatment will continue.

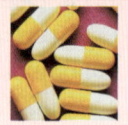

For example, antibiotics can be used to treat very serious, life-threatening infections but they can also cause diarrhoea. The benefit, treating the infection, outweighs the side effect, diarrhoea, so the treatment will continue.

...and Risks

All forms of treatment have associated risks as well as the chance of possible side effects.

For example, there are lots of risks associated with surgery — complications on the operating table, the risk of picking up a serious bacterial infection, or the patient reacting badly to the anaesthetic. There are also some risks associated with fitness programmes — such as straining a muscle.

Because of the risks involved, informed consent (permission to do it) must be given by a patient before a treatment or programme can begin. The health or fitness practitioner has to tell the patient all about the treatment, the risks involved, the possible side effects, the benefits and any alternatives. If the patient decides to go ahead they may have to sign a consent form.

The Type of Treatment Depends on the Target

A practitioner will choose the treatment or fitness programme to suit the target. Here are some different targets:

1) Enhanced fitness — when the client is aiming to improve their fitness. This might mean different things for different people, e.g. running faster or increasing flexibility.
2) Cure — often the repair of damaged tissues, e.g. the healing of a sprained ligament or a broken bone.
3) Recovery and Rehabilitation — when the patient is brought back to the same level of function and fitness as before an injury or illness. This might involve a training programme where the patient undertakes progressively more difficult tasks, slowly rebuilding their strength or flexibility.

Different methods can be used to reach the same target. For example, if a client wishes to lose weight a fitness professional may suggest a diet, or increased exercise, or a combination of the two.

Treatment Doesn't Always Mean Cure

The aim of a treatment, if possible, is cure. But some illnesses or injuries can never be cured. Instead, the treatment will focus on managing the symptoms and helping the patient to lead as healthy or as pain-free a life as possible. Here are some examples:

1) Asthma is a disorder that causes the airways to constrict (narrow). The symptoms can be treated by using inhalers but the patient can't be cured.
2) Lots of people suffer from chronic back pain that can't be cured. Pain relief, physiotherapy and special treatments like supportive chairs and mattresses can help reduce the pain and symptoms.

Boredom — the dangerous side effect of revision...

Sorry, not a lot of fun stuff on this page — but you've still got to learn it, learn it, learn it.

Module 1 — Life Care

Treatment

When designing a treatment or fitness programme there are lots of ways to achieve the desired goal.

Treatment Could Involve Surgery, Exercise or Diets

There are lots of different types of treatment available. Here are a few examples:

Surgery
1) Stomach stapling — can be used to help increase weight loss for health reasons.
2) Heart surgery — e.g. can replace valves, clear blocked arteries.

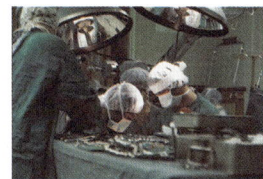

Exercise regime
1) General exercise regime — to improve overall health and fitness.
2) Specific regimes — e.g. to increase strength for a weight lifter, or improving lap times for a runner.

Diet
1) Athlete's diets — e.g. low fat, high carbohydrate.
2) Health diets — e.g. to loose weight for surgery or because weight is dangerously high.
3) Special diets — e.g. to avoid nuts or lactose.

Physiotherapists Treat Skeletal-muscular Injuries

Serious injuries to the skeletal or muscular system will be treated by a physiotherapist.

1) A physiotherapist will treat the injury, e.g. with cortisone injections to reduce pain and swelling, or with laser treatment to speed up healing.
2) They will also give advice on the best exercises to do to rehabilitate after an injury. These may be graded exercises, which steadily build up the strength of a muscle or joint.

See p.16 for more on the skeletal system.

For example, for a sprained ankle, the treatment might involve the RICE method:

REST — to avoid any further damage. This is especially important for the first 24 hours.
ICE — to help to reduce swelling (e.g. using a bag of frozen peas wrapped in a tea towel).
COMPRESSION — a firm bandage is placed around the injured part to help reduce swelling and prevent further damage from excessive movement of the injured joint.
ELEVATION — raising an injured limb as high as possible to help reduce swelling.

Or for a damaged knee the exercises to strengthen the knee might include:

1) Standing up and tensing the muscles without moving the knee.
2) Sitting with the lower leg hanging loose, then slowly raising and lowering the lower leg by bending the knee.
3) Stepping up and down, onto and off a low box.
4) Standing, and bending and straightening the legs at the knees.

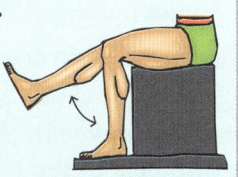

Stomach stapling — don't try this at home...

Remember that the different types of surgery, exercise regimes and diets we've listed at the top of the page are only examples — there are loads more to choose from. You might be asked to give one example of each in the exam so make sure you know them like the back of your hand.

Module 1 — Life Care

Treatment

It's really important for health and fitness practitioners to monitor their patients throughout the treatment process and for a while afterwards to make sure that they stay fit and healthy.

The Treatment May Need to be Modified

Health and fitness practitioners monitor patients for a number of reasons — to ensure the treatment is working, to check that they're making progress, to check for side effects and to provide encouragement. Practitioners may decide that the treatment needs to be modified. This could be for a number of different reasons, for example...

1) Because it's not producing any improvement, e.g. an antibiotic isn't clearing an infection.
2) Because it's causing damage, e.g. exercises that are too difficult and are causing injury.
3) Because it's producing side effects that are dangerous or outweigh the benefits, e.g. patients with arthritis are often prescribed aspirin but this can sometimes lead to bad stomach problems.

Monitoring should continue even after a treatment is completed — to check improvement is maintained.

> Here are some examples of how patients are monitored during and after treatment:
>
> 1) An athlete has torn her heel tendon. She has to rest it and then start a series of exercises, gradually stretching the heel more and more. Her trainer regularly checks and records the amount of stretch at the heel and checks for signs that the tear isn't getting worse — like stiffness or pain. The athlete will be monitored for a few weeks after the treatment is complete to make sure everything is still OK.
>
>  2) Midwives closely monitor both the mother and baby throughout the pregnancy, during the birth and afterwards — ante natal and post natal care. It involves things like blood tests, ultrasound scans and blood pressure checks.

Monitoring Techniques Need to be Accurate and Reliable

Assessment of progress always depends on the accuracy and reliability of the monitoring procedures:

ACCURACY — the results should be as close to what's actually happening as possible, e.g. if a doctor is monitoring someone's weight they need to be sure the scales they are using are accurate.

RELIABILITY — the results should be consistent, e.g. again when monitoring someone's weight, they should be weighed on the same scales and wearing the same amount of clothes to get a fair comparison.

Practitioners Need to Keep Records

Practitioners always keep records of their clients' details. This is important for:

1) Remembering the essential background information they used to plan the programme or treatment — they'll see lots of clients and it'd be hard to remember everyone's details.
2) Remembering the treatment or fitness plan.
3) Monitoring changes — to see if the client is making progress.
4) Sharing information — most professionals work as part of a larger team, e.g. doctors may work with physiotherapists and nurses. It's important that all the members of the team can look at all the information so they know what treatment or programme has been advised and can assist in the care of the patient or client.

My idea of a fitness programme — running to the pie shop...

It can be really important to see your health or fitness practitioner often when you're trying to stick to a personal programme. Sometimes repeated exercises can get boring (just like revising) and a bit of encouragement can make a big difference. Now go work those brain cells and learn this page.

Module 1 — Life Care

Prioritising Treatment and Resources

When lots of people need treatment, like in an emergency situation with many casualties, or when dealing with everyone who uses the NHS, health and fitness practitioners need to prioritise who to treat.

In Emergency Care it's Important Who's Treated First

When emergency care is needed, for example in an accident and emergency department or the site of a bus crash, it's important for health professionals to prioritise treatment. This means assessing which patients need help first and which ones have less serious injuries, so can wait a little longer to be helped.

1) Patients with breathing or circulatory problems are treated first — they're the most seriously injured.
2) Time is really important — the quicker someone is treated the better their chances of survival.
3) Patient's with major blood loss, head injury or serious broken bones are treated next.
4) People with minor injuries, like cuts or bruises, are treated last.
5) Elderly patients and young children are also given priority over people with the same severity of injury, as they're generally weaker.

Managers Have to Prioritise Resources

The NHS is funded by tax-payers and funds are limited. The funding pays for many things, including:

1) Staff wages
— e.g. doctors, nurses.
2) Medicines
3) Buildings
4) Equipment
— e.g. MRI and X-ray machines.
5) Support services
— e.g. security, waste removal.
6) Staff training
7) Cleaning
— e.g. the buildings, bed sheets etc.
8) Administration
— e.g. computers, secretaries etc.
9) Public information programmes
— e.g. for vaccination programmes.
10) Uniforms

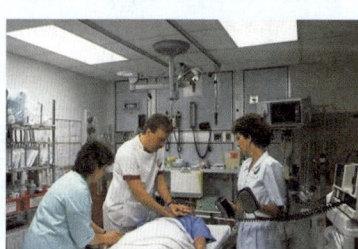

1) Every part of the NHS (e.g. each hospital) has to balance the money that they're given with the money they spend.
2) If they over-spend the debt will be passed to the following year — but they won't get any extra money.
3) This means that the pressure is on all health organisations to keep within their budgets. It's the job of the managers within these organisations to distribute and manage the money available to them and make sure the facilities are used in the most efficient and effective way.
4) Cuts may be made in services to keep within budget — e.g. hospital managers might have to choose between redecorating part of the hospital or closing a ward.
5) It's not just health professionals that have to worry about funding. Fitness professionals will have to make similar decisions — e.g. they may have to choose between some new running machines or new showers.

Doctor, doctor, I feel like a pair of curtains...*

Deciding what order to treat people in is, just like my dad always says, all about getting your priorities right. The same thing applies when making decisions in your own life, for example, choosing between going out with your friends and doing homework or whether to buy some elephants or a house. Tricky.

*Pull yourself together man.

Module 1 — Life Care

Health and Fitness Practitioners

There are many different types of health and fitness practitioner. But regardless of their job it's helpful if all health care professionals and fitness practitioners have certain personal qualities and professional skills.

Heath and Fitness Practitioners Must be Professional

To be professional they have to follow good practice. This involves...

Trust me, I'm a doctor!

...developing personal relationships

Health and fitness practitioners should be able to build up a personal relationship with the patient but remain professional and not become emotionally involved — this could prevent them from making the best decisions.

...having a good understanding of their area of knowledge

This allows them to make good judgements — they need to be able to tell when the evidence doesn't agree with what the patient or client is saying, e.g. a client might say that they've been sticking to their diet but the scales say they've gained weight, so the evidence doesn't agree.

...considering the whole person

They should be able to consider the whole person — this means taking into account the effects of family, workplace and environment on their patients' or clients' health and fitness.

...working as a team

Health and fitness practitioners have to work well as part of a team. This is because loads of different practitioners will work with a patient or client, e.g. doctors, nurses and physiotherapists will all have to work together when treating someone with a broken leg.

Following Good Practice Requires Some Personal Qualities

1) Empathy — they should have an understanding of their patients' and clients' feelings.
2) Good communication — health and fitness practitioners need good communication skills for a number of reasons:
   - It's important that health and fitness practitioners are able to explain things in a way that the patient or client understands fully what they have to do or what's going to happen.
   - They also need to be able to ask questions in a way that gets the required information from the patient or client.
   - Communication with other health and fitness practitioners is important when working as part of a team.
   - Taking down patient notes is an important part of communication (see p.10).
   - Listening skills are important too. Professionals need to be able to understand what the patient or client is saying. Sometimes patients are confused and very young children can't always explain things — someone else may need to reinterpret what is said.
3) Tact — be good at handling difficult or delicate situations, e.g. when delivering bad news.
4) Good personal manner — this encourages patients and clients to have confidence and trust them.
5) Patience — patients and clients often won't follow advice or treatment regimes, even when it's really good for them.

Tact — useful for sticking posters to the wall...

These skills are really important for anyone who wants to be a health or fitness practitioner, but they're also really important for loads of other jobs too, e.g. if you want to join the police or be a chef.

Module 1 — Life Care

The Blood and Blood Vessels

Now that you know who does what it's probably a good idea to have a look at some of the science behind their work. You may remember blood samples and what they can tell you about the body from p.7, well now it's time to take a closer look at blood and just how it's transported around the body.

Blood is a Fluid Made up of Cells, Platelets and Plasma

1) Red blood cells — they transport oxygen from the lungs to all the cells in the body.
2) White blood cells — they help to fight infection.
3) Platelets — these help the blood to clot at the site of a wound.
4) Plasma — this is the liquid that carries everything about.

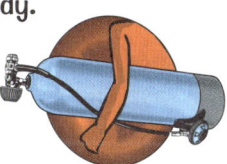

Blood is Carried Around the Body in Blood Vessels

There are three different types of blood vessel:

1) ARTERIES — carry the blood away from the heart.
2) CAPILLARIES — involved in the exchange of materials at the tissues.
3) VEINS — carry the blood to the heart.

Blood Vessels are Designed for Their Function

ARTERIES CARRY BLOOD UNDER PRESSURE

1) The heart pumps the blood out at high pressure, so the artery walls are strong and elastic.
2) The walls are thick compared to the size of the lumen (the hole down the middle). They contain thick layers of muscle to make them strong.

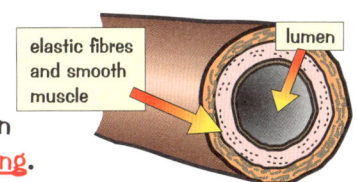

CAPILLARIES ARE REALLY SMALL

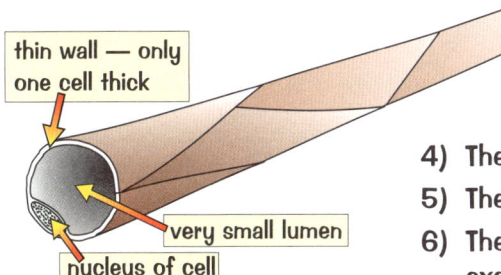

1) Arteries eventually branch into capillaries.
2) Capillaries are really tiny — too small to see.
3) They carry the blood really close to every cell in the body to exchange substances with them.
4) They have permeable walls, so substances can move in and out.
5) They supply food and oxygen and take away wastes like CO_2.
6) Their walls are only one cell thick. This increases the rate of exchange by decreasing the distance over which it happens.

VEINS TAKE BLOOD BACK TO THE HEART

1) Capillaries eventually join up to form veins.
2) The blood is at lower pressure in the veins so the walls don't need to be as thick as artery walls.
3) They have a bigger lumen than arteries to help the blood flow despite the lower pressure.
4) They also have valves to help keep the blood flowing in the right direction.

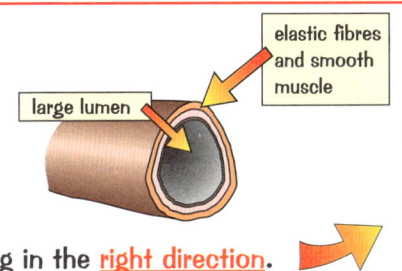  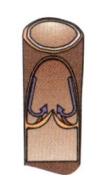

Learn this page — don't struggle in vein...

This is more like it, a bit of proper biology to sink your teeth into — it only gets better from here on in.

Module 1 — Life Care

The Heart

Blood doesn't just move around the body on its own, of course. It needs a pump.

The Heart is a Really Important Organ

1) It's important to look after your heart — if it stops pumping, you're in really big trouble.
2) Heart disease (which often leads to a heart attack) is one of the main causes of death in the Western world.
3) A lot of time and resources go into preventative care against heart disease and researching the factors that can increase a persons risk — such as high blood pressure, unhealthy diet and smoking.
4) Heart function can be monitored — by ECGs and ultrasound (p.5)
5) A damaged heart can sometimes be repaired but it means having surgery so it's better just to keep it in tiptop condition.

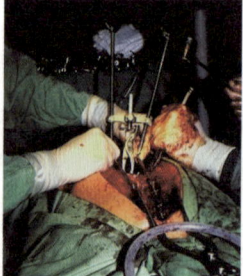

Learn This Diagram of the Heart with All Its Labels

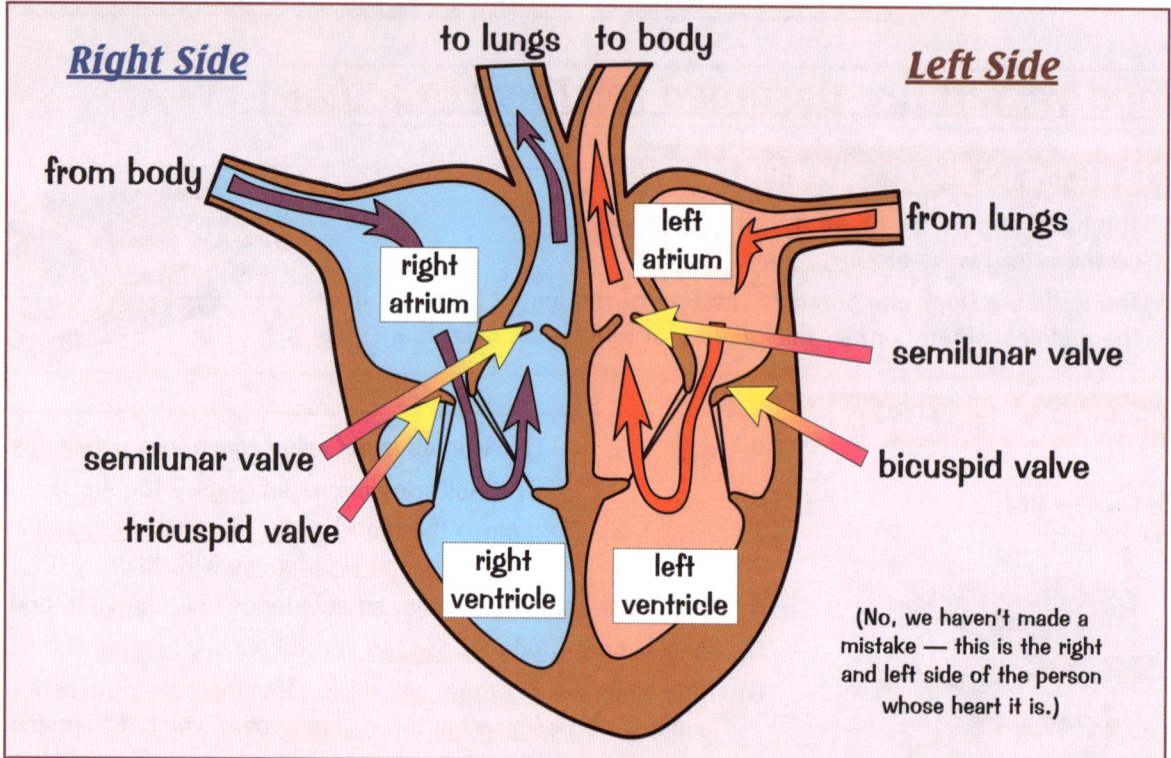

(No, we haven't made a mistake — this is the right and left side of the person whose heart it is.)

1) The right atrium of the heart receives deoxygenated blood (blood without any oxygen) from the body.
2) The deoxygenated blood moves through to the right ventricle, which pumps it to the lungs.
3) The left atrium receives oxygenated blood (oxygen rich blood) from the lungs.
4) The oxygenated blood then moves through to the left ventricle, which pumps it out round the whole body.
5) The left ventricle has a much thicker wall than the right ventricle. It needs more muscle because it has to pump blood around the whole body, whereas the right ventricle only has to pump it to the lungs.
6) The valves prevent the backflow of blood.

Okay — let's get to the heart of the matter...

The human heart beats 100 000 times a day on average. You can measure it by taking your pulse, p.4.

Module 1 — Life Care

The Breathing System

Doctors and sports scientists monitor people's breathing systems for all sorts of reasons, like looking for an infection or checking it's working efficiently during exercise. So they need to understand all about it.

The Breathing System is in the Top Part of Your Body

There are a few parts you need to know...

1) The lungs are the organs where gas exchange happens — oxygen goes into the blood and carbon dioxide moves out.
2) The trachea (the pipe connecting your mouth and nose to your lungs) splits into two tubes called 'bronchi' — one goes to each lung.
3) The bronchi split into progressively smaller tubes called bronchioles that end with small sacs called alveoli — this is where gas exchange occurs.
4) The ribs protect the lungs and the heart etc. They're also important in breathing (see below).
5) The intercostal muscles are the muscles in between the ribs.
6) The diaphragm is the large muscle at the bottom of the lungs, which is also important for breathing.

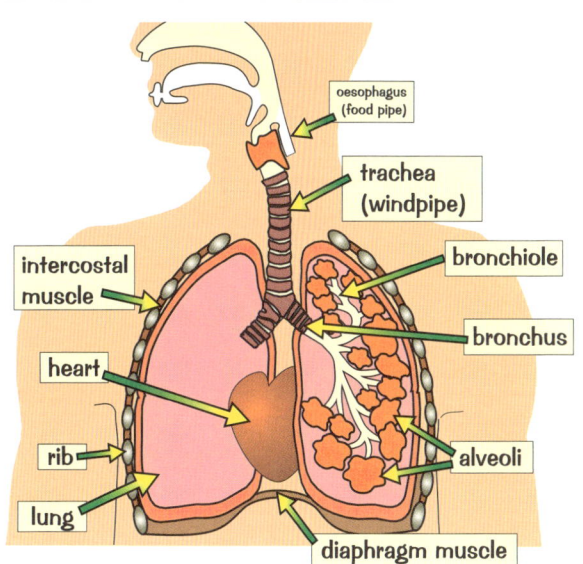

Breathing In and Out Uses Muscles

The diaphragm and intercostal muscles play an important role in breathing in (inhaling) and out (exhaling).

Breathing In...

1) The intercostal muscles and diaphragm contract.
2) The ribcage moves up and out.
3) The lung volume increases.
4) This draws air in.

...and Breathing Out

1) The intercostal muscles and diaphragm relax.
2) The ribcage drops down and in.
3) The lung volume decreases.
4) Air is forced out.

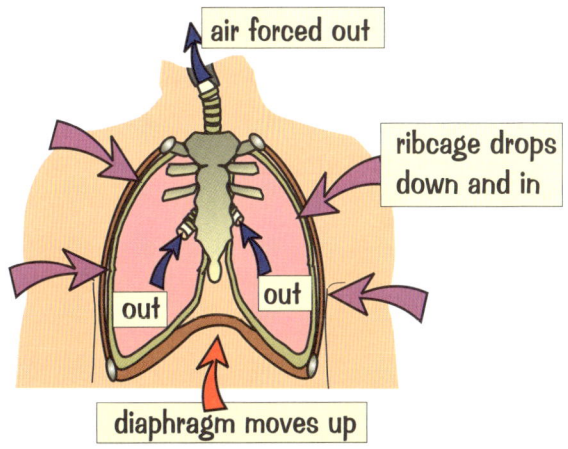

Now take a deep breath and learn these facts...

If you're asthmatic, you've probably been to the doctors loads of times to have your breathing system monitored. This helps them to work out the amount of medication you need to get it working properly.

Module 1 — Life Care

The Skeletal System

Health professionals study the skeletal system for loads of different reasons — e.g. some need to know the skeleton inside-out to analyse X-rays (see p.7), and physiotherapists deal with all sorts of muscular and skeletal problems so need to understand how the two work together.

The Skeleton has Different Functions

The skeleton does a lot more than you might think.
You need to know what it does and learn the names of the most important bones. The main functions are:

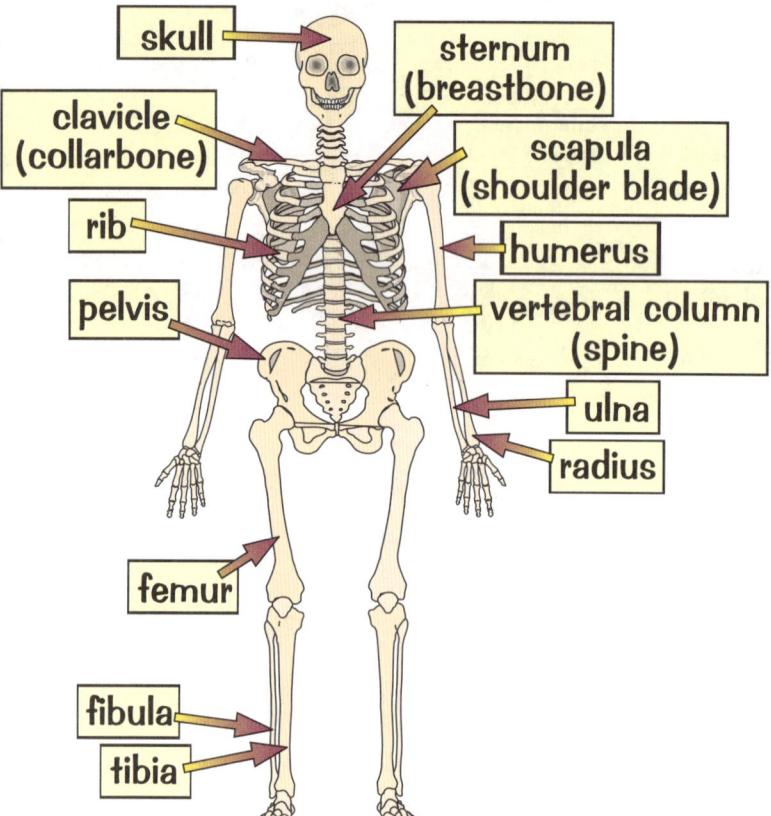

Support
1) The skeleton is a rigid frame for the rest of the body — it supports the soft tissues.
2) Without the skeleton, we'd collapse like jelly.

Protection
1) Bones are very tough.
2) They protect delicate organs — like the brain, heart and lungs.

Movement
1) Bones on their own can't move.
2) Muscles, attached by tendons, can move various bones (see below).

Muscles and Bones are Connected by Tendons and Ligaments

1) Bones are attached to muscles by tendons (which also attach muscles to other muscles).
2) Muscles move bones at a joint by contracting (becoming shorter).
3) Tendons can't stretch much so when a muscle contracts it pulls on the bone.
4) The bones at a joint are held together by ligaments.
5) Ligaments have tensile strength (i.e. you can pull them and they don't snap easily) but they are pretty elastic (stretchy).

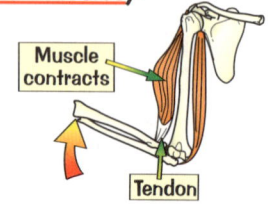

The muscle contracts, pulling on the tendon, which lifts the lower arm.

What's a skeleton's favourite instrument?... a trom-bone...

The skeleton gives the body its shape and has loads of jobs to do. It's made up of various kinds of bones, all meeting at joints. Lots of jobs also means lots of things that can go wrong — broken bones (p.7), twisted joints, dislocations... the list is endless.

Module 1 — Life Care

Pregnancy

It's far from easy growing a whole new person. No wonder so many people help to look after you when you're pregnant. Gynaecologists, obstetricians, midwives, doctors, nurses, and so on, all get to have a good poke around to check everything's going well.

The Female Reproductive System Makes Eggs (ova)

1) An egg (ova) is produced every 28 days from one of the two ovaries.
2) It passes into the oviduct (fallopian tube) where it may meet sperm, which have entered the vagina during sexual intercourse.
3) If it isn't fertilised by sperm, the egg will break up and pass out of the vagina.
4) If it is fertilised the new cell will travel down the fallopian tube to the uterus (womb) and attach itself to the endometrium (uterus lining) where it begins to grow and develop into a fetus (baby).

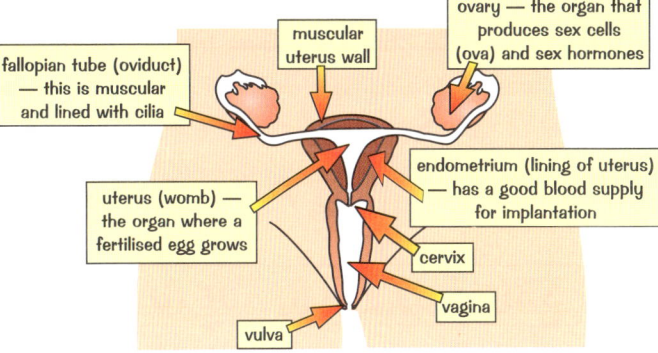

The Female Body Changes During Pregnancy and Birth

Changes during pregnancy

1) Uterus stretches — to allow room for the fetus (baby) to grow.
2) Amnion membrane forms — this surrounds the fetus and is full of amniotic fluid to protect the fetus against knocks and bumps.
3) Placenta develops — this lets the blood of the fetus and mother get very close to allow the exchange of food, oxygen and waste.
4) Umbilical cord develops — to connect the placenta to the fetus.
5) Breasts enlarge — the breasts get ready to start producing milk.

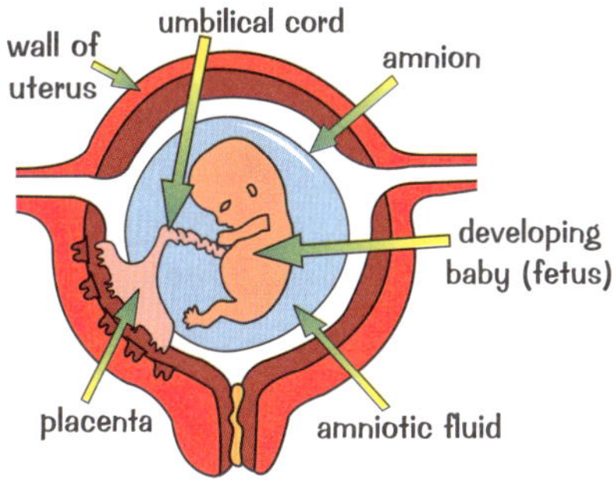

Changes during birth

1) Amnion breaks — and the amniotic fluid flows out.
2) Uterus contracts — the muscles of the uterus start to contract to push the baby out.
3) Placenta comes out — after the baby is born the placenta comes away from the lining of the uterus and is pushed out of the body (called the afterbirth).
4) Milk is produced — to provide the new baby with food.

This is what women are talking about when they say 'my waters have broken'.

The Female Body Functions Differently During Pregnancy

Carrying a baby can be hard work for the body:
1) The mum puts on weight — due to a larger uterus and breasts, and extra fat stored for breast feeding.
2) Heart rate increases — to help supply the body with all the extra energy it needs.
3) The kidneys have to work harder — to filter the extra waste that's coming from the baby.

Female or not — you've still got to know all this...

Having a baby is tough. Not just because you have to look after a screaming and pooing baby but because it's hard work for a woman's body. A healthy woman's body should be able to cope, but it's really important to have regular ante and post natal medical checks to keep an eye on mum and baby.

Module 1 — Life Care

Controlling Body Temperature

Keeping your body at the right temperature is really important. Loads of different health practitioners, like those working in accident and emergency departments, mountain rescue services or the coastguard, often have to deal with temperature-related health problems (e.g. hypothermia).

Body Temperature is Around 36.5-37 °C

1) The reactions in your body work best at about 37 °C.
2) This means that you need to keep your body temperature around this value — within 1 or 2 °C of it.
3) A part of your brain acts as your own personal thermostat. It receives messages from temperature receptors in the skin that provide information about skin temperature.

The Skin has Tricks for Altering Body Temperature

To keep you at this temperature your body does these things:

When You're TOO HOT:

1) More sweat is produced from sweat glands in the skin. The water in the sweat evaporates, taking heat with it. This helps cool you down.
2) Blood vessels (see p.13) close to the skin's surface get bigger in diameter. This means that more blood gets to the surface of the skin. The warm blood then loses some of its heat to the surroundings.
(This is why you look red when you're hot — it's the increased blood flow to the surface of the skin.)

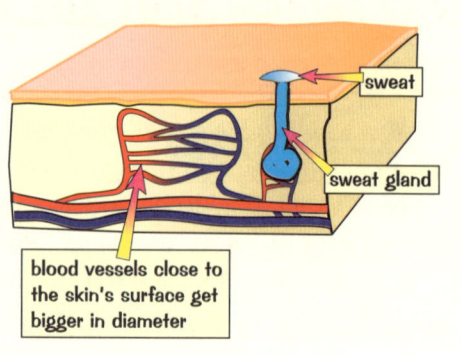

When You're TOO COLD:

1) Less sweat is produced, so heat isn't lost when the water in it evaporates (because there's not much evaporation going on).
2) Blood vessels close to the skin's surface get smaller in diameter. This means that less blood gets to the surface of the skin. This stops the blood losing its heat to the surroundings. (This is why you look paler when you're really cold — there's very little blood going to the surface of the skin.)
3) You shiver (your muscles contract), which generates heat.

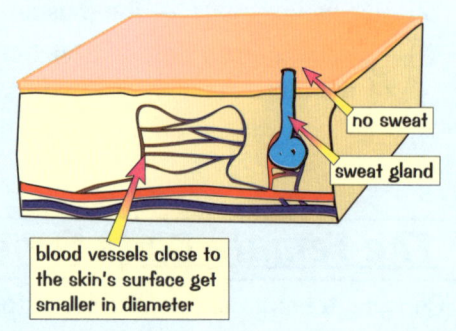

Sweaty and red — I'm so attractive in the heat...

If you get way too hot you could get heat exhaustion — you feel really tired and a bit sick, and if it's untreated you could die... scary. It's a similar story if you get too cold (the fancy name for this is hypothermia) — you can slip into a coma and die. Getting too cold also isn't great for your fingers, toes and nose either — if the blood supply is cut off for too long the cells in the tissues die. This causes frostbite (where the fingers and toes go all black and manky) and it's quite common in mountaineers.

Module 1 — Life Care

The Kidneys

The kidneys are really important — they control the content of the blood. Your kidneys can fail though — people with kidney failure can use a kidney dialysis machine to replace some functions of the kidney.

Kidneys Basically Act as Filters to "Clean the Blood"

The kidneys perform three main roles:

1) Removal of urea from the blood.
2) Adjustment of ions in the blood.
3) Adjustment of water content of the blood.

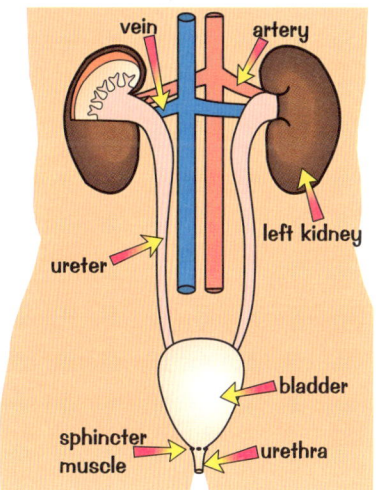

1) Removal of Urea

1) Urea is produced as a waste product from the reactions going on in the body.
2) Urea is poisonous. It's released into the bloodstream by the liver. The kidneys then filter it out of the blood and it's excreted from the body in urine.

2) Adjustment of Ion Content

1) Ions such as sodium are taken into the body in food and then absorbed into the blood.
2) If the ion content of the blood is wrong this could cause too much water to enter or leave body cells. Having the wrong amount of water can damage cells.
3) Excess ions are removed by the kidneys. For example, a salty meal will contain far too much sodium and so the kidneys will remove the excess sodium ions from the blood.
4) Some ions are also lost in sweat (which tastes salty, you may have noticed).

3) Adjustment of Water Content

Water is taken into the body as food and drink and is lost from the body in three main ways:
   1) In urine
   2) In sweat
   3) In the air we breathe out.

The body has to constantly balance the water coming in against the water going out. Your body can't control how much you lose in your breath, but it can control the other factors. This means the water balance is between:
   1) Liquids consumed
   2) Amount sweated out
   3) Amount excreted by the kidneys in the urine.

On a cold day, if you don't sweat, you'll produce more urine which will be pale and dilute.
On a hot day, you sweat a lot and produce less urine which will be dark-coloured and concentrated.
The water lost when it's hot has to be replaced with water from food and drink to restore the balance.

Adjusting water content — blood, sweat and, erm, wee...

If your kidneys fail, urea, ions and water all accumulate in the blood (this makes sense if you think about it — they're not being filtered out properly). High urea levels in a blood test can indicate kidney damage.

Module 1 — Life Care

The Kidneys

Now that you know what the kidneys do, you need to know how they do it.

Nephrons Are the Filtration Units in the Kidneys

The kidneys work like a big filtering system, removing unwanted substances from the blood. There are three main steps — ultrafiltration, reabsorption and release of wastes...

1) Ultrafiltration:

1) A high pressure is built up when the blood from the body enters the kidneys. This squeezes water, urea, ions and sugar out of the blood and into a part of the nephron called the Bowman's capsule (see below)

2) The membranes between the blood vessels and the Bowman's capsule act like filters. Big molecules like proteins and blood cells can't move out — they stay in the blood.

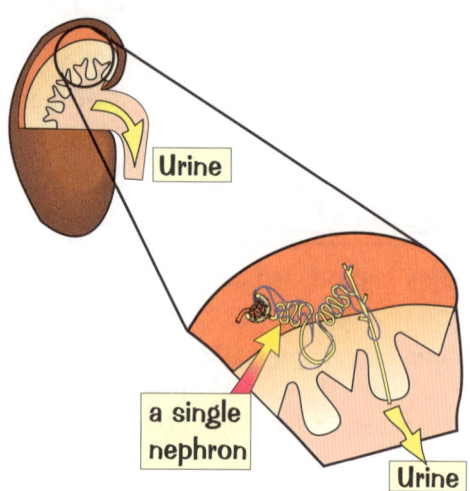

The presence of blood or protein in urine can be used to diagnose kidney damage — see p.7.

2) Reabsorption:

As the liquid flows along the nephron, useful substances are reabsorbed back into the blood:

1) All the sugar is reabsorbed.
2) Sufficient ions are reabsorbed. Excess ions are not.
3) Sufficient water is reabsorbed.

3) Release of wastes:

The remaining substances (including urea) continue out of the nephron, into the ureter and down to the bladder as urine.

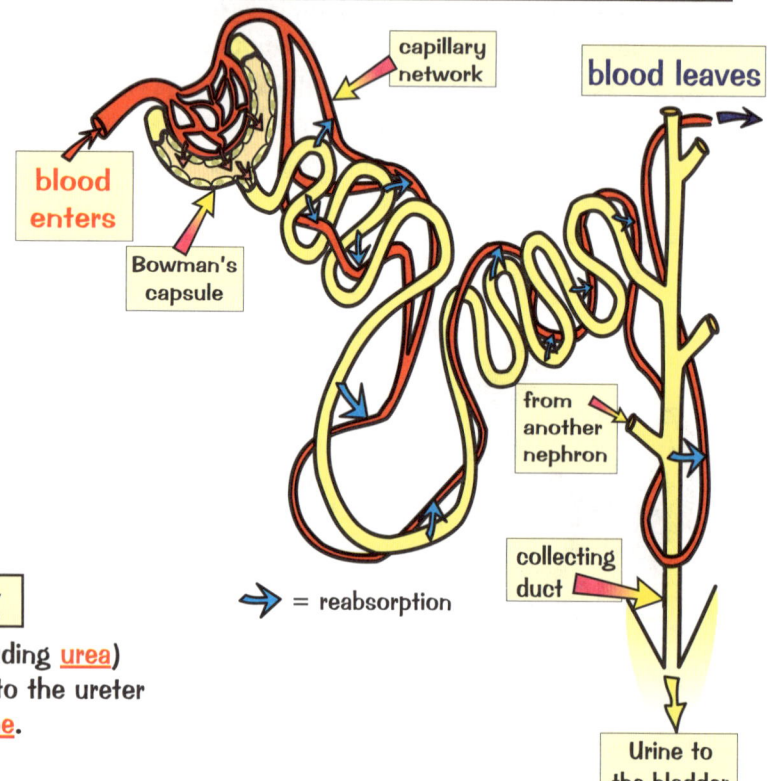

Let's see how much you've absorbed then...

The kidneys are pretty complicated organs as you can see. Do the usual thing — sit and learn it, then cover the page and sketch out the diagrams and scribble all the important details. Then try again until you get it all. But only scribble out very rough diagrams — just to show the important bits.

Module 1 — Life Care

Revision Summary for Module 1

That wasn't such a bad section to start on. Now you know how the healthy human body works and all about the people, organisations and techniques used to keep it healthy... you could almost be a doctor (well, maybe after your A-levels and then five years at Uni, but let's not dwell on details).
Here are a few questions to check that you do know it...

1) Describe three features of the National Health Service.
2) Name and describe the role of two professionals who work in health care or fitness.
3) Describe two ways that health care information is passed on to the public.
4) List three questions a health or fitness practitioner might ask you when taking a medical history.
5) What is a sphygmomanometer used to measure?
6) What is the formula for calculating body mass index?
7)* Cecil is 180 cm tall and weighs 85 kg. Calculate his BMI.
8) What is an electrocardiograph used to study?
9) Give one use for an ultrasound scan.
10) Give two reasons why a person's pulse rate might be weak?
11) What's a person's normal core body temperature?
12) If a person's body mass index is 21 are they underweight, OK, overweight, obese or severely obese?
13) List two diseases that blood tests may be used to diagnose.
14) Why would a treatment that is producing a side effect be continued?
15) List two targets of a treatment or fitness programme.
16) How would a physiotherapist treat a sprained ankle?
17) Give two reasons why a treatment may be modified.
18)* The following people are brought into the accident and emergency department of a hospital after being involved in a car accident.
    Susan (26) has a few cuts and bruises but no major injuries.
    Gareth (27) is complaining of chest pains and has difficulty breathing.
    Gerald (74) is complaining of chest pains and has difficulty breathing.
    Angela (31) has lost quite a bit of blood but the bleeding has been stopped.
    In what order should the casualties be treated?
19) Name two qualities or skills that health and fitness practitioners should possess.
20) Describe how the structures of arteries, veins and capillaries are adapted to their function.
21) Name two valves found in the heart.
22) What do the valves in the heart do?
23) What is the name of the part of the breathing system where gas exchange occurs?
24) Describe the relationship between ligaments, tendons, muscles and bones.
25) What is the name of the organ that produces sex cells (ova) in females?
26) Describe two changes that happen to the body during pregnancy.
27) Describe how the body responds to being too hot.
28) How does shivering help to warm you up?
29) Name the three main roles of the kidney.
30) What is a nephron?
31) What substances pass from the kidneys to the bladder?

* Answers on p.132.

Module 1 — Life Care

Module 2 — Agriculture and Food

Products from Organisms

This module is all about growing plants, raising animals and cultivating microorganisms to make food. Yum.

Products From Organisms Come From Gathered Harvests...

Gathered harvests are where the whole organism survives — something they produce is collected. Here are some examples:

Milk
E.g. from cows and goats.

Fruit and Nuts
From many different plants. See page 27 for more on fruit.

Wool
E.g. from sheep.

Extracellular protein from microorganisms
E.g. chymosin used during cheese making (see p.37).
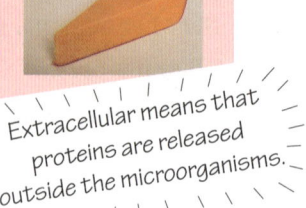

Extracellular means that proteins are released outside the microorganisms.

...and Whole Organism Harvests

Whole organism harvests are where the whole organism is used or consumed. Here are some examples:

Meat
Farm animals e.g. cows and pigs (see page 32).

Crops
E.g. vegetables, sugar beet and wheat (see page 26).

Food from microorganisms
E.g. meat substitutes for vegetarians (see page 36).

Living Organisms Are Used for Other Products or Tasks

We don't just use living organisms for food — they're used for many other tasks too.

1) **Producing fuels for transport** — e.g. sugar crops and microorganisms are used in the production of gasohol, microorganisms are used to make biogas and vegetable oils are used for biodiesel.
2) **Waste treatment** — microorganisms are used during sewage treatment.
3) **Food processing** — e.g. bacteria are used to make yoghurt and cheese (see p.37).
4) **Environmental management** — e.g. biological control, which is the use of predators to control pests (see p.29).

Everyone's a fruit and nut case...

Humans first started planting crops over 10,000 years ago, which makes farming one of the oldest traditional jobs. Agriculture is very important — it involves growing plants, raising animals and culturing microorganisms to make food and other products. Loads of people in the UK work in agriculture.

Agriculture in the UK

A lot of the food we eat in the UK is produced by British farmers. This requires a lot of land. There are different types of farming, such as arable or raising cattle. Yee haarr.

Agriculture is Growing Living Organisms for Their Products

Agriculture is the posh word for farming. There are five main types of agriculture:

1. Arable Farming

Arable farming involves growing crops for humans and animals to eat, and for other uses like making biofuels. People who work in the arable farming sector will do jobs involving:

1) Ploughing — turning the soil and sometimes adding fertilizer to get it ready for planting crops.
2) Agricultural engineering — looking after farming equipment like combine harvesters and tractors.
3) Planting, irrigating and harvesting — planting seeds, watering the crops and collecting the produce.

You may be asked to interpret some data on agriculture in the exam. So here's some on arable farming in the UK. The table shows the area of land used for growing three different crops over three years.

	Thousand Hectares		
	Dec '04	Dec '05	Dec '06
Wheat	1834	1771	1850
Barley	391	393	389
Oats	63	87	106

© Crown Copyright March 2007
Estimates made for holdings not surveyed or not responding
Department for Environment, Food & Rural Affairs, Foss House, Kings Pool,
1-2 Peasholme Green, YORK, YO1 7PX

From the table you can see that:

1) Wheat covers the largest area of land every year.
2) The area of land used for barley has stayed fairly constant.
3) The area of land used for growing oats has increased.

2. Horticulture

Horticulture is growing flowers and plants for gardens. It involves work similar to arable farming, e.g. ploughing, planting and harvesting but also things like collecting and storing seeds.

3. Beef Cattle, Sheep and Pig Farming

This means rearing cattle, sheep and pigs for meat and other products like leather and wool. Jobs include feeding and looking after the animals and, on sheep farms, shearing animals.

4. Dairy Cattle

Dairy cattle produce milk, which is also used to make milk products such as cheese and yoghurt. Jobs on a dairy farm are similar to those on cattle, sheep and pig farms but also include milking the cows and maintaining equipment that's used for milking.

5. Poultry Farming

Poultry are domesticated birds that are kept for food and eggs. These include chickens, turkeys and ducks. Jobs include feeding and slaughtering animals and also collecting eggs, by hand or machine.

What's big, red and will kill you if it falls out of a tree...?*

Data on agriculture could come in many different forms — like articles, flow charts, diagrams and tables (like the one above). There's lots more data interpretation still to come in this section, you lucky people.

*A combine harvester

Module 2 — Agriculture and Food

Agriculture in the UK

You've learnt a bit about the food, glorious food, that's grown in this country, but how does it get from the field to your kitchen — the chain of food production, that's how.

The Chain of Food Production — From The Farm to Your Fridge

The chain of food production includes every stage from growing the food to getting it to your home.

1) **GROWING** — crops and animals are grown on farms. Microorganisms are grown in fermenters in factories.

2) **TRANSPORTING** — the harvested product may be transported from the farm to another site for processing.

3) **PROCESSING** — the product may be processed, e.g. milk needs to be pasteurised. Microorganisms can be used in processing (see biotechnology below).

4) **STORING** — if not all the processed product is required immediately, some of it will have to be stored until it is needed, e.g. supermarket chains store goods at large distribution centres before they're taken to individual supermarkets.

5) **DELIVERING** — finally the processed product will be delivered to the shops for you to buy and take back to your home.

Biotechnology Can be Used in Food Production

Biotechnology includes the use of microorganisms during food processing and production, see p.36-37. For example:

1) Yeast is used in the brewing and wine industries to make alcohol.
2) Yeast is also used in bread making.
3) Bacteria are used to turn milk into cheese and yoghurt.
4) Fungi make mycoprotein — meat substitutes for vegetarians.

Chocolate to mouth — my favourite food chain...

The term 'chain of food production' is used by people working in agriculture and food production to describe the stages involved in food production. So make sure you learn all the stages and don't forget how important those little microorganisms can be in food production. Tasty.

Module 2 — Agriculture and Food

Regulating Agriculture and Food

Not all jobs in agriculture involve dealing with food and its production. There are also jobs in organisations that are responsible for the regulation of agriculture — they protect public health and the environment.

Agriculture and Food Production is Regulated

Agriculture is regulated for three important reasons:

1) Health and safety — farms and factories involved in food production are checked regularly to make sure they're working in a safe manner and are looking after the health of the workers.
2) Animal welfare — by law animals must be treated humanely, including on the farm, at market, during transportation and at slaughter.
3) Environmental protection — it's important to make sure farming methods don't harm the environment, e.g. fertilizers can cause problems if they get into the water system.

There's more on the FSA on p.43.

The FSA and Defra are two organisations that help to regulate agriculture:

The Food Standards Agency (FSA) was set up by the Government but it's independent of it. They help regulate the production, storage and transport of foods to protect consumer interests and public safety.

The Department for Environment, Food and Rural Affairs (Defra) is the Government department responsible for farming and food production. Defra looks after the interests of everyone involved in farming, agriculture and the environment, and works towards sustainable development (see page 41).

Enforcement Officers Monitor the Food Chain

Enforcement officers work for many different organisations. They're responsible for making sure that rules and regulations are followed throughout the food chain. Here are some examples:

1) Factory inspectors — make sure that workplaces stick to health and safety rules.
2) Environmental health practitioners — visit food factories, shops, restaurants, houses and offices to make sure that they're safe and hygienic. They can withdraw products or close premises if they are a danger to public health. They also monitor pollution levels and help protect the environment.

There Are Organisations That Support the Food Industry

Some organisations promote the products of particular parts of the food industry. They also carry out research and provide practical advice to producers in that part of the industry.

1) The Milk Development Council — runs marketing campaigns to promote milk and other dairy products to the public. They also help dairy farmers increase their profit.
2) The British Potato Council — advertises and promotes potatoes in the UK and abroad. It's funded by potato producers and commercial potato buyers.
3) The Meat and Livestock Commission — aims to improve the efficiency of the UK livestock industry and to promote British meat in the UK and abroad.
4) ADAS — gives advice and information on all aspects of farming, e.g. animal welfare.

Support the potato industry — eat chips...
Potatoes were the first vegetable grown in space — aboard the Columbia Space Shuttle in 1995.

Module 2 — Agriculture and Food

Products from Plants

The next few pages are on plants and all the wondrous products they produce — food for people and animals, wood, fabrics, biofuels and not forgetting pretty flowers. It's always nice to get flowers.

Plants Provide Food

Lots of the food that we get from plants doesn't need any processing at all. Here are some examples:

For people
- Potatoes — everyone loves potatoes.
- Lettuce — watery goodness.
- Apples — from orchards.

For farm animals
- Grass — sheep munch on grass.
- Silage — made from grass and is used to feed cattle over winter.
- Hay — horses love hay.

Some Plant Material Has to be Processed Before it Can be Used

Some plant material is processed to turn it into a useful product. Here are some examples:

Sugar

1) Sugar beet is a vegetable that's used to make sugar.
2) After being harvested it's transported to factories where it's cut into chips and put in tanks of water. The sugar leaks out of the chips and into the water.
3) The chips are removed and crushed to squeeze all the sugar juice out of them.
4) The sugary water is filtered and evaporated, leaving behind the sugar crystals. The crystals are then dried and packaged as bags of sugar ready to be sold.

Flour

1) The grains from cereal crops are ground between stones or steel wheels to produce flour. This is called milling.
2) Which parts of the grain are milled determines the type of flour produced, e.g. white or whole grain.

Vegetable oil

1) Vegetable oil can be extracted from plant seeds, (e.g. sunflower or rape seeds) or fruit (e.g. olives).
2) The plant material is crushed and squashed and the oil is separated.
3) The oil can also be extracted chemically.

Plants Provide Other Useful Products

We don't just eat plants, we get other products from them as well:

1) Materials — e.g. wood from trees is used to make furniture and paper.
2) Fibres and fabric — e.g. cotton from the cotton plant and linen from the flax plant.
3) Biofuels — these are fuels made from biological products, e.g. ethanol from the sugar extracted from sugar beet and biodiesel from the processed oils of vegetables.

Hippies love biofuel — it's flower power...

Plants are such handy things. Look around your room, I bet there'll be loads of products in it that have come from plants — the bread in that mouldy sandwich under your bed, those stinky cotton socks in your washing basket and probably some of your furniture too.

Module 2 — Agriculture and Food

The Plant Life-Cycle

Fruits and seeds are harvested from many plants. But they can only be produced in flowering plants.

The Life-Cycle of a Flowering Plant Has Five Main Stages

1) Pollination
The transfer of pollen (male sex cells) into the female parts of the flower, e.g. by insects.

2) Fertilisation
The male and female sex cells join together.

3) Production of seeds and/or fruit
The seed is formed and in some plants a fruit develops around the seed.

5) Germination of seeds
The seed starts to grow into a new plant.

4) Dispersal of seeds and/or fruit
Small, dry seeds are blown away by the wind. Fruits may be eaten by animals and the seeds scattered in their poo.

A Germinating Seed Needs Water and Oxygen

Seeds will often lie dormant until the conditions around it are right for germination. There are three things that seeds need to start germinating:

1) Water — to activate the enzymes that break down the food reserves in the seed.
2) Oxygen — for the process that provides the energy for growth.
3) A suitable temperature — for the enzymes inside the seed to work. This depends on what type of seed it is.

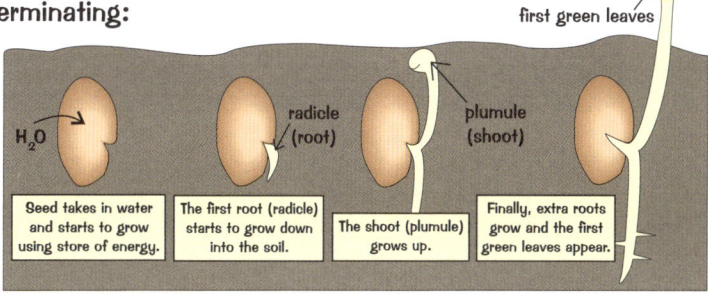

Germination Rate is the Number of Seeds Likely to Germinate

Germination rate is the number of seeds of a plant type (or batch) that are likely to germinate under the right conditions. It's often given as a percentage. Germination rates can be used by farmers or gardeners to calculate how many seeds they need to plant to grow a certain number of plants.

In the exam you might be asked to interpret some data on germination rates. Here's an example:

Farmer Froggart wants to grow a field of peas. A seed company sends him some details about three species of pea plant, including germination rates. Which species should farmer Froggart use if he wants the most number of plants from the fewest number of seeds?
Answer — species A, as it has the highest germination rate.

Species	Germination rate (%)
A	89
B	70
C	76

Daleks love gardening — ex-germinate, ex-germinate...

You can improve germination rates by selectively breeding plants with good quality seeds, see p.31.

Module 2 — Agriculture and Food

Plant Growth

Plants need food to grow. Photosynthesis is the process that produces 'food' in plants. The 'food' it produces is glucose. Farmers who understand photosynthesis can give their crops the perfect growing conditions to maximise their profits.

Four Things are Needed for Photosynthesis to Happen:

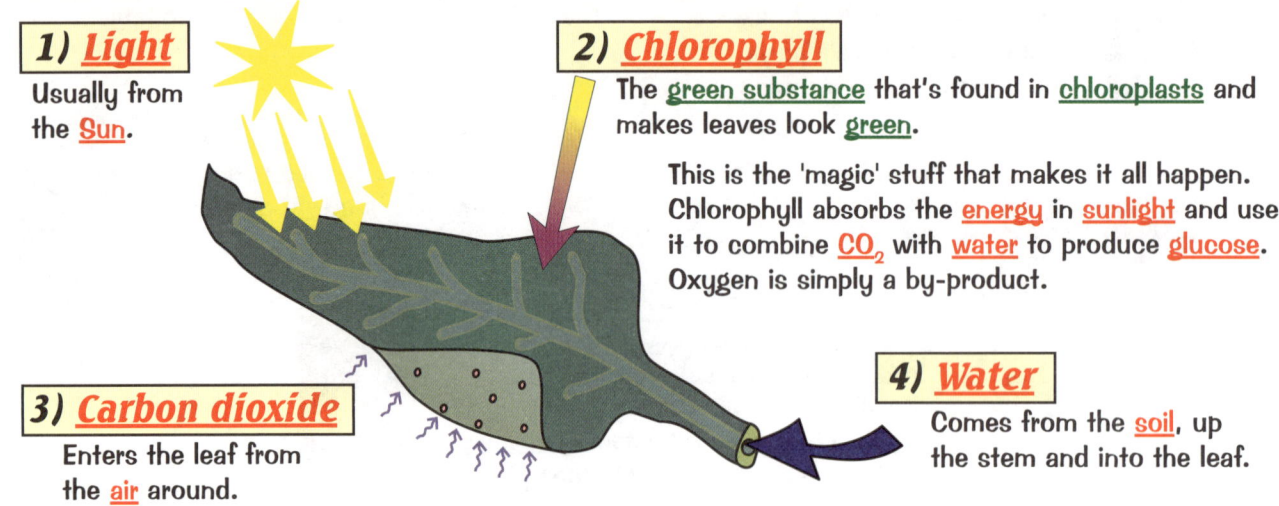

1) Light — Usually from the Sun.

2) Chlorophyll — The green substance that's found in chloroplasts and makes leaves look green.

This is the 'magic' stuff that makes it all happen. Chlorophyll absorbs the energy in sunlight and uses it to combine CO_2 with water to produce glucose. Oxygen is simply a by-product.

3) Carbon dioxide — Enters the leaf from the air around.

4) Water — Comes from the soil, up the stem and into the leaf.

Photosynthesis Can be Written as an Equation:

carbon dioxide + water —SUNLIGHT/chlorophyll→ glucose + oxygen

You Can Artificially Create the Ideal Conditions for Photosynthesis

The problem is, some of the things needed for photosynthesis aren't always naturally available in the right amounts. Photosynthesis can be helped along by artificially creating the ideal conditions in glasshouses (big greenhouses to you and me) or polytunnels (big tube-like structures made from plastic).

1) Light is always needed for photosynthesis, so commercial farmers often supply artificial light after the Sun goes down to give their plants more time to photosynthesise.

2) Farmers can increase the level of carbon dioxide in glasshouses, e.g. by burning fuel that produces carbon dioxide as a by-product.

3) Keeping plants enclosed in a glasshouse also makes it easier to keep them free from pests and diseases.

4) Glasshouses also trap the Sun's heat to keep the plants warm.

5) If the farmer can keep the conditions just right for photosynthesis, the plants will grow much faster and high quality crops can be harvested more often.

Strawberry fields forever — well, all year round at least...

It's not just poor GCSE students who need to learn about how plants photosynthesise. Farmers use this information to get the most out of their crops. Those who got stuck in at school know how to grow things like lettuce and even strawberries all year round — even in the UK's cold, dark, rubbish climate.

Module 2 — Agriculture and Food

Crop Yield

Farmers want high yields from their crops. The higher the yield, the more money they'll make.

Pests Reduce Crop Yields

Pests reduce crop yields by damaging seeds, fruits, flowers, stems, leaves and roots.
1) They may damage the actual harvest (e.g. fruit), which means that they have to be thrown away.
2) They may slow the growth of the crop (e.g. by damaging leaves), which means less of the crop grows.
3) They spread diseases from one plant to another (e.g. when collecting nectar or pollen).

Chemicals or Predator Organisms Can be Used to Control Pests

If insect pests get into glasshouses they can be a big problem — it's warm and there's lots of food about.
1) Chemical control uses pesticides to kill pests.
2) Natural predators can also be used to kill pests.
   For example — aphids are pests that eat roses and vegetables. Ladybirds are aphid predators so people release them into their glasshouses to keep aphid numbers down.

Using chemical control or natural predators in glasshouses has advantages and disadvantages:

	Chemical control	Natural Predators
Advantages	Cost efficient. Easy to apply to all plants.	Less polluting. Usually only affects pest animal.
Disadvantages	Could remain on food. Could kill harmless animals, e.g. pollinating insects.	Won't kill all pests. Takes management and training. Predators could escape into the natural environment.

Crop Yields Can be Measured Using Wet Mass

1) Wet mass is the mass of fresh plant material — including all the water in the plant tissues. Potato and pea yields are measured as wet mass.
2) Some crop yields are measured by dry mass — the water is removed from the plant tissues before it's weighed. Tea and cereal grain yields are measured as dry mass.
3) Yields are usually measured as the amount of harvestable material produced from one plant or from an area.

You may be asked to interpret data on crop yields in the exam.

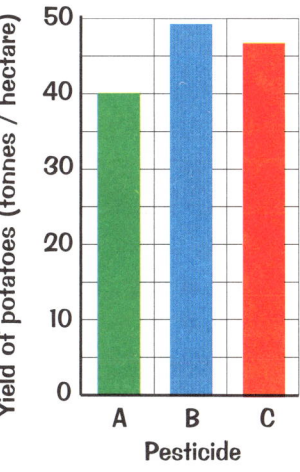

Graph to show the effect of pesticide on potato yields.

> Here's a graph that shows the yield of potatoes (wet mass) in tonnes produced per hectare, when three different pesticides are used.
> From the graph you can see that using Pesticide B gives a greater crop yield than using pesticide A or C.

Don't get bugged by biological pest control...

Yield is a measure of quantity but remember the quality of the crop is important too. The quality may affect how much money the farmer can get for his crop — the higher the quality, the higher the price.

Module 2 — Agriculture and Food

Growing Plants

Farmers need to understand what plants need to grow so they can increase yields.

Plants Can be Grown With or Without Soil

1) The growing media for most plants is soil. Sometimes compost (decayed plant matter) is added to the soil to improve it. (Some seeds are grown in pure compost to start with.)
2) Plants can also be grown without soil in a nutrient solution. This is called hydroponics (see below).

Whatever the growing media is, it needs to contain everything the plants need to grow...

Plants Need Water, Nutrients and the Right pH to Grow

1) Water — water is needed for photosynthesis (see page 28). Plants take up water through their roots.
2) Nutrients — plants need essential nutrients to help them grow (e.g. nitrates, phosphates and potassium, which help with good root, shoot and flower growth). These are taken up along with water through their roots.
3) pH — the availability of nutrients in the growing media is affected by pH. Different plants grow well at different pHs, e.g. potatoes like slightly acidic soil, sugar beat likes neutral to alkaline soil.

A Good Soil Contains a Mixture of Materials

1) A good soil contains a lot of nutients. The nutrient content of the soil can be improved mixing in compost (which is high in nutrients). Farmers can also add fertilizers (which contain lots of nutrients) to the soil — this helps the plants to grow bigger and quicker.
2) A good soil also holds water and nutrients — making them available for the plant. How well a soil's able to do this depends on:
   - The soil structure — good soils have an equal mixture of sand, silt and clay particles.
   - The humus content — a good soil has a high humus content. Humus is organic material formed from the decomposition of dead plants and animals — it's natural compost.
3) A good soil structure also supports the plant (stops it from falling or blowing over).

Hydroponics is Growing Plants Without Soil

Most commercially grown tomatoes and cucumbers are grown in circulating nutrient solutions (water and fertilizers) instead of in soil — this is called hydroponics.

There are advantages and disadvantages of using hydroponics instead of growing crops in soil:

ADVANTAGES	DISADVANTAGES
Takes up less space so less land required.	It can be expensive to set up and run.
No soil preparation or weeding needed.	Need to use specially formulated soluble nutrients.
Can still grow plants even in areas with poor soil.	Growers need to be skilled and properly trained.
Many pest species live in soil, so it avoids these.	There's no soil to anchor the roots so plants need support.
Mineral levels can be controlled more accurately.	

Plants without soil? It's not like when I was a lad...

Plants need three things to grow — a water supply, a source of minerals and nutrients, and the right pH. You can buy grow bags for some plants, e.g. tomatoes. These contain growing media especially made for that plant. All you have to do is add the plant and some water, and Bob's your uncle, yummy toms.

Module 2 — Agriculture and Food

Cuttings and Tissue Culture

Some plants are just better than others — they might produce tastier fruit or be more resistant to pests. You can make a genetically identical copy (a clone) of a good 'un using cuttings or tissue culture.

You Can Take Cuttings to Make Genetically Identical Plants

The easiest way to make lots of genetically identical plants is to take cuttings from a good parent plant.

1) You have to snip bits off the parent plant, usually a stem with buds and leaves on, and pot them up.
2) Each cutting will grow into a new plant that's genetically identical to the parent.
3) The plants can be produced quickly and cheaply.

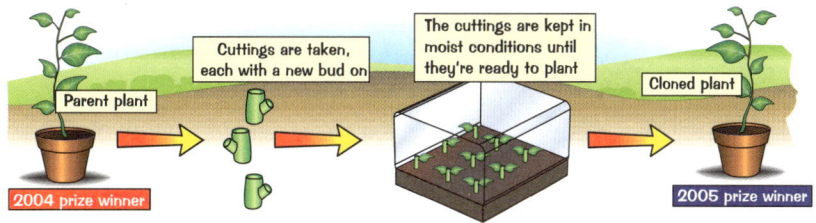

Tissue Culture Only Uses a Few Plant Cells

You can also grow genetically identical plants using tissue culture.

1) You remove a small amount of tissue from the parent plant. Because you only need a tiny amount, you can remove several pieces of tissue to give several clones. You get the best results if you take tissue from fast-growing root and shoot tips.
2) You grow the tissue in a medium containing nutrients and growth hormones. This is done under aseptic (sterile) conditions to prevent growth of microbes that could harm the plants.
3) As the tissues produce shoots and roots they can be moved to potting compost to carry on growing.

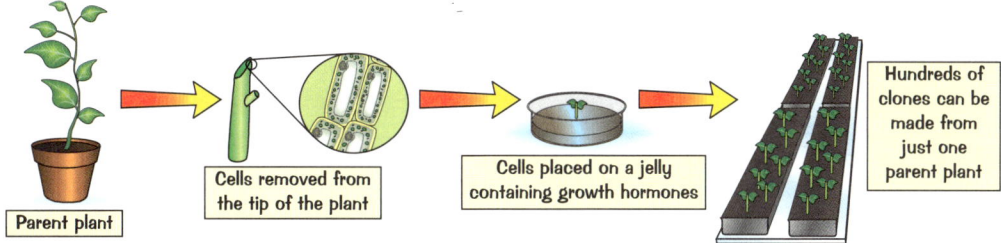

Producing Identical Plants Has Pros and Cons

1) You can be sure of the characteristics of the new plants because they'll be genetically identical to the parent — so you'll only get good ones, and won't waste time and money growing duds.
2) It's possible to mass-produce plants that are difficult to grow from scratch.
3) No fertilisation or pollination is needed to produce seeds for new plants.
4) The main draw back is a reduced gene pool:

Alleles are different versions of the same gene.

> A "reduced gene pool" means fewer alleles in a population — which will happen if you're cloning from the same plants or animals (see p.35) all the time. If a population is identical and a new disease appears, all the plants or animals could be wiped out — there may be no allele in the population giving resistance to the disease.

Stop cloning around — just learn it...

Tissue culture allows plant growers to make big money — a lot of the house plants for sale at garden centres are grown using tissue culture. It can also be used to try and save endangered species.

Module 2 — Agriculture and Food

Products from Animals

We get a lot of products from animals — not just meat.

Animals Can Provide Food, Textiles and Fertilizers

Farm animals provide us with lots of different types of food and lots of other useful products.

Food
E.g. meat, eggs, milk and dairy products.

Textiles
E.g. leather (made from animal hides) and wool.

Fertilizers
E.g. manure is a rich fertilizer made from the droppings of farm animals. Bonemeal is a fertilizer made from the bones of animals.

Some Animal Products Are Processed Before They're Used

We get lots of different meats from animals, e.g. bacon, pork chops and steaks, but we can't just eat a cow, skin and all. In the exam you may have to interpret information on how animals and their products are processed into the food we eat. So here's an example of how meat is processed:

1) Slaughterhouse (abattoir) — the animals are transported from the farm to the slaughterhouse. They are killed and the meat goes through the first stages of processing, which involves:

   - stunning and slaughtering the animals
   - removing the skin/feathers, which can be taken away for further processing
   - inspection of the carcass for quality and safety
   - breaking down the carcass into different parts, e.g. cattle are split into quarters

2) Butchers — prepare the cuts and sell the meat.

Four Factors Affect Animal Growth

Farmers can increase animal growth if they understand what animals need to grow.

1) Warmth — animals grow faster if they don't waste energy keeping warm.
2) Shelter — animals grow faster if they have shelter to keep them warm.
3) Food and water — both food and water are needed to provide energy to grow.
4) Good health — pests and diseases can weaken animals, slowing down growth or killing them.

In the exam you might be asked to interpret data related to animal growth and product yield.

E.g. Farmer Giles tested three different types of feed to see which would give the greatest product yield in his pigs. Three types of feed were fed to three groups of pigs and the average change in mass of the pigs was calculated for each group. Using the table you can see that to get the greatest product yield from his pigs farmer Giles should use feed C.

Type of feed	Average change in mass of the pigs (kg)
A	66
B	70
C	77

My brother talks a whole load of manure...

Over 20 different cuts of meat come from pigs including ham, ribs, chops, shoulders, trotters and not forgetting bacon. Mmmmmmmmmmmmmmmmmmmmmmmm, bacon...

Module 2 — Agriculture and Food

Intensive and Organic Farming

Farmers use different methods to rear animals — like organic or intensive methods.

Animals Can be Reared Intensively or Organically

Intensive Farming

Intensive farming is where the animals are kept inside in limited space with automatic systems to control light, temperature and ventilation. This means that they don't waste energy keeping warm or moving around and so they grow faster on less food. They are given concentrated feeds and often hormones to increase their growth rates even more.

Organic Farming

Organic farming is an alternative to modern farming. It uses more traditional methods than intensive farming. Organically-reared animals have lots of space to roam about and are fed a diet of organically grown food. Because the yields are lower organic food is more expensive to buy.

Intensive Farming Raises Ethical Issues

There are some ethical concerns about intensive farming:
1) Some people think that forcing animals to live in unnatural conditions is cruel.
2) The crowded conditions on factory farms create a favourable environment for the spread of diseases, like avian flu and foot-and-mouth disease.
3) Animals kept in crowded conditions can suffer from stress.

Organic Farming Has Advantages and Disadvantages

ADVANTAGES

1) Organic farming uses fewer artificial chemicals, so there's less risk of toxic chemicals remaining on food.
2) For a farm to be classed as organic, it will usually have to follow guidelines on the ethical treatment of animals. This means no battery farming.

DISADVANTAGES

1) Organic farming takes up more space than intensive farming — so more land has to be farmland, rather than being set aside for wildlife or for other uses.
2) It's more labour-intensive. This provides more jobs but it also makes the food more expensive.
3) For a certain area of land, you can't grow as much food as you can with intensive farming.

My dad grows AAA's — he runs a battery farm...

For products to be labelled organic, the company selling them has to abide by certain rules on animal welfare and feeding practices set down by the EU and groups like The Soil Association.
The Soil Association is an organisation that certifies farms and products as organic (see page 40). About 80% of all organic food sold in the UK is Soil Association approved. That's a lot of grub.

Module 2 — Agriculture and Food

Sexual Reproduction in Animals

Farmers use science and technology for animal reproduction and breeding programmes. One use is artificial insemination — the insertion of sperm from a male into a female, which leads to fertilisation without all the bother of sexual intercourse.

Sexual Reproduction in Mammals Has Five Main Stages

1) Formation of gametes
The male (sperm) and female (egg) sex cells, called gametes, are formed.

2) Fertilisation
The male and female sex cells join together inside the female to form a zygote.

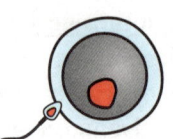

3) Internal development
During the pregnancy the zygote grows to become a fully developed fetus (baby).

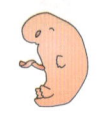

4) Birth
When the fetus has developed enough, chemical signals start the birth and the baby is eventually born.

5) Growth and development
The baby grows and develops into an adult mammal.

Farm Animals Can be Bred Using Artificial Insemination

Artificial insemination (AI) can be used for many animals but it's most commonly carried out in cattle. Artificial insemination involves four stages:

1) Selection of animals — animals with 'good' characteristics, e.g. high meat or milk yields, high fertility rates, good mothering skills, are selected.
2) Collection of sperm — the sperm is collected into a device that stimulates the male to ejaculate and then keeps the sperm at the right temperature.
3) Storage of sperm — the sperm is checked for quality, to make sure it will fertilise the female. It's then placed in disposable plastic straws, which are frozen in liquid nitrogen (-196 °C) until the sperm are required.
4) Insertion of sperm — to inseminate the female a long pipette is used to insert the contents of the straw. The female must be inseminated at the right time, just before she is about to release an egg, to increase the chances of fertilisation happening.

Artificial Insemination has Advantages over Natural Mating

Advantages of artificial insemination include:
1) Reduced cost — it's cheaper and safer for the farmer to buy semen than keep a male animal.
2) Decreased risk of disease — the risk of exposure to sexually-transmitted diseases is reduced.
3) Increased quality — the sperm is of known quality from a tested, high quality bull.

A.I. — I thought that was something to do with robots...

Artificial insemination can be done alongside embryo transfer, which is on the next page. On you go...

Module 2 — Agriculture and Food

Selective Breeding and Embryo Transplants

Selective breeding and embryo transplants are ways for humans to develop crops or herds with useful characteristics.

Selective Breeding is Very Useful in Farming

Selective breeding is when humans select the plants or animals that are going to breed and flourish, according to what we want from them. It's also called artificial selection.
Here's the basic process involved in selective breeding:

1) From the existing stock, the organisms that have the best characteristics are selected.
2) They're bred with each other.
3) The best of the offspring are selected and bred.
4) This process is repeated over several generations to develop the desired traits.
5) The characteristics that are 'best' will vary, but it usually means things like:

- High yield of meat, milk, grain, etc, so it will increase productivity.
- Good health and disease resistance.
- Qualities like a good temperament and high fertility.
- Qualities like pretty flowers and smell for plants.

6) The main draw back is a reduced gene pool (see page 31).

You Need to Know About Embryo Transplants

Normally, farmers only breed from their best animals. However, such traditional methods would only allow the prize female to produce one new offspring each year. These days the whole process has been transformed using embryo transplants:

1) Sperm cells are taken from the prize male and egg cells are taken from the prize female.
2) The sperm are used to artificially fertilise an egg cell.
3) The fertilised egg divides to give a ball of genetically identical cells, which develops into an embryo.
4) The embryo is then split into separate cells. Each cell grows into a new embryo, which is a clone of the original one.
5) These embryos are implanted into lots of females, called 'surrogate mothers', where they grow. They can also be frozen for use at a later date.
6) The offspring are clones of each other, NOT clones of their parents.
7) The advantage of this is that hundreds of "ideal" offspring can be produced every year from the best male and female animal, and the original prize female can keep producing prize eggs all year round.
8) The big disadvantage (as usual) is a reduced gene pool (see page 31).

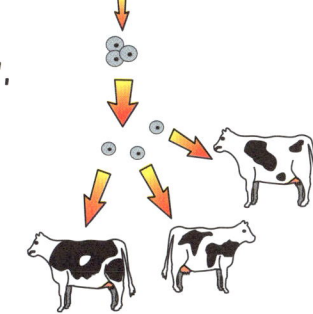

Selective breeding — sounds like a night out at my local disco...

Selective breeding's not a new thing. People have been doing it for yonks. That's how we ended up with something like a poodle from a wolf. Somebody thought 'I really like this small, woolly, yappy wolf — I'll breed it with this other one'. And after thousands of generations, we got poodles. Hurrah.

Module 2 — Agriculture and Food

Products from Microorganisms

Microorganisms can help us make some really tasty food products — and it's another ideal topic for examiners to give you some info to interpret. There are loads of examples on these two pages...

Microorganisms Can Help Us Make Lots of Useful Products

Microorganisms include bacteria, fungi (including yeasts) and viruses.
We can make useful products from (or with the help of) microorganisms. For example:

Food
E.g. bread, cheese, yogurt and mycoprotein.

Alcohol
For drink, e.g. beer and wine, or fuel, e.g. ethanol (which is mixed with petrol to make gasohol).

Enzymes
E.g. chymosin, used in cheese making.

1) Microorganisms convert sugar into other substances during respiration (a process that releases energy). There are two types — aerobic (with oxygen) and anaerobic (without oxygen).
2) In industry, this process is called fermentation.
3) Microorganisms need the right conditions for fermentation, i.e. a food source, the right temperature, and oxygen if it's respiring aerobically.

Yeast Grow Quickest When Respiring Aerobically

Some products are made from the microorganisms themselves, e.g. mycoprotein. Others are a product that they make, e.g. yeast extract. Either way, you want the microorganisms to grow as fast as possible — and that's by aerobic respiration.

Learn this equation for aerobic respiration: sugar + oxygen → carbon dioxide + water

Mycoprotein

Mycoprotein is a product from fungi that's used to make meat substitutes for vegetarians, e.g. Quorn™.

1) The fungus is grown in fermenters (see diagram) using sugar for food. The sugar is obtained by digesting maize starch with enzymes.
2) The fungus respires aerobically, so oxygen's supplied, together with nitrogen and other minerals. The mixture's also kept at the right temperature and pH.
3) When the fungi has grown, it's extracted and dried.
4) It's then processed further by adding flavourings and other ingredients.

Enzymes break down the starch into sugars.

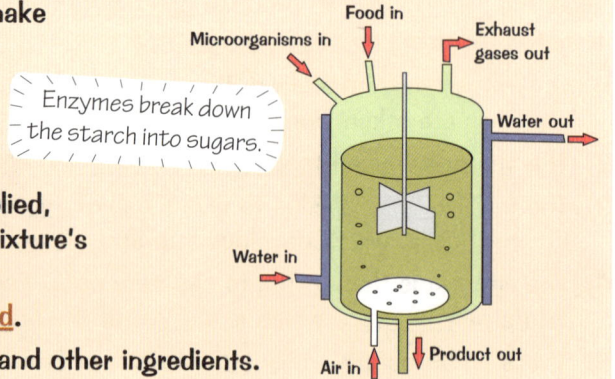

Anaerobic Fermentation in Yeast Produces Carbon Dioxide

Anaerobic fermentation by yeast helps us make bread.
Learn the equation for anaerobic respiration in yeast: sugar → ethanol + carbon dioxide

Bread

1) Grains are milled to produce flour (see p.26).
2) Yeast and sugar is added to the flour to make dough.
3) The yeast feed on the sugar, producing carbon dioxide that makes the bread rise.

Module 2 — Agriculture and Food

Products from Microorganisms

Fermentation doesn't only occur in yeast. Bacteria do it too — only their anaerobic fermentation is ever so slightly different.

Anaerobic Fermentation in Bacteria Produces Acid

Anaerobic fermentation in some bacteria (e.g. *Lactobaccili*) help us make cheese and yoghurt. Anaerobic respiration in these bacteria produces lactic acid.

Here's the equation to learn: sugar → lactic acid

Cheese

You need to know the steps involved in cheese making, so here goes...

1) A culture of bacteria is added to warm milk.
2) They turn the sugar in the milk into lactic acid, which causes the milk to curdle.
3) Enzymes (e.g. chymosin) are often added to help produce solid curds in the milk.
4) These curds are separated from the liquid whey.
5) The curd is left to ripen for a while before it's processed.

Yoghurt

Yoghurt is basically fermented milk. Here's how it's made:

1) Milk is pasteurised (heated) to kill any unwanted microorganisms. All the equipment is also sterilised (see p.38). Then the milk's cooled.
2) A culture of bacteria is added and the mixture is incubated (heated to about 40 °C) in a fermenter.
3) The bacteria turn the sugar in the milk into lactic acid, causing the milk to clot and solidify into yoghurt.
4) Flavours (e.g. fruit) and colours are sometimes added before the yoghurt is packaged.

Genetically Modified Organisms Make Useful Proteins

We can produce large amounts of useful proteins (e.g. chymosin) from microorganisms by modifying their genetic material.

1) A gene for a useful protein is selected and added into the genetic material of another organism.
2) The genetically modified (GM) organism can then produce this protein.
3) You can get large amounts of the protein by growing the GM organisms on a large scale. Easy.

Chymosin

1) The enzyme chymosin is used in cheese making — it clots the milk. Scientists have genetically modified yeast to produce this enzyme.
2) Chymosin is traditionally taken from the lining of a calf's stomach — so by using chymosin from genetically modified organisms, cheese suitable for vegans can be produced.

The world's fastest yoghurt — pasteurised before you see it...

You still need to stop some microorganisms infecting your food — that's why milk is pasteurised.

Module 2 — Agriculture and Food

Growth of Microorganisms

Not all microorganisms are nice, friendly, useful creatures — some are evil little critters...

Microorganisms Can Cause Disease and Food Spoilage

1) Some bacteria and fungi can cause food to "go off" — this is called food spoilage.
2) Food can be spoilt by visible growth, e.g. mould on bread.
3) Food spoilage is also caused by waste products. Microorganisms can break down the food and feed on it, producing waste products that contaminate the food.
3) Some microorganisms can make you ill if you ingest them — causing food poisoning.
4) And of course, other microorganisms cause other diseases, e.g. the flu virus causes flu.

Contamination Has to be Avoided in Food Production

When you're growing specific microorganisms for food production you don't want other types sneaking in and messing things up.

1) Contamination in food production could allow dangerous microorganisms to grow in the food.
2) Aseptic techniques are used to make sure things are kept clean and sterile.
3) There are several ways you can make things sterile, e.g. using heat or chemicals, which kills the microorganisms. It's important to sterilise all equipment before and after use, and mixtures can be boiled — this is done before the useful microorganism is added, or else it'd be killed as well.

You Can Monitor Population Growth

You need to know three ways to measure the number (or population) of microorganisms in a sample:

COLONY COUNTS

1) A sample of the stuff you're growing is diluted and spread over an agar plate. This is then incubated to allow the microorganisms to grow.
2) Each microorganism will produce a colony (a clump of cells). By counting the number of colonies, you can calculate how many microorganisms were in the original sample.
3) If there are too many colonies to count, you do it again with a more diluted sample.

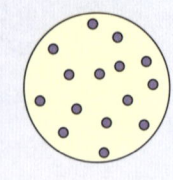

TURBIDITY

1) This is a measurement of the cloudiness of a liquid — the more microorganisms in a liquid the more cloudy it will be.
2) The amount of light that travels through the liquid can be measured. The more cloudy a liquid is, the less light can pass through it — this can give an indication of the number of microorganisms in it.

The graph shows that the turbidity of a sample increases over time indicating an increase in population. The maximum rate of growth occurs where the line is the steepest, between 3 and 6 hours.

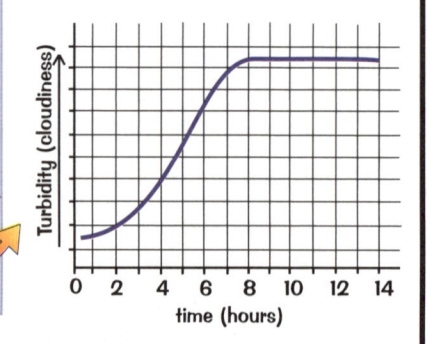

BIOMASS

The amount of organic material (biomass) in a sample can be weighed. The biomass gives an indication of the number of microorganisms that are growing.

Avoid contamination — don't put red socks in with your whites...

You need to be able to interpret data on the population growth of microorganisms. So you might be given data produced by measuring colony counts, turbidity or biomass to look at. Good clean fun.

Module 2 — Agriculture and Food

Testing Food

Food and other products from organisms must be tested to ensure that they're safe to eat and they're the correct quality.

The Quality and Safety of Food is Very Important

1) If the food is unsafe it could cause food poisoning.
2) If the product isn't the right quality the customers aren't getting what they've paid for.

There are Three Types of Testing Techniques...

Qualitative These tests usually give you a yes/no answer (they don't give you a number answer). Here are some examples:

1) You can tell if plants lack a certain mineral by their appearance, e.g. if a plant can't get enough of the mineral nitrogen it will have stunted growth and yellow older leaves.
2) In brewing you can see when fermentation is complete — gas bubble production slows down.
3) Inspecting a crop for damage can give a good indication of its quality.
4) The quality of dyes can be determined simply by looking at their colour.
5) You can usually tell if food has 'gone off', e.g. it's green and furry.

Semi-Quantitative These tests give you an estimate of something (but they aren't as accurate as quantitative tests — see below).
E.g. soil pH can be measured using test strips that indicate pH to within 1 or 2 pH units (see page 51).

Quantitative These tests measure something and give you an accurate number. Here are some examples:

1) Soil pH can be measured accurately using a pH meter (to within 0.1 pH units).
2) The level of alcohol in beer can be determined using a hydrometer.
3) Percentage germination rate (a measure of seed quality) can be determined by growing seeds (see p.27).
4) The concentration of dyes present in foods can be measured using a colorimeter (see p.52).
5) Carbohydrate and protein levels in cereal grains can be measured using chemical tests.

Different Conditions Affect the Quality of Food

In the exam you might need to interpret data on the effects of poor storage, transport, preparation and cooking of food. Here's an example of how storage affects the quality of milk:

1) The graph shows the result of an experiment to investigate the freshness of milk that had been stored at different temperatures.
2) The amount of bacteria was measured after 24 hours using colony counts (see p.38).
3) The graph shows that the higher the temperature the milk's stored at, the more live bacteria are present in the milk.
4) Line X shows the amount of bacteria that would cause milk to be regarded as unsafe to sell. From the graph you can tell that milk would be unsafe to sell if stored above 8 °C for 24 hours.

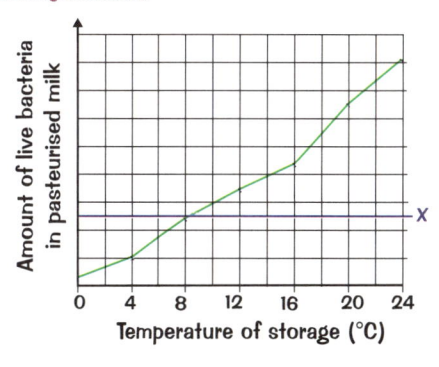

Exams — your very own testing technique...

This page might look horrific but don't worry, it's all pretty easy stuff — just read it through carefully.

Module 2 — Agriculture and Food

The Food Market

The '<u>market</u>' is a strange concept — it's not where you go to buy organic sausages and have a nice cup of hot soup, it's a bit more abstract than that... The <u>food market</u> is basically a description of the all the <u>interactions between the buyers and sellers of food products</u>.

Price is Influenced by Different Factors

The price of an item of food can vary according to....

SUPPLY AND DEMAND

1) The <u>amount</u> of a product <u>that can be bought</u> (supply) and the <u>amount people want to buy</u> (demand) will affect the <u>price</u> of a product.
2) When a product is readily available or there's <u>more</u> than is wanted (not enough demand) it will be <u>cheaper</u>.
3) If there is an increase in demand for a product and there <u>isn't much available</u> (supply) then it'll be <u>more expensive</u>.

> Here's a nice example: bananas
> Bananas are great, everyone wants some.
> But what if they didn't? If lots of people decided not to buy them, the price would go down — the <u>supply</u> would be higher than the <u>demand</u>.
> What if there was a huge banana shortage? There wouldn't be enough bananas for the banana fans, so the price would rise — the <u>demand</u> would be higher than <u>supply</u>.

GOVERNMENT INTERVENTION

1) The <u>government provides money</u> (known as <u>subsidies</u>) to the <u>producers</u> in some <u>industries</u>, e.g. dairy farming — this keeps the <u>price</u> of the product <u>lower</u> than it would otherwise be.
2) Subsidies may be given to make sure some products continue to be made in the <u>UK</u>, providing <u>jobs</u>. Without subsidies some industries in the UK would be <u>outcompeted</u> by other countries.

Marketing Products is Important

<u>Marketing</u> is important as it lets people know what products are <u>available</u> to buy.
1) Producers can use <u>advertising</u> to tell you about their product.
2) They can also make their products <u>look nice</u> — so people will want to buy them.

Quality Marks Indicate Certain Standards

<u>Quality marks</u> on products tell you that the product you're buying has reached a certain standard. Here are <u>two examples</u> of quality marks...

Lion Quality Stamp

This shows that the eggs have come from hens <u>vaccinated</u> against <u>Salmonella</u>.

Soil Association Organic Standard

Soil Association
the heart of organic food & farming

This shows that the food has been produced and processed to strict <u>organic standards</u>.

These quality marks may also <u>increase the market value</u> of a product — simply because people are willing to pay more for products that they know are of a <u>good quality</u> and are <u>safe</u>.

Quality stamps are really rather eggciting...

There are quite a few things that affect how much you'll pay for a product — not just how much it costs the producer to make. Something to think about next time you're shopping for eggs...

Module 2 — Agriculture and Food

Sustainable Agriculture

Farming has a big effect on the environment so producers need to think about their impact.

Sustainable Agriculture — Responsible Farming

> Sustainable agriculture — a way of farming that allows the production of crops or livestock without damaging the environment.

So basically its making sure we farm responsibly so we don't ruin things for future generations.

The Quality of Soil Needs Protecting

Soil is really important in farming so farmers need to protect and improve it.
1) Plants take essential nutrients from the soil in order to grow and reproduce, see p.30.
2) When plants die they're broken down by microbes — so the nutrients are returned to the soil, ready for other plants to use.
3) But if the plants are taken away by the farmer (for us and other animals to eat) then the nutrients are also taken away.
4) This means the nutrients in the soil aren't naturally replaced, and the farmer has to use other methods to replace them...

- Planting legumes — these plants can put nutrients back into the soil (as nitrogen compounds). This graph shows that the longer these crops are grown, the more nitrogen compounds are present in the soil.
- Fertilizers — these put nutrients directly back into the soil, however it's important to make sure their production doesn't have a bad impact on the environment and their use doesn't harm wildlife.

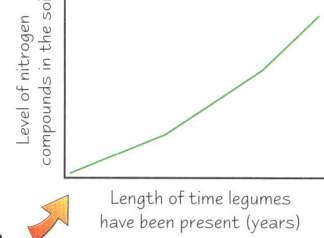

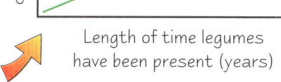

Non-Renewable Resources are Running Out

1) Non-renewable resources are natural resources that will one day run out. These include some fuels, and chemicals used to make synthetic fertilizers and pesticides.
2) Farmers should reduce their dependence on non-renewable resources by:
   - Using renewable resources, e.g. energy from wind, sun and waves, and natural fertilizers like manure.
   - Using less fuel, synthetic fertilizers and pesticides.

Farming has Other Harmful Effects on the Environment

1) If farmers use too much fertilizer it can run into rivers — this can cause the death of many fish.
2) Pesticides can build up to toxic levels in predator animals.
3) Farming destroys the natural habitat of wildlife — to make way for crops. There are a few ways farmers can try to reduce the damage to wildlife:
   - Growing hedgerows between fields provides a valuable habitat for wildlife, especially insects, and can reduce soil erosion.
   - Farmers can set aside large areas of land that they don't use for farming.

Sustainable farmers can keep it up for longer...

This module's full of opportunities for examiners to get you to interpret data — and this page's no different. Start by learning what sustainable agriculture is, then go on to how it cn be done.

Module 2 — Agriculture and Food

Revision Summary for Module 2

Hmm... so this whole farming lark, what's that all about? Well, if you don't know, you haven't read this section properly, and your first task is to go back and read it all again. However, if you think you know your stuff, here are some delightful questions for you...

1) Name two products that come from gathered harvests.
2) Name two products that come from whole organism harvests.
3) Name two jobs an arable farmer might do.
4) What is horticulture?
5) What are the five stages in the chain of food production?
6) Suggest two uses of biotechnology to produce food.
7) Why is it important to regulate agriculture?
8) Name an organisation that supports part of the food industry and describe its role.
9) List three food products produced by plants.
10) What are the five stages in the life-cycle of a flowering plant?
11) What three things does a seed need to germinate?
12) What is the word equation for photosynthesis?
13) Describe one way that farmers can increase the amount of carbon dioxide in glasshouses.
14) Describe two ways that pests reduce crop yields.
15) How are potato yields measured?
16) Describe the properties of a 'good soil'.
17) What is hydroponics? Give two advantages of hydroponics.
18) Describe how tissue culture can be used to clone plants.
19) Give one disadvantage of cloning plants.
20) Name two products produced from animals.
21) What four factors affect animal growth?
22) Give one ethical concern about intensive farming.
23) Give a disadvantage of organic farming.
24) Describe the four stages involved in artificial insemination.
25) Suggest one benefit of artificial insemination compared to natural mating.
26) List two characteristics a farmer may look for in dairy cows that he wants to selectively breed.
27) What is the big advantage of using embryo transplants in cows?
28) Name two useful products from microorganisms.
29) Write down the word equation for aerobic respiration in yeast.
30) What is mycoprotein?
31) Write down the word equation for anaerobic respiration in bacteria.
32) Describe how microorganisms can be modified to produce useful proteins.
33) Why are aseptic techniques used in food production?
34) Describe one way that the population of microorganisms can be estimated.
35) Describe two quantitative testing techniques.
36) How does supply and demand affect the price of products?
37) Name two quality marks used in the food market and describe what they indicate.
38) What is meant by sustainable agriculture?

Module 2 — Agriculture and Food

Module 3 — Scientific Detection

The Work of Scientific Detectives

This module's all about the people and organisations that collect and analyse scientific evidence. Scientific detectives are involved in areas like law enforcement, environmental protection and consumer protection.

CSIs and Forensic Scientists Work in Law Enforcement

Crime scene investigators (CSIs) work closely with the police to record the details of a crime scene and collect any useful evidence. Forensic scientists look for and examine evidence that might be useful for solving crimes — they go to crime scenes, work in laboratories and appear as witnesses in court.

THE FORENSIC SCIENCE SERVICE is a government-owned company that supplies forensic science services to police forces in England and Wales, such as:

1) Identifying and analysing blood and other bodily fluids.
2) Identifying and comparing fibres, plant and animal materials.
3) Examining and comparing chips of paint and glass fragments.
4) Collecting and comparing fingerprints.
5) Comparing bullets found at crime scenes to those test-fired from suspects' guns.

Environmental Protection Officers Protect the Environment

Environmental protection officers collect and analyse evidence about the environment, and do work that protects and improves our environment. They work outdoors, in laboratories and in offices.

THE ENVIRONMENT AGENCY is a government-funded organisation that aims to make the environment a better place for people and wildlife — for example by:

1) Monitoring and improving air, water and soil quality.
2) Investigating and monitoring pollution.
3) Protecting wildlife.
4) Reducing the risk of flooding.
5) Protecting rivers and lakes from pollution.
6) Working with industries and businesses to reduce waste and pollution, and increase recycling.
7) Taking legal action against offenders who break environmental protection laws.

Public Analysts Work in Consumer Protection

Public analysts make sure that things used by the public meet certain safety standards and laws. This includes food, drinking water, toys, cosmetics and medicines. They work in local authorities and in organisations like the Food Standards Agency.

THE FOOD STANDARDS AGENCY is a government department that works to protect public health and interest about food — for example by:

1) Developing policies relating to food safety.
2) Providing advice to food manufacturers and suppliers.
3) Monitoring and improving food hygiene practices.
4) Testing foods to ensure they are safe to eat and labelled correctly.
5) Taking legal action against offenders who break food safety laws.

Science detectives — real-life Poirots...

So if you're a dab hand at science and murder in the dark a career as a scientific detective is for you.

Good Laboratory Practice

Good laboratory practice is needed to produce and analyse quality evidence that's valid and reliable. Of course you know all about good lab practice and follow it all the time at school but here goes anyway...

Good Laboratory Practice Increases Reliability

Good laboratory practice involves:

1) Using common practices and procedures — this means that different scientists and different laboratories perform experiments, like food testing in the same way.

2) Following health and safety regulations — like wearing protective clothing and disposing of chemical waste properly. This reduces the chance of samples being contaminated, which can invalidate results.

3) Checking and maintaining all equipment regularly — so the equipment is kept in good condition and is able to produce reliable measurements and results.

4) Training staff and offering continued professional development — so staff always know about the latest and best methods to use.

Results are reliable if an experiment is repeated by different people and the results stay the same.

Good laboratory practice

Bad laboratory practice

Public Labs are Accredited to Show Their Results are Reliable

1) Public laboratories can be accredited — in the UK by UKAS (United Kingdom Accreditation Service).

2) Accreditation shows that the lab meets internationally agreed standards, the staff should always work to a good level and the results produced should be reliable.

3) This means anyone looking at the results from an accredited lab can be pretty sure the experiments were carried out in a standard way and the results can be trusted.

Proficiency Tests are Used to Check Reliability

Proficiency testing compares test results from different labs to check they're reliable. Proficiency testing can be used to:

1) Check that a lab can do standard tests.
2) Check the performance of individual workers.
3) Check that instruments are working properly.
4) Look at new test methods.

In proficiency testing, different laboratories are sent samples of the same material to test. The reliability is checked by comparing results from the different laboratories — each lab is sent a sample of the same material so they should all get the same results.

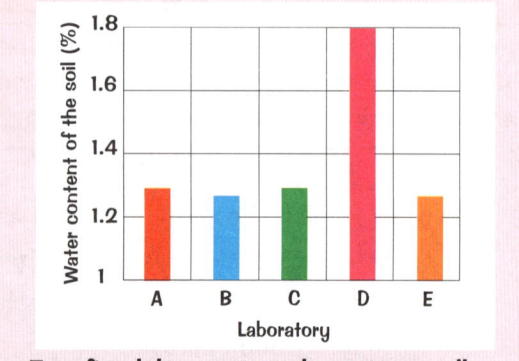

E.g. five labs were each sent a small sample of soil to test the water content. The results from lab D are different.

Tamoto techkup — a sauce of error...

There are loads of great reasons to learn good laboratory practice — passing your GCSE exams for one.

Module 3 — Scientific Detection

Visual Examination

Visual examination is a simple, quick and low-tech method of examining evidence. Scientific detectives often do this when they are on location — e.g. a crime scene investigator examining a crime scene, an environmental protection officer at a flood site, or a food hygiene inspector visiting a restaurant.

A Permanent Record is Made During a Visual Examination

When a scientific detective visually examines evidence, a permanent record must be taken for future use. This can be done by:
1) Writing a description.
2) Drawing pictures.
3) Taking photographs.
4) Recording video.

For example, crime scene investigators will take photographs and record a video of a crime scene before collecting any evidence. Written notes and sketches will also be made so there's a record of evidence even if the photos or video become damaged.

Visual Examination Involves Identifying Important Features

When you make a visual examination of evidence you need to look for important features. This means looking for features like the size, shape, colour and location of evidence. For example:

1) A tyre print found at a crime scene — look at the depth, width and pattern.

2) Chemical barrels found near a polluted river — look at the size, colour, any labels, if they are intact and how near they are to the site of pollution.

Objects and Images Can be Compared to See If They Match

1) Visual examinations are often used to compare pieces of evidence to see if they match. The important features are compared to see what points are the same or different, e.g. the pattern of a footprint found at a crime scene may be compared to the pattern of a footprint made by some suspects' shoes.

2) Often the best way to compare things is to record the size by measuring it with a ruler or tape measure, e.g. using a measuring tape that has 1 cm graduations, if the top of a footprint is half-way between the 25th and 26th graduation, it's approximately 25.5 cm long.

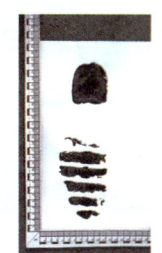

Shoe print from crime scene | Print from shoe 1 | Print from shoe 2

3) In some cases the area needs to be calculated.
4) Areas are calculated using formulas:
   - The area of a square or rectangle = length × width
   - The area of a circle = $\pi \times r^2$ (where r = radius)
5) E.g. a pool of blood found at a murder scene may have its area measured to see how much blood the victim lost, or the area of an oil slick may be measured to tell how bad the spill is.

Comparing footprints — mine's bigger than yours...

In the exam you could be asked to suggest what evidence might be collected from, e.g. a crime scene.

Module 3 — Scientific Detection

Light Microscopes

Light microscopes are used to see more detail than can be seen with the naked eye. Scientists use them all the time 'cause they're such handy little gadgets.

Learn the Parts of a Light Microscope and Their Purpose

1) **Eyepiece lens** — looked through to see the image and also magnifies the image.
2) **Tube** — light travels through the tube from the mirror, or built-in light, to the eye.
3) **Objective lens** — magnifies the image. Usually there are three different objective lenses (e.g. ×4, ×10 and ×40).
4) **Stage** — supports the slide.
5) **Clip** — holds the slide in place.
6) **Mirror or built-in light** — shines light through the slide so it can be seen more easily.
7) **Handle** — to carry the microscope with.
8) **Focusing knob** — moves the stage up and down to bring the image into focus.

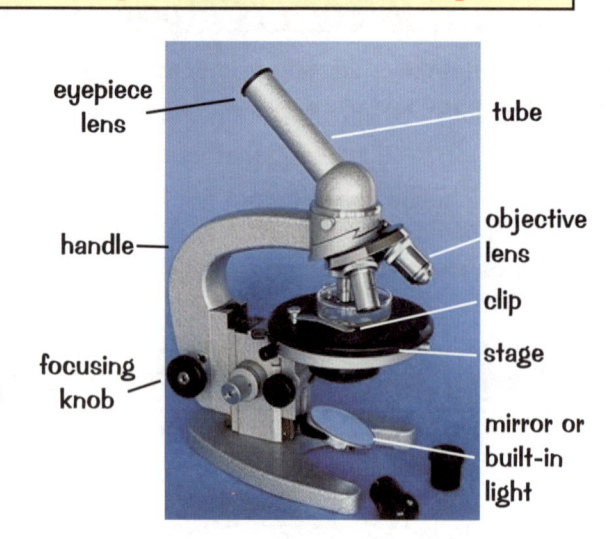

Microscopes Increase Magnification and Resolution

MAGNIFICATION

Microscopes use lenses to magnify images. This means they make them look bigger. E.g. if a lens has a '×10' magnification, it makes something look ten times bigger.

RESOLUTION

Microscopes also increase the resolution of an image. This means they increase the detail you can see. Using the focusing knob on a microscope, you can change the distance between the slide and the objective lens to make the details appear clearer.

Magnifying Power is Eyepiece × Objective Lens Magnification

You can work out the magnifying power of a microscope by multiplying the magnification of the eyepiece lens by the magnification of the objective lens:

Magnifying Power = Eyepiece Lens Magnification × Objective Lens Magnification

For example:

Eyepiece lens magnification	Objective lens magnification	Magnifying power
×10	×4	×40
×10	×10	×100
×10	×40	×400

A typical team of scientists at work with their jolly microscopes — remember, there's no 'I' in 'team'.

Revise this — and make light work of it in the exam...

You need to know all the parts of the light microscope and what they do. You also need to learn how to work out the total magnifying power. Bet you can hardly wait, you lucky things.

Module 3 — Scientific Detection

Light Microscopes

Light microscopes are used by scientists to examine all sorts of things — e.g. bacteria, hairs or soil. Seeing these things **bigger** and with **more detail** helps scientists to describe the main features.

Samples Need to be Prepared Before Investigation

You can't just slap a piece of evidence underneath a microscope — it has to be on a slide.

1) Use a pipette to put one drop of mountant (a clear, gloopy liquid) in the middle of the slide — this secures the sample in place. Sometimes water can be used.
2) Use forceps to place your sample on the slide (e.g. a hair for forensic examination).
3) Make sure the mountant is holding the sample in place, and it's positioned so it will all be under the cover slip.
4) Sometimes a drop of stain (e.g. methylene blue) is added to make the sample easier to see under a microscope.
5) Place the cover slip at one end of the sample, holding it at an angle with a mounted needle.
6) Carefully lower the cover slip onto the slide. Press it down gently with the needle so that no air bubbles are trapped under it.

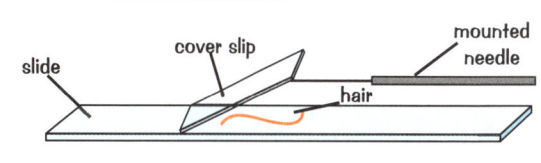

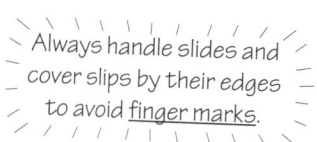

Always handle slides and cover slips by their edges to avoid finger marks.

You Will Have to Interpret Images from a Light Microscope

In the exam you may have to look at a drawing, sketch or photograph from a light microscope, together with a scale, and answer questions about the different features you can see. Here are two examples:

Example 1: This slide shows bacteria found in a sample of food collected by a food hygiene inspector.
1) First think about the main features of the slide.
   • Three different types of bacteria are shown — A, B and C.
2) Then count the numbers of different features.
   • There are — 3 of A, 4 of B and 3 of C.
3) Next measure all the main features.
   • A have a diameter of about 1 μm. B are about 1½ μm long and less than ½ μm wide. C are about 2 μm long and 1 μm wide.
4) Finally identify the features using reference samples.
   • A are cocci. B are bacilli. C are bacilli with flagella.

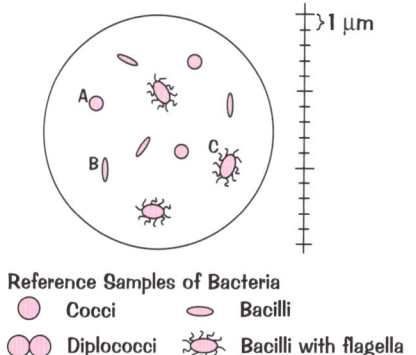

Reference Samples of Bacteria
○ Cocci   ⬭ Bacilli
⊙⊙ Diplococci   🦠 Bacilli with flagella

Example 2: This picture shows a bullet found by a crime scene investigator.

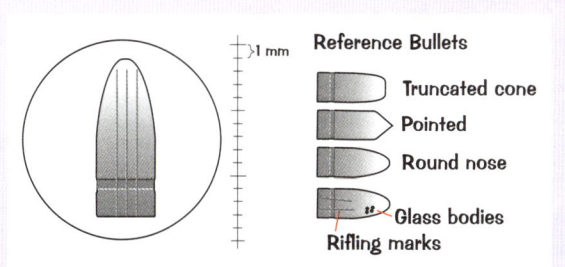

Reference Bullets
— Truncated cone
— Pointed
— Round nose
— Glass bodies
Rifling marks

1) Describe the main features.
   • rounded tip and lines along its length.
2) Count the numbers of features.
   • three straight lines.
3) Measure the main features.
   • about 12 mm long and 5 mm wide, and the lines are about 1 mm apart.
4) Identify the features using reference samples.
   • round-nosed bullet with rifling marks.

Cover, slip — I thought this was science, not cricket...

Don't worry too much about interpreting any images in the exam — all the info you'll need will be given to you. Make sure you read the scales correctly though, and don't forget to include any units.

Module 3 — Scientific Detection

Electron Microscopes

Electron microscopes are much more powerful than light microscopes — they can magnify samples up to two million times. But they're really, really, really expensive.

Electron Microscopes Use a Beam of Electrons Instead of Light

1) The sample material to be looked at is sliced into very thin sections and placed in a vacuum.
2) Some materials have to be processed before they're sliced — e.g. by freezing or coating them with a metal.
3) A beam of electrons is then fired at the sample.
4) The machine then creates an image called an electron micrograph on a computer screen.

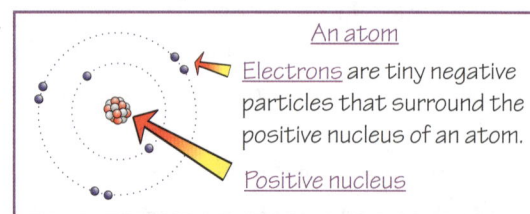

An atom
Electrons are tiny negative particles that surround the positive nucleus of an atom.
Positive nucleus

Electron Microscopes Show a Lot of Detail but are Expensive

Electron microscopes show loads more detail than light microscopes — they have a higher magnification. But they're much more expensive and preparing the samples is more difficult too.

Light microscope
- Lower magnification
- Less detail
- Cheap
- Simple sample preparation
- Can see colour

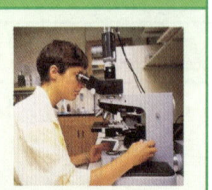

Electron microscope
- Higher magnification
- More detail
- Expensive
- Complex sample preparation
- Can't see colour

You Should Look for the Main Features on Electron Micrographs

You interpret a picture from an electron microscope (an electron micrograph) in the same way as a picture from a light microscope (see previous page). You describe, count and measure all the main features in the picture and then use a reference sample to identify each of them. Here's an example I made earlier:

This electron micrograph shows a sample of pollen from the back garden of a house that was burgled. Pollen are big enough to be seen under a light microscope but to identify the different types of pollen you need to use an electron microscope to get a detailed picture of the surface of the pollen.

1) Describe the main features — there are three different types of pollen.
2) Count the number of different features — 8 of A, 3 of B and 1 of C.
3) Make measurements of the main features — A is 7.5 µm, B is 15 µm, C is 17.5 µm
4) Use reference samples to identify the main features — A is daisy pollen, B is hornbeam tree pollen and C is cherry blossom pollen.

Reference pollen:
5 µm
Daisy
Hornbeam tree
Cherry blossom

EYE OF SCIENCE / SCIENCE PHOTO LIBRARY

Electron microscopes can't see colour — this picture has had some false colour added to make it easier to identify the different features.

Elect Ron Microscope — your Science Party candidate...

Electron microscopes are used to look at lots of different things, not just pollen — for example, forensic scientists use them for looking at paint layers from cars and really small fragments of glass.

Module 3 — Scientific Detection

Chromatography

Chromatography is used a lot in the chemical industry — it's a <u>method</u> for <u>separating chemical mixtures</u>. It's pretty useful in <u>forensics</u>, e.g. to <u>compare ink samples</u> to <u>detect forgeries</u> (fake documents).

Chromatography Can be Used to Detect Forgeries

Chromatography can be used to <u>analyse</u> loads of different <u>unknown mixtures</u>, e.g. identifying <u>banned</u> colours in <u>food</u>, a source of <u>pollution</u> in a lake, or the <u>inks</u> used in a suspected <u>forgery</u>. Most <u>inks</u> are made up of a <u>mixture of dyes</u>. A forged document will probably use <u>different ink</u> from an <u>official document</u> (so it'll contain a different mixture of dyes).

Here's how you do <u>paper chromatography</u>...

1) Draw a <u>line</u> across the bottom of a sheet of <u>filter paper</u> (in pencil).
2) Add <u>spots of ink</u> to the line at regular intervals.
3) Tape the top of the paper to a pencil and <u>hang</u> the sheet in a <u>beaker of solvent</u>, e.g. <u>water</u>.

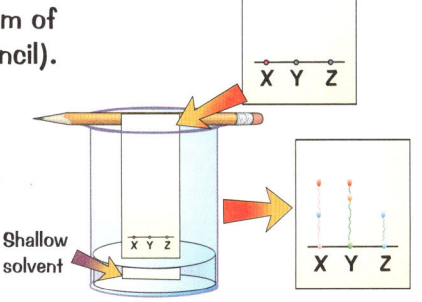

4) The <u>solvent</u> used depends on what's being tested. Some compounds <u>dissolve</u> well in <u>water</u>, but sometimes other (<u>non-aqueous</u>) solvents, like ethanol, need to be used.
5) The solvent <u>seeps</u> up the paper, carrying the ink dyes with it.
6) Each different dye will move up the paper at a <u>different rate</u> and form a <u>spot</u> in a different place.

> Thin-Layer Chromatography (TLC) is very similar to paper chromatography. The main difference is that instead of paper it uses a <u>thin layer of gel or paste</u> (e.g. silica gel) on a <u>glass plate</u>.

In both types of chromatography the dyes are separated by the movement of a <u>solvent</u> (called the <u>mobile phase</u>) through a <u>medium</u> of filter paper or gel (called the <u>stationary phase</u>). The dyes move between the mobile and stationary phases as they move up the paper (or gel). The different dyes move up at <u>different rates</u> because they have <u>different solubilities</u>. The <u>more soluble</u> dyes spend more time in the mobile phase and so move up the paper (or gel) <u>faster</u> than the less soluble ones, who spend more time in the stationary phase.

Unknown Compounds are Compared to Reference Material

You can <u>compare</u> the dyes in an unknown ink to the dyes in <u>known inks</u> to see which ink it is. The <u>pattern</u> of dye spots will match when two inks are the same (the spots will be the same distance apart).

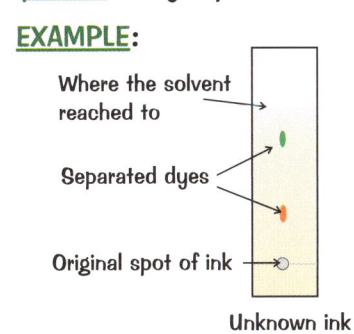

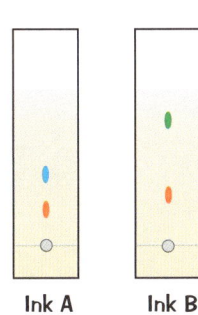

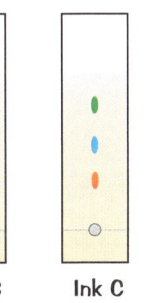

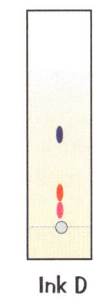

EXAMPLE:

Where the solvent reached to
Separated dyes
Original spot of ink

Unknown ink   Ink A   Ink B   Ink C   Ink D

You can see from the <u>position</u> of the <u>spots</u> on the filter paper that the unknown ink has the <u>same composition</u> as <u>ink B</u>.

> There's a <u>third type</u> of chromatography, <u>gas chromatography</u> — it's a bit more <u>high-tech</u> than the other two. It has a <u>greater separating power</u> and can be used to separate <u>very small samples</u> of gases, liquids or volatile solids (a solid that gives off a vapour). Gas chromatography tells you <u>how much</u> of a compound is present (<u>quantitative data</u>), in contrast to TLC and paper chromatography, which only tell you <u>which</u> compounds are present (<u>qualitative</u>).

Module 3 — Scientific Detection

Electrophoresis

Electrophoresis is another really useful technique — it lets you produce a DNA profile. DNA profiles can be used by the police to catch criminals who leave DNA at the scene of a crime, which is handy.

All Organisms Contain DNA

1) Remember that DNA is the genetic material found in every cell nucleus. It's a bit like a blueprint for how to make an organism.
2) DNA in humans is unique — no two humans in the world have the same DNA (with the exception of identical twins, who have identical DNA).
3) DNA can be extracted from small biological samples, e.g. hair, skin flakes, blood, semen and saliva, because they all contain cells.
4) Different species have different DNA (e.g. you can tell the difference between DNA from humans, DNA from cows and DNA from microorganisms).

DNA Profiling Can Pinpoint an Individual or Organism

1) DNA taken from a crime scene is usually compared with a DNA sample taken from a suspect.
2) It can also be used in paternity tests — to check if a man is the father of a particular child. This is because children inherit some of their DNA from their mum and some from their dad — so their DNA profiles will be similar to those of their parents.
3) It can also be used to test food — you can test whether a pork sausage contains any beef.
4) Whatever's being tested the method used is pretty much the same — good old electrophoresis.

HOW IT WORKS

1) First you have to extract the DNA from the cells in the blood, semen etc.
2) The DNA is then cut up into fragments.
3) This produces lots of different sized bits of DNA. The number of each size will be different for everyone and everything, because of the way it's cut.
4) The bits of DNA are suspended in a gel, and an electric current is passed through the gel.
5) Electrophoresis is a bit like chromatography (see p.49). The different fragments move at different rates based on their size and charge.
6) The DNA is then treated to make it visible.

Here's an example:
1) A drop of blood was found at a crime scene.
2) Forensic scientists ran a DNA profile for the blood.
3) They also ran DNA profiles for two suspects.
4) Matching DNA samples have the same pattern of bands. So here you can see that the blood from the crime scene has come from suspect 2.

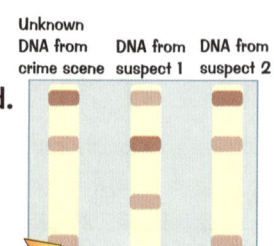

So the trick is — frame your twin and they'll never get you...

Identical twins have exactly the same DNA so they can't be identified from each other by DNA fingerprinting — the patterns produced would be the same. It's the perfect crime I tells ya.

Module 3 — Scientific Detection

Colour Matching

There are lots of tests that scientists use that involve colour changes — e.g. testing for acids and alkalis, or for the presence of particular chemicals.

Litmus Turns Red in Acids and Blue in Alkalis

Litmus is a dye that changes colour in acids and alkalis.
It is usually put onto filter paper so it can be used easily.

1) Blue litmus paper turns red in acids.
2) Red litmus paper turns blue in alkalis.

The litmus test is an example of a qualitative test.
If you use litmus paper to test a gas you wet it first, so the gas dissolves in the water on the paper.

A qualitative test tells you what is present, e.g. an acid or an alkali. A quantitative test tells you how much is present, i.e. it gives you a number.

Universal Indicator Measures pH

Universal Indicator is a useful combination of dyes that's used to estimate the pH of a substance.

1) pH is a measure of acidity.
2) The pH scale goes from 0 to 14.
3) If something is neutral it has pH 7.
4) Anything less than 7 is acid.
   Anything more than 7 is alkaline.

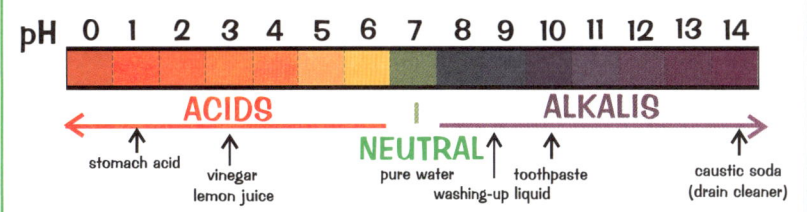

pH 0 1 2 3 4 5 6 7 8 9 10 11 12 13 14

← ACIDS | ALKALIS →
NEUTRAL
stomach acid, vinegar, lemon juice — pure water — toothpaste, washing-up liquid — caustic soda (drain cleaner)

Using Universal Indicator solution is an example of a semi-quantitative test — it tells you how acidic a substance is (gives you a number) but it isn't very precise (e.g. it can only tell you if something is pH 8 or pH 9, but not if it's pH 8.65 or pH 8.75).

For example, a public analyst tested some tap water samples using Universal Indicator solution. The samples changed the following colours:
The scientist compared the colours with a pH colour chart to find out:

1) Which samples were acidic — A and B
2) Which samples were neutral — C
3) Which sample was the most acidic — B
4) The pH of each sample — A was pH 6, B was pH 4 and C was pH 7.

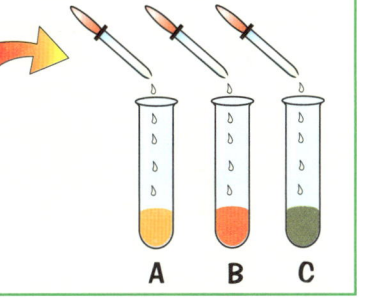

Colour Test Kits are Used to Test for Diabetes and Pregnancy

There are lots of different colour test kits that test for the presence of particular chemicals.
Two examples used in medical diagnosis are:

Clinisticks — used to test for glucose in urine. They contain a dye that changes colour if glucose is present. If glucose is present in your urine, it can mean that you have diabetes (a disease where your body can't regulate its blood sugar level properly).

Pregnancy tests — these contain a chemical that turns blue in the presence of HCG (a hormone found in your urine when you're pregnant). Different tests display the results in different ways — you might have to look for a blue line or a blue dot on the test strip.

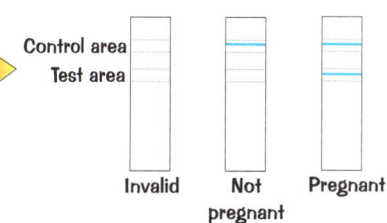

Control area
Test area
Invalid — Not pregnant — Pregnant

If you don't know these tests, urine big trouble...

People who have diabetes can also use a colour test kit to see how much glucose they have in their blood — they can then use this information to decide how much insulin to inject. Nifty.

Module 3 — Scientific Detection

Colorimetry

You can measure some colour changes more accurately using colorimetry. It can tell you how much of a chemical is in a solution — it gives you a number, so it's a quantitative test.

Colorimeters Measure the Intensity of Colour

Colorimeters are machines that measure colour. They work like this:

1) Light is passed through a solution.
2) Some of the light is absorbed by the solution — darker colours absorb more light than lighter colours.
3) The colorimeter measures the amount of light that passes through the solution and uses this to work out how much light was absorbed.
4) A reading of absorbance is given (the amount of light absorbed).
5) The higher the absorbance, the darker the colour of the solution.

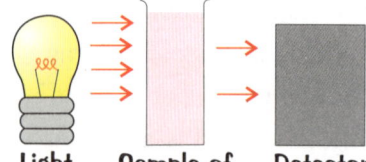

Samples are Compared to Standard Reference Solutions

You can work out the concentration of a coloured chemical in a solution by comparing it to reference solutions using a colorimeter. Reference solutions are samples of known concentration. To find the unknown concentration of a sample, you have to draw a calibration graph. Here's an example:

An environmental scientist needs to know the concentration of iron in a sample of polluted water.

1) The scientist mixes the water with a chemical that turns red when iron is present. The darker the red colour, the more iron is present.
2) She then puts a colourless solvent (pure water) in the colorimeter to set the meter to zero.
3) She measures the absorbance of some reference solutions and plots the absorbance readings against the known concentrations.
4) Next a line of best fit is drawn — this is a line that goes through, or as near to, as many of the points as possible.
5) Then she tests the polluted water in the colorimeter. It has an absorbance reading of 0.8.
6) She uses the calibration graph to work out the concentration of iron — she draws a line from the absorbance reading across to the line of best fit, then draws a line down and reads off the concentration.
7) The concentration of iron in the polluted water is just under 5 parts per million — 5 parts of iron in a total of 1 million parts.

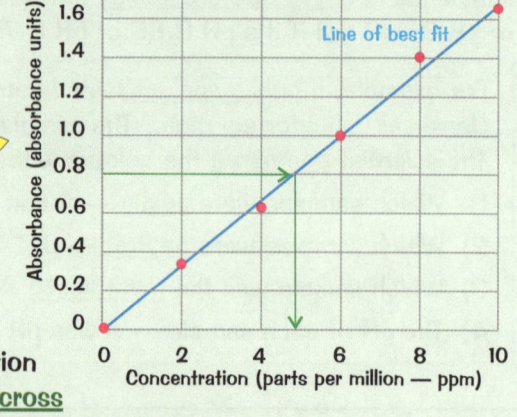

Colorimetry Takes a Long Time but the Results are Quantitative

Both colorimetry and colour matching have advantages and disadvantages —

Colour Matching	Colorimetry
• Qualitative or semi-quantitative • Quicker • Can be done anywhere • Cheaper	• Quantitative • Slower • Can only be done in a lab • More expensive

Did you hear about the biologist that had twins?*

You may have to draw a calibration graph in the exam, so make sure you understand how to use them.

Module 3 — Scientific Detection

*She called one Henry and the other Reference Sample.

Scientific Evidence

Being a good scientific detective is all about producing reliable evidence using good scientific practice all the way through — from collecting and analysing your samples to understanding what it all means.

Samples Need to be Collected and Stored Properly

When collecting samples for analysis you should:
1) Make sure they are representative.
2) Prevent them from deteriorating by storing them appropriately.
3) Avoid contamination of samples.
4) Prevent tampering with samples.

For example, when crime scene investigators are collecting evidence from a crime scene:
1) They stop unauthorised people entering the crime scene — to stop evidence being removed or planted.
2) They wear protective clothing — to prevent contamination.
3) They collect and store each piece of evidence separately — to stop items contaminating each other.
4) They collect representative samples — e.g. soil that is typical of the crime scene area.
5) They store evidence in sealed bags or pots — to stop it being contaminated or tampered with.

Scientists Use Standard Procedures for Analysis and Testing

Standard procedures are agreed ways of working (see p.44) — they're chosen because they are safe, effective and accurate methods to use. It means that everyone carries out an analysis in the same way. For example:

A food scientist is testing a sample of food to find out the types and numbers of bacteria it contains. The scientist uses standard procedures to prevent contamination, such as:

- Wearing gloves when handling the food sample and doing tests.
- Keeping the food sample in a container with a lid.
- Sterilising the sample bottle lid when it is removed.
- Sterilising all equipment before and after each use.
- Sealing and labelling bacterial culture plates.
- Not opening culture plates once they're sealed.

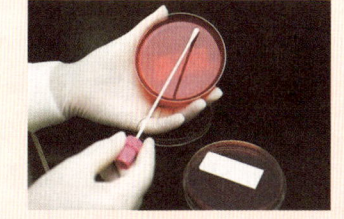

The scientist records all the standard procedures used, so that it's clear how the tests were performed.

Measuring Equipment is Calibrated Before Being Used

Scientists have to calibrate measuring instruments to check they're working properly. They do this by using the machine to measure standard reference materials. Before scientists use measuring instruments they check they're calibrated correctly. Surprise, surprise, here are some examples:

1) Top pan balance — place something of known mass on the balance and check the amount shown matches the known weight.
2) pH meter — the probe is added to a solution of known pH. If the machine shows an incorrect pH level the meter can be adjusted.

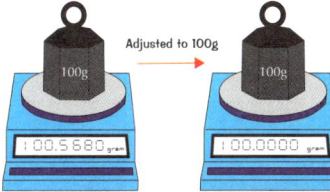

Avoid contamination — don't put red socks in with your whites...

It's pretty important to avoid contamination. E.g. if a suspect somehow got back into the crime scene then any evidence linking them to the crime might be invalid. The Police can't be sure what was originally there.

Module 3 — Scientific Detection

Scientific Evidence

Once they've analysed their evidence, scientific detectives need to present and interpret their data. Drawing conclusions from evidence can be tricky — e.g. you have to be careful not to accuse an innocent person of murder, the wrong company of polluting a river, or the wrong restaurant of food poisoning.

You Can Manipulate Data Using Calibration Graphs or Formulae

To make experimental data useful, it often has to be manipulated using calibration graphs (see page 52) or formulae. For example, suppose the Food Standards Agency is checking the fat content of a chocolate bar to make sure it's labelled correctly. To increase the reliability of the data, the average value of three bars is calculated. To find the average (or mean):

ADD TOGETHER all the data values and DIVIDE by the total number of values in the sample.

Chocolate bar	Amount of fat per 100 g
A	34.3 g
B	33.6 g
C	33.5 g

So, (34.3 + 33.6 + 33.5) ÷ 3 = 101.4 ÷ 3 = 33.8 g.

You Should Present Data in Tables, Graphs or Drawings

Scientific data should be presented in tables, graphs or in suitable drawings. They should have:

1) A title — explaining what data is shown.
2) Clear labels — e.g. the columns and rows of a table and the axes of graphs should be labelled.
3) Units of measurement — such as cm or ppm.

Table to show the percentage colourings in three sweet brands

Sweet brand	% colourings
A	18%
B	47%
C	35%

Bar chart to show the percentage colourings in three sweet brands

Evaluate Findings by Thinking About the Quality of Data

To objectively evaluate data you need to:
1) Identify outliers in data — results that don't seem right.
2) Explain the significance of findings — what is shown by the results.
3) Assess uncertainties — possible errors in the results.
4) Decide whether conclusions are valid and justifiable — is the data good enough to prove anything?

An environmental scientist is investigating arsenic pollution in a river. He thinks a factory on the river may be the source of the pollution. The scientist:

1) Collects water samples from different places on the river.
2) Uses colorimetry to test the samples for arsenic.
3) Manipulates his results using a calibration graph to find out the arsenic concentration of each water sample.
4) Presents his results in a graph and a pretty picture.
5) He evaluates his findings like this:

Drawing to show the relative levels of arsenic in the water at different places along a river

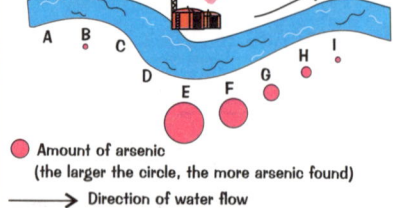

● Amount of arsenic (the larger the circle, the more arsenic found)
→ Direction of water flow

Graph to show the concentration of arsenic in the water at different places along a river

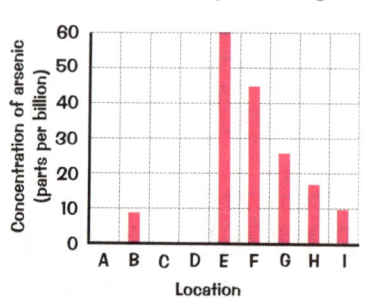

- He identifies outliers in the data — the water at location B contains arsenic even though it is before the factory.
- He explains the significance of his findings — the river water contains much more arsenic after the factory, so the factory might be the source of the pollution.
- He assesses uncertainties — he used standard procedures and believes his results are reliable and accurate, but there is the chance of a random error in measurement.
- He makes his conclusion — it seems likely that the factory is the source of the pollution (but there may be other explanations).

Module 3 — Scientific Detection

Revision Summary for Module 3

My favourite part of any section — the end. But it's not over yet for all you budding scientific detectives — there's still this beautiful revision summary to get through. If your memory fails you, then have a look back through the section. If you forget a single detail you might miss a vital clue in the investigation — and how else are you going to work out who did it?

1) Name two pieces of evidence a crime scene investigator may collect at a crime scene.
2) Name one organisation an environmental protection officer may work for.
3) Name two ways you can follow good laboratory practice.
4) What is meant by reliable results?
5) Give two ways you could make a permanent record during a visual examination.
6) When making a visual examination, what should you look for?
7) What is the job of the focusing knob on a light microscope?
8)* What is the magnifying power of a microscope with a ×10 eyepiece and a ×40 objective lens?
9) How would you secure a sample on a slide?
10) What can be used to identify specific features from a picture or photograph from a light microscope?
11) Give one way a sample for an electron microscope may be processed before being sliced.
12) Which type of microscope, light or electron, gives a higher magnification?
13) How are dyes separated in chromatography?
14) What type of chromatography gives you quantitative data?
15) Name two kinds of samples that DNA can be extracted from.
16) What is the name of the method used in DNA profiling to separate the DNA pieces?
17) Which type of colour test substance, litmus or Universal Indicator, gives a purely qualitative result?
18) Give two examples of colour test kits used in medical diagnosis.
19) What does a colorimeter measure?
20) Are the results from a colorimetry test qualitative, semi-quantitative or quantitative?
21) What are standard procedures?
22) How would you calibrate a piece of measuring equipment?
23) List two ways you could present data.
24) What is meant by an outlier in a set of data?

* Answers on p.132.

Module 3 — Scientific Detection

Module 4 — Harnessing Chemicals

Chemistry and Symbols

Chemists do love their symbols. There are two different kinds of symbol on this page — symbols to show different chemicals and symbols to show danger.

Elements Can be Represented by Words or Symbols

Writing out the full names of chemicals all the time can be quite time consuming. That's why scientists invented chemical symbols — they mean you can write down any element using only one or two letters. Symbols come in really handy sometimes — and there's plenty of them throughout the section.

The symbols for all the elements can be found in the periodic table. Unfortunately for you, there's a list of 11 that you're expected to know. Make sure you can give the element's chemical symbol if you're told its name (and vice versa).

| C — Carbon | Ca — Calcium | Cl — Chlorine | Mg — Magnesium | H — Hydrogen |
| K — Potassium | N — Nitrogen | Na — Sodium | O — Oxygen | S — Sulfur | Zn — Zinc |

A Formula Shows All the Atoms in a Compound

Compounds are substances that contain more than one kind of atom bonded together.

1) Carbon dioxide is a compound — it contains carbon atoms and oxygen atoms joined together.
2) In fact, every molecule of carbon dioxide contains 1 carbon atom and 2 oxygen atoms.

There you go... a molecule of carbon dioxide — one carbon atom and two oxygen atoms.

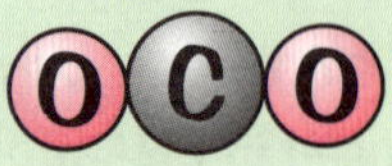

3) Using chemical symbols, this would be: CO_2
Easy.

An atom of carbon... ...and two atoms of oxygen.

You Need to Learn the Common Hazard Symbols

Lots of chemicals can be bad for you or dangerous in some way.
These hazard symbols might just save your skin...

Oxidising
Provides oxygen which allows other materials to burn more fiercely.
Example: Liquid oxygen.

Highly Flammable
Catches fire easily.
Example: Petrol.

Toxic
Can cause death either by swallowing, breathing in, or absorption through the skin.
Example: Hydrogen cyanide.

Harmful
Like toxic but not quite as dangerous.
Example: Copper sulfate.

Corrosive
Attacks and destroys living tissues, including eyes and skin.
Example: Concentrated sulfuric acid.

Irritant
Not corrosive but can cause reddening or blistering of the skin.
Examples: Bleach, children, etc.

H_2O, CO_2, FBI, DVD, WLTM, GSOH...

You might come across these symbols outside chemistry lessons as well... Think about the news — there's always lots of talk about levels of CO_2 in the atmosphere. Similarly, hazard symbols don't just crop up in the lab — you see them in workshops, and in your home on bottles of cleaning chemicals.

Laboratory Equipment

The kind of equipment you use in chemistry lessons at school is the same kind of stuff that professional scientists working in a hospital or a forensic lab might use. Make sure you know about these bits of kit...

Equipment for Measuring Out and Transferring Chemicals

Burette
Used to dispense a measured volume of liquid. Their most common use is in titrations (see p.64). Always read the volume from the bottom of the meniscus — get your head and eyes down to that level. You should fill pipettes and burettes to about 3 cm above the desired amount, then carefully drop the level down to what you need. It's also important to clamp the burette properly so that it doesn't fall over and smash.

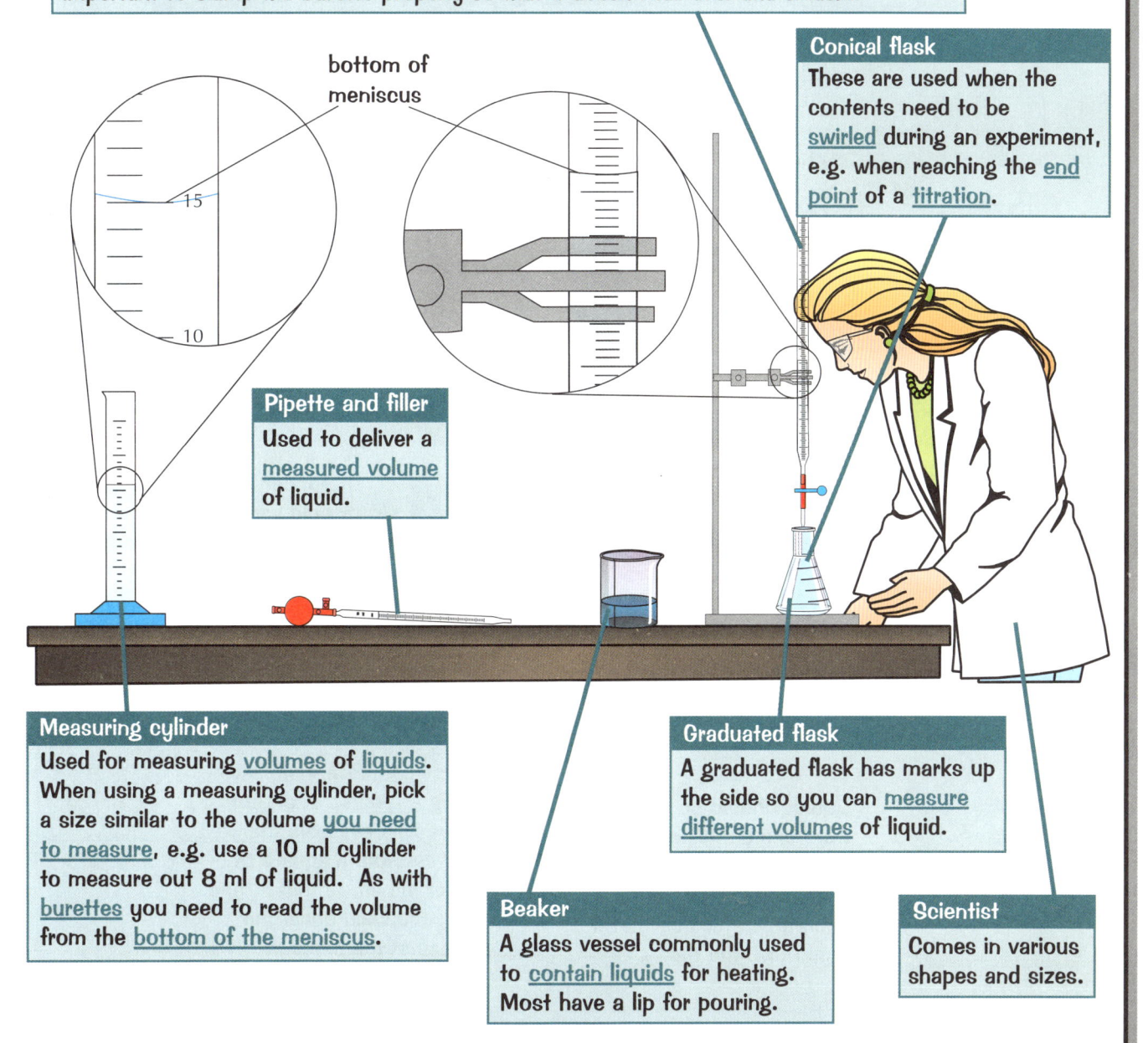

bottom of meniscus

Conical flask
These are used when the contents need to be swirled during an experiment, e.g. when reaching the end point of a titration.

Pipette and filler
Used to deliver a measured volume of liquid.

Measuring cylinder
Used for measuring volumes of liquids. When using a measuring cylinder, pick a size similar to the volume you need to measure, e.g. use a 10 ml cylinder to measure out 8 ml of liquid. As with burettes you need to read the volume from the bottom of the meniscus.

Graduated flask
A graduated flask has marks up the side so you can measure different volumes of liquid.

Beaker
A glass vessel commonly used to contain liquids for heating. Most have a lip for pouring.

Scientist
Comes in various shapes and sizes.

Everyone has a degree these days — even flasks...

Most of this kit should look pretty familiar to you — it's the kind of stuff you use in pretty much all experiments to measure out chemicals, carry out chemical reactions and that kind of thing. Scientists in hospitals and labs will use the same apparatus in their research — it's all really standard equipment.

Module 4 — Harnessing Chemicals

Laboratory Equipment

Here are some more bits of chemistry equipment that scientists might have to use in their day-to-day work. You should be able to recognise these and know what they're used for.

You Need to Know the Names of These Pieces of Equipment

A magnetic stirrer contains a magnet that is spun around by a motor. A flask sits on the stirrer and a small plastic-coated magnet or "flea" is put inside. As the magnet spins, the flea spins with it, stirring the contents of the flask.

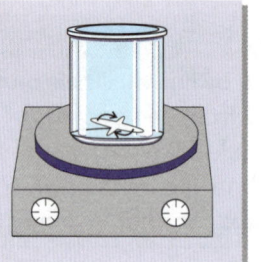

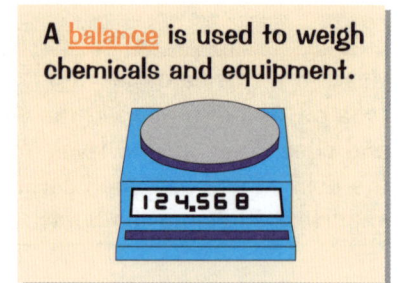

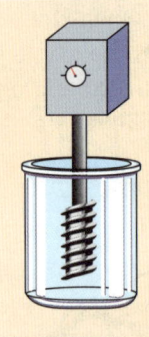

A balance is used to weigh chemicals and equipment.

An immersion heater is an electrically heated metal coil (like the element in a normal kettle). It's dipped into a liquid to heat it from the inside.

A heating mantle is an electric device for heating round-bottomed flasks. It's used to heat flammable liquids because it's safer than using a Bunsen burner.

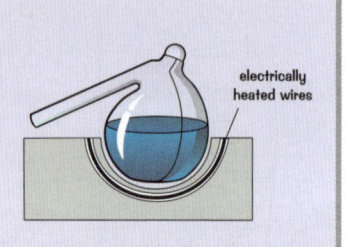

A hot water bath is used when chemicals need to be kept at a constant temperature. An electric heating element at the base is connected to a thermostat so that the water in the bath is always at the same temperature.

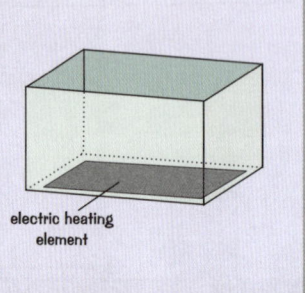

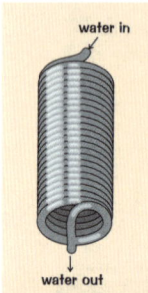

A heating/cooling coil is a coil of copper or glass tubing. Hot or cold water flows through the coil. It can be immersed in a liquid, or fitted into a tube so that a gas can flow over it.

Liquids should be poured from one container to another using a glass rod. The liquid should be poured carefully so that it runs down the rod.

Solids can be transferred using a funnel. If one of these isn't available then you can fold a square of paper in half, unfold it, and pour the solid down the crease in the paper

There's more to lab equipment than safety goggles...

In the exam, you could be asked to name any of the pieces of equipment on this page. Or, you could be asked to describe how you'd transfer solids or liquids between containers without spilling them. Make sure you learn the details on this page carefully or you'll just be spilling easy marks away.

Module 4 — Harnessing Chemicals

Acids and Alkalis

Chemicals (including those in your kitchen, or garden shed) can be acidic, basic or neutral.

pH is a Measure of Acidity or Alkalinity

The acidity (or alkalinity) of a chemical is measured on the pH scale.

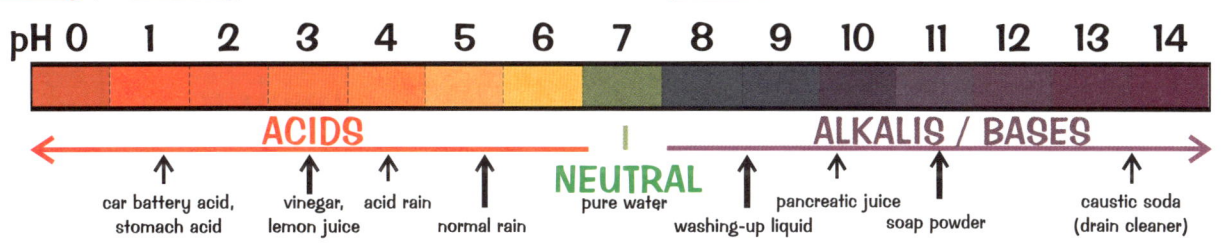

pH 0 1 2 3 4 5 6 7 8 9 10 11 12 13 14

← ACIDS | ALKALIS / BASES →

NEUTRAL
- car battery acid, stomach acid
- vinegar, lemon juice
- acid rain
- normal rain
- pure water
- pancreatic juice
- washing-up liquid
- soap powder
- caustic soda (drain cleaner)

1) An acid is a chemical with a pH below 7.
2) Alkalis or bases are chemicals with a pH above 7. Ammonia gas is a base. Metal oxides and hydroxides are also bases (the ones that dissolve are alkalis).

   Alkalis are just soluble bases.

3) Solutions that are neither acids nor alkalis are called neutral, and have a pH of exactly 7.
4) A solution's pH can be measured with a pH meter (like the one on the right) or by adding Universal Indicator to the solution. Universal Indicator is a combination of dyes, and gives the colours in the pH scale shown above.

The Reaction of an Acid with an Alkali is Called Neutralisation

Alkalis react with acids to form neutral ionic compounds called salts, plus water.

This equation is really worth remembering:

ACID + ALKALI → SALT + WATER

E.g. hydrochloric acid + sodium hydroxide → sodium chloride + water
     (an acid)   (an alkali)   (a salt)

This kind of reaction is called neutralisation, since the pH of the salt solution is 7.

The Name of the Salt Depends on What's Reacting

The name of the salt produced in a neutralisation reaction depends on the acid and alkali used. Take a look at the three examples below.

1) Hydrochloric acid (HCl) produces chloride salts. Here's an example:

   hydrochloric acid + sodium hydroxide → sodium chloride + water

2) Nitric acid (HNO_3) produces nitrate salts. Have a look at this:

   nitric acid + magnesium oxide → magnesium nitrate + water

3) Sulfuric acid (H_2SO_4) produces sulfate salts. You guessed it — here's another example:

   sulfuric acid + calcium hydroxide → calcium sulfate + water

The first part of a salt's name comes from the alkali. The second part comes from the acid.

Neutral — I don't mind either way...

Neutralisation is a reaction that you'll find popping up time and time again — it doesn't just go on in the lab or during large-scale chemical synthesis. Taking indigestion tablets causes a neutralisation reaction in your stomach. The tablets contain a base that neutralises excess hydrochloric acid.

Module 4 — Harnessing Chemicals

Reactions of Acids

You also need to know about the reactions of acids with metals and metal carbonates. These reactions are similar to the ones on the previous page — they each make a salt.

Metal + Acid → Salt + Hydrogen

Here's another one of those really important equations. Learn it...

ACID + METAL → SALT + HYDROGEN

You can see this reaction happening if you put a small volume of hydrochloric acid into a test tube and add a piece of magnesium. You'll see little bubbles of gas rising to the surface — that's hydrogen.

Naming the salt is done in exactly the same way as on the previous page. Just follow these rules...

Hydrochloric acid will always produce chloride salts
- hydrochloric acid + magnesium → magnesium chloride + hydrogen
- hydrochloric acid + zinc → zinc chloride + hydrogen

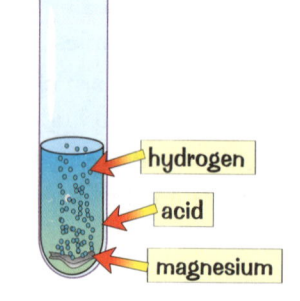

Sulfuric acid will always produce sulfate salts
- sulfuric acid + magnesium → magnesium sulfate + hydrogen
- sulfuric acid + zinc → zinc sulfate + hydrogen

The first part of the salt's name is the metal. The second part comes from the acid.

Metal Carbonate + Acid → Salt + Water + Carbon Dioxide

Again, this reaction produces a salt, but this time, carbon dioxide and water are produced too.

ACID + METAL CARBONATE → SALT + WATER + CARBON DIOXIDE

Writing equations for these reactions is just as easy as it was for acid-metal reactions.

Hydrochloric acid will always produce chloride salts
- hydrochloric acid + magnesium carbonate → magnesium chloride + water + carbon dioxide
- hydrochloric acid + zinc carbonate → zinc chloride + water + carbon dioxide

Sulfuric acid will always produce sulfate salts
- sulfuric acid + magnesium carbonate → magnesium sulfate + water + carbon dioxide
- sulfuric acid + zinc carbonate → zinc sulfate + water + carbon dioxide

Examples of salts — salt on my chips, salt on my crisps...

If you've ever descaled a kettle, you'll know that there's a lot of fizzing. That's actually an acid (the descaler) reacting with a carbonate (the scale) — the fizzing is the carbon dioxide escaping.

Module 4 — Harnessing Chemicals

Solutions

When it comes to solutions, concentration is really important. So pay attention...

A Solution Means a Solute is Dissolved in a Solvent

1) A solution is a mixture of a solute and a solvent.
2) The solute is the thing (often a solid) being dissolved, and the solvent is the liquid it dissolves in. For example, when you dissolve salt in water, salt is the solute and water is the solvent.
3) The concentration of a solution tells you how much solute is dissolved in a volume of solution. There's an easy formula:

$$\text{concentration} = \frac{\text{mass (of solute)}}{\text{volume (of solution)}}$$

Remember: $1 \text{ cm}^3 = 1 \text{ ml}$
1 litre = 1000 cm^3 (or 1000 ml)

4) Concentration is usually measured in: g/cm^3 — grams of solute per cm^3 of solution.
   or: g/litre (g/l) — grams of solute per litre of solution.

Making a Solution of Known Concentration

Scientists working in labs (e.g. in hospitals or chemical analysis centres) need to know how to make solutions of particular concentrations. You might have to do this too. So here's how...

Example: Describe how to make 0.5 litres of sodium chloride solution with a concentration of 30 g/l.

First, the theory: You know that one litre of solution would contain 30 g of sodium chloride. So 0.5 litres of solution would need half this amount — 15 g.

Next, the practice: First things first — check whether there are any hazards associated with sodium chloride, and make sure you take any necessary precautions.
1) Add 15 g of sodium chloride (the solute) to a graduated flask.
2) Add some distilled water (the solvent) to the flask and then stir until all the sodium chloride has dissolved.
3) Add some more distilled water to make up the volume to the exact amount you need (0.5 litres).

One important thing here... you mustn't start with 0.5 litres of water and add 15 g of sodium chloride. This will make the total volume a little bit more than 0.5 litres. Which isn't what you want.

Use the Concentration Formula to find Mass

You can rearrange the concentration formula to get: **mass = concentration × volume**

Example: How many grams of sodium chloride are in 400 cm^3 of a 0.25 g/cm^3 solution?
Answer: Mass = concentration × volume = 0.25 × 400 = **100 g**

Example: How many grams of calcium chloride are in 2000 cm^3 of a 4 g/litre solution?
Answer: Be very careful with the units — you've got volume in cm^3, but concentration in g/litre. So, convert everything to litres first. Volume = 2000 cm^3 = 2 litres. This means that... mass = concentration × volume = 4 × 2 = **8 grams**

Learning this takes some mental concentration...

With orange squash, you can just keep adding water till it tastes about right. You can't do that in GCSE Applied Science — because the solution you're making might well be poisonous, and because the concentration has to be spot on, not just 'about right'. So measure everything very carefully.

Module 4 — Harnessing Chemicals

Making Insoluble Salts

Insoluble chemicals are chemicals that don't dissolve. They're often made by mixing two solutions. In the lab, you do the mixing in a beaker. In industry, you might use a container the size of a house.

Insoluble Chemicals are Produced by Precipitation Reactions

1) In a precipitation reaction, two solutions are mixed together to form an insoluble product.
2) The insoluble substance formed is called a precipitate — it turns the solution cloudy because it doesn't dissolve (this usually happens pretty quickly).
3) Suppose you want to make some lead iodide — a bright yellow, insoluble solid. One way to do this is to mix together a solution of lead nitrate and a solution of sodium iodide. Put one solution into a small beaker and carefully add the other solution. Give it a good stir to make sure it's all mixed together. A yellow substance will form immediately — this is the precipitate.

lead nitrate + sodium iodide → lead iodide + sodium nitrate

Another example of a similar reaction is the reaction between solutions of barium chloride and sodium sulfate, which produces insoluble barium sulfate:

barium chloride + sodium sulfate → barium sulfate + sodium chloride

Notice how the different bits of the reactants basically just "swap partners".

Insoluble Chemicals are Separated by Filtering and Drying

Filtering   Because it's insoluble, the precipitate can be separated from the solution by filtering.

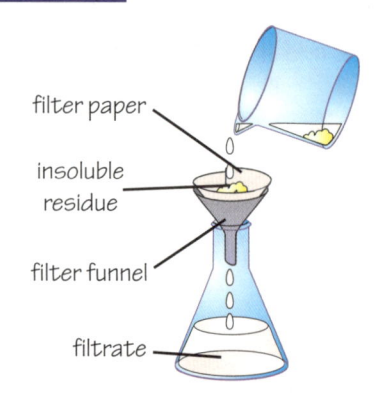

1) Put a folded piece of filter paper into a filter funnel and stick the funnel into a conical flask.
2) Pour the contents of the beaker into the middle of the filter paper. (Make sure that the solution doesn't go above the filter paper — otherwise some of the solid could dribble down the side.)
3) Swill out the beaker with distilled water and tip this into the filter paper — to make sure you get all the product from the beaker.
4) The solid left in the filter paper is the insoluble residue (lead iodide).
5) The liquid that collects in the conical flask is called the filtrate.

Rinse and dry   Chances are, the lead iodide on your filter paper will be a bit impure (and soggy).

1) First you need to rinse the contents of the filter paper with distilled water to make sure that all the soluble compounds have been washed away. Then just scrape the lead iodide onto some fresh filter paper. 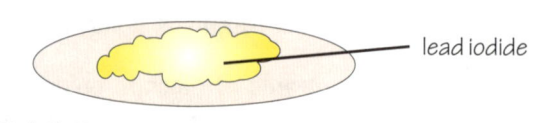
2) Now you need to dry it. There are a couple of different ways of drying the product. It can simply be left on the side to dry, but many industrial laboratories have ovens used for drying chemicals, and others have desiccators — pots that contain chemicals that absorb the water from other substances.

Precipitation — I thought that was rain...

Insoluble chemicals are pretty simple to separate out — just remember to filter, rinse and dry.

Module 4 — Harnessing Chemicals

Making Soluble Salts

If the salt you're trying to get is soluble, then there's no way you're going to be able to separate it from the solution using filtration. This time, you need to use evaporation and crystallisation...

Add an Excess of the Insoluble Reactant

This technique involves mixing a soluble substance with an insoluble one to give a soluble product.

1) Because your product is soluble, you can't separate it out by filtration. But, you can use filtration to remove any insoluble reactant left over — that's the idea here.

2) For example, soluble copper chloride is made by reacting insoluble copper oxide with hydrochloric acid. Just add copper oxide powder to some hydrochloric acid.

copper oxide + hydrochloric acid → copper chloride + water
base + acid → salt + water

3) You must add an excess of the insoluble reactant (i.e. more than could possibly react). Keep adding more and stirring until no more will react (you must see bits of copper oxide sitting on the bottom of your beaker).

4) Because you've added excess copper oxide, you know all the hydrochloric acid must have reacted. This is dead important — you'd have a helluva job removing any unreacted acid.

5) But you can easily remove the excess copper oxide — by filtration (see page 62). Collect the filtrate (the liquid that passes through the filter paper) in an evaporating basin. This will be a pure solution of copper chloride. It's a good idea to rinse the residue and filter paper with distilled water to make sure you've got all the product.

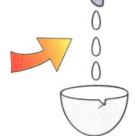

Evaporation and Crystallisation Produce a Solid Product

Your next job is to get rid of the solvent (water) — this will leave you with pure, solid copper chloride.

> If some of the water is removed, so that there is not enough to dissolve the product completely, solid particles called crystals will form — this is known as crystallisation. Removing more water causes more solid to form. The solid left after the water has gone is called the residue.

1) If you're in a hurry to make your product then you should put the evaporating basin containing the solution onto a tripod and gauze and remove all the water by heating with a Bunsen burner, as shown in the diagram.

2) This way, the water will have evaporated in a few minutes and when the basin is cool enough to pick up, you can collect the result of all your hard work — but, be warned, it may not look very impressive.

3) This is because most crystals grow quite slowly, so a rapid crystallisation like this produces lots of little crystals.

4) If you want to make really big crystals then you'll have to wait for the water to evaporate slowly.

Look into my crystal ball — you'll be making a solid product...

Water naturally turns into a vapour and drifts away — this is called evaporation, and should be a pretty familiar process to you. For example, it's the way puddles of rainwater disappear. Water evaporates faster at higher temperatures — the hotter it is, the faster those puddles of rain will disappear.

Module 4 — Harnessing Chemicals

Titrations

Here's the last method you'll need to know about for producing a pure salt.
It's the trickiest of the lot — this is because your reactants and product are all soluble.

Titrations Can Be Used to Produce a Pure Salt

When your reactants and product are all soluble, you can't get rid of anything by filtering.
And it's no good adding an excess of anything — you'd struggle to get rid of it later.
So what you have to do is add just the right amount of each reactant. For example,
in an acid-base titration, you need to add just the right amounts of acid and alkali.

1) When a soluble salt is made by reacting an acid with an alkali, it's important that exactly the right amount of each is added — so that the final solution contains only the salt and water.

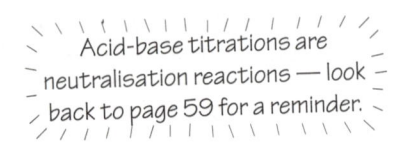

Acid-base titrations are neutralisation reactions — look back to page 59 for a reminder.

2) This is done by carefully mixing a suitable acid and alkali until the pH is 7. You can use the titration apparatus shown in the diagram.

3) For example, if you wanted to produce sodium chloride, you could titrate hydrochloric acid with sodium hydroxide:
hydrochloric acid + sodium hydroxide → sodium chloride + water

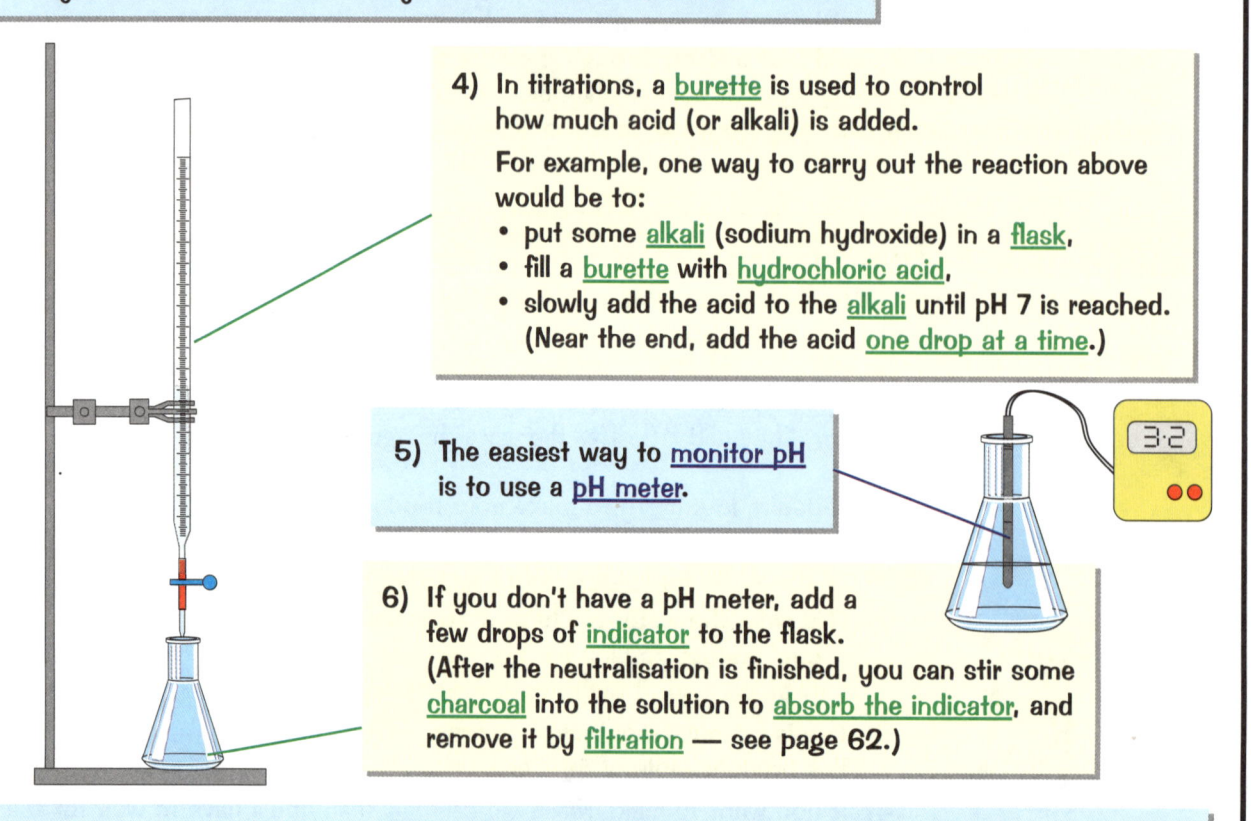

4) In titrations, a burette is used to control how much acid (or alkali) is added.
For example, one way to carry out the reaction above would be to:
- put some alkali (sodium hydroxide) in a flask,
- fill a burette with hydrochloric acid,
- slowly add the acid to the alkali until pH 7 is reached. (Near the end, add the acid one drop at a time.)

5) The easiest way to monitor pH is to use a pH meter.

6) If you don't have a pH meter, add a few drops of indicator to the flask.
(After the neutralisation is finished, you can stir some charcoal into the solution to absorb the indicator, and remove it by filtration — see page 62.)

7) Crystals of the pure salt can be made by evaporating the water in the same way as on page 63.

Pure salt — I prefer salt and vinegar...

There are different ways of obtaining your solid product depending on whether it's soluble or insoluble. You could be asked to describe how you'd obtain a sample of a certain salt, and you'd need to be able to choose the right method depending on its solubility. So make sure you've got this stuff learnt.

Module 4 — Harnessing Chemicals

Organic and Inorganic Chemicals

Chemicals are often put into different 'families' — where chemicals in the same family have something in common. Two big families that are often used are 'inorganic chemicals' and 'organic chemicals'.

Chemicals Can be Inorganic Or Organic

INORGANIC
1) Most inorganic chemicals don't contain carbon.
2) Things like rocks, minerals and ores (things that have never lived) are made up of inorganic chemicals.
3) For example, iron (from iron ore) and potassium sulfate are both obtained from rock — and both of these chemicals are inorganic.

ORGANIC
1) Most chemicals that contain carbon are organic chemicals.
2) Organic chemicals often come from living things, or from things that were once living. For example, coal and crude oil formed over millions of years from the remains of dead plants, so chemicals obtained from coal or crude oil are generally organic.

So if a chemical contains no carbon, it's inorganic and probably comes from 'never-lived' material. If it contains carbon, it's probably organic and derived from something that is (or was once) alive.

'Derived from' just means 'obtained from'. E.g. an organic chemical like ethene (C_2H_4) isn't actually contained in crude oil, but it's made from a chemical that is.

Organic Chemicals are Divided into Smaller Groups

There are loads of different kinds of organic chemical...

1) **Hydrocarbons** are compounds that only contain hydrogen and carbon. So, if the formula for a compound only has Cs and Hs in it, you'll know it's a hydrocarbon, e.g. ethene (C_2H_4).

Organic chemicals can also be divided into separate families based on their functional groups. Functional groups are characteristic groups of atoms that make all members of a family react in a similar way. You can often recognise functional groups from a compound's chemical formula.

2) **Alcohols** have an -OH functional group.

—O—H

Alcohols all have the same general formula — $C_nH_{2n+1}OH$. For example, an alcohol with 2 carbons has the formula C_2H_5OH.

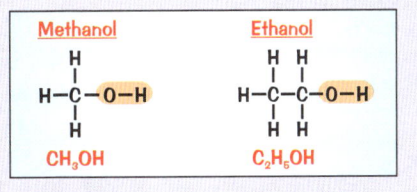

Methanol — CH_3OH
Ethanol — C_2H_5OH

Don't write CH_4O instead of CH_3OH — it doesn't show the functional -OH group.

3) **Carboxylic acids** have a -COOH functional group.

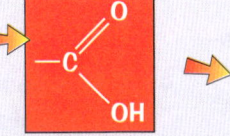

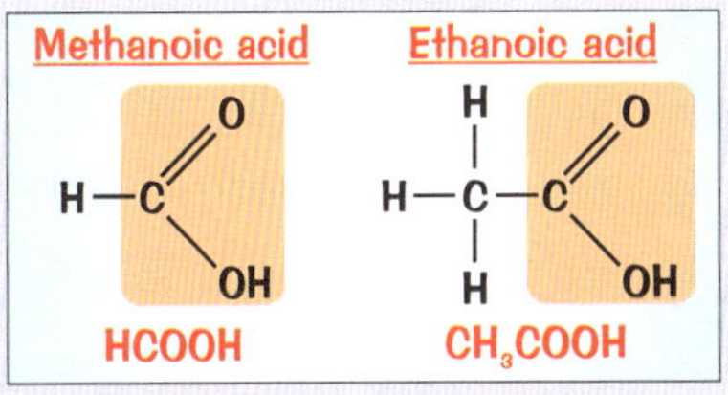

Carboxylic acids are often called organic acids (as they're built around carbon atoms).

Methanoic acid — HCOOH
Ethanoic acid — CH_3COOH

Organic chemicals — useful and tuneful...

Not to confuse you or anything, but... many chemicals contained within living things don't contain any carbon and aren't organic (e.g. HCl in stomach acid). So, just because a chemical is part of an animal or a plant doesn't immediately make it organic — it's whether it's built around carbon atoms that's vital.

Module 4 — Harnessing Chemicals

Making Esters

Esters are organic chemicals used to flavour sweets, as fragrances for perfumes, as hardening agents in paints, as solvents for glues and nail varnish... yep, they're important. And so is how they're made.

Esters are Made in a Non-Aqueous Solution...

1) The reaction between an alcohol and a carboxylic acid produces an ester and water.
2) The carboxylic acid is dissolved in the alcohol with which it is being reacted — this is a non-aqueous solution (aqueous solutions have water as the solvent).

...by Heating an Alcohol and a Carboxylic Acid Under Reflux

Making esters can be slow (no good for companies, whose aim is to make stuff as quickly as possible). But you can speed the reaction up using a catalyst (see p.69). However, this introduces other problems.

1) The reaction takes place very slowly at room temperature — it would take several days to complete.
2) It would be impossible for a company to make a profit at this rate so a catalyst (usually sulfuric acid) is added, and the reacting mixture is heated to speed things up (see page 69 for more information on reaction rates).
3) As the reaction mixture gets hot, the chemicals begin to evaporate. This is where the problem lies — the vapours will escape. However, this can be easily solved by fitting the flask with a special tube known as a condenser.
4) Any vapours that enter the condenser are cooled by water flowing around it. This turns them back into a liquid and they fall back into the flask — this is called reflux.

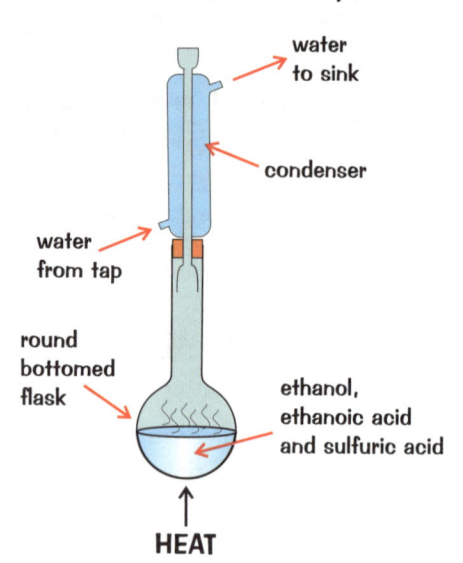

Esters are Purified by Distillation

you know which chemical is currently boiling from the temperature of gases entering the condenser

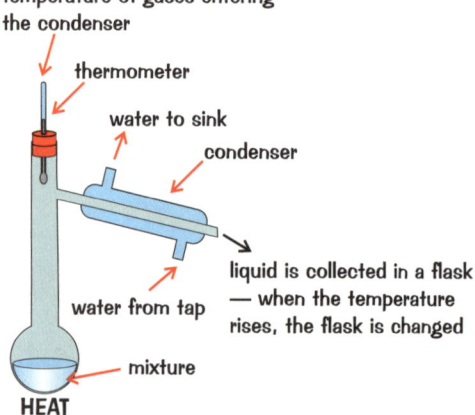

1) In this reaction, not all the acid and alcohol react (that's just the way it is with some reactions). So after refluxing, there'll be ester, water and some unreacted alcohol and carboxylic acid in the flask.
2) To get a pure ester, the mixture is separated by distillation. Distillation involves heating the mixture, and relies on the fact that different chemicals have different boiling points.
3) At lower temperatures, the vapour given off contains mostly the chemical with the lowest boiling point.
4) This vapour condenses (becomes liquid) in a condenser, and is collected — this is the distillate.
5) By repeating this process at different temperatures, you can collect the different chemicals in the mixture as they boil off.

Refluxing — I think relaxing sounds better...

... and you can relax once you've learnt this. You might not have heard of esters before, but there's nothing too tricky about them. You mix an alcohol with a carboxylic acid using reflux to cool any vapours, and then purify what you've produced using distillation. Don't worry, it's all on this page.

Module 4 — Harnessing Chemicals

Mixtures

Loads of everyday things are mixtures of some kind, where one substance is finely dispersed in another. Remember... there are no chemical bonds between the different substances in a mixture.

An Emulsion is a Cloudy Mixture of a Liquid in Another Liquid

1) An emulsion is made from tiny droplets of one liquid dispersed in another, where the liquids won't dissolve in each other, e.g. oil and water.
2) Emulsion paint, mayonnaise and some salad dressings are examples of emulsions.
3) Emulsions are cloudy, and will eventually separate if left for a while. E.g. you can make salad dressing from olive oil and vinegar. You shake it up to make a cloudy liquid then drench your lettuce with it. But if you come back to it tomorrow lunchtime, the oil will have separated out and be sitting on top of the vinegar, so you'll have to shake it up again.
4) Emulsions like mayonnaise have emulsifiers (or emulsifying agents) added to them. Emulsifiers are molecules that help the two liquids in an emulsion mix together and stop them from separating out.

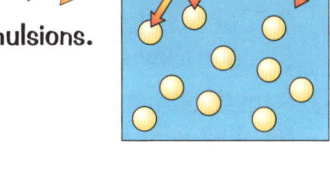

A Suspension is a Cloudy Mixture of a Solid in a Liquid

1) A suspension is a mixture of small solid particles (e.g. silt) mixed in with a liquid (e.g. water).
2) The particles don't mix completely — they don't dissolve and there are no chemical bonds.
3) The particles aren't small enough to stay floating around — eventually they will separate, and the solid particles gradually settle to the bottom.
4) Muddy water is a great example of a suspension — get a jar of muddy water, leave it on the side for an hour or two, and you'll end up with clear water with a layer of sludge at the bottom. Nice.
5) Ice cream is another example — tiny crystals of ice suspended in cream.

Some Solids can also be Mixtures

Many everyday solids that you use will also be mixtures.
1) Drugs like cold medicines often contain a mixture of pain killers and decongestants (amongst other things).
2) Many cosmetics (like lipstick) are solid mixtures.
3) In the exam they might ask you to interpret information about the composition of different mixtures.

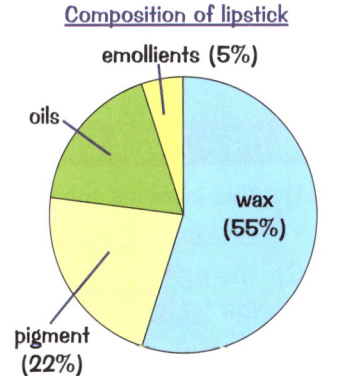

Composition of lipstick
- emollients (5%)
- oils
- wax (55%)
- pigment (22%)

Example Use the pie chart on the right to answer these questions.
1) What is the percentage of oils in lipstick? (Ans: 18%)
2) What percentage of lipstick is wax and pigment? (Ans: 77%)

Who knew lunch involved quite as much chemistry...

An excuse to eat ice cream — tell your parents it's ground-breaking research into particulate bonding in suspensions. They wouldn't want to hinder your educational development now would they...

Module 4 — Harnessing Chemicals

Rates of Reaction

It's important to be able to control and measure the rate of chemical reactions, especially in industry.

Reactions Can Go at All Sorts of Different Rates

The rate of a chemical reaction is how fast the reactants are changed into products — the reaction is over when one of the reactants is completely used up.

1) One of the slowest is the rusting of iron (it's not slow enough though — what about my little Mini).
2) A moderate speed reaction is a metal (like magnesium) reacting with acid to produce a gentle stream of bubbles.
3) A really fast reaction is an explosion, where it's all over in a fraction of a second.

Three Ways to Measure the Speed of a Reaction

The speed of a reaction can be observed either by how quickly the reactants are used up or how quickly the products are formed. It's usually a lot easier to measure products forming. The rate of reaction can be calculated using the following equation:

$$\text{Rate of Reaction} = \frac{\text{Amount of reactant used or amount of product formed}}{\text{Time}}$$

There are different ways that the speed of a reaction can be measured. Have a look at these three:

1) PRECIPITATION

1) This is when the product of the reaction is a precipitate, which makes the solution cloudy.
2) Observe a marker through the solution and measure how long it takes for it to disappear.
3) The quicker the marker disappears, the quicker the reaction.

2) CHANGE IN MASS (USUALLY GAS GIVEN OFF)

1) Measuring the speed of a reaction that produces a gas can be carried out on a mass balance.
2) As the gas is released, the mass disappearing is measured on the balance.
3) The quicker the reading on the balance drops, the faster the reaction.

3) THE VOLUME OF GAS GIVEN OFF

1) This involves the use of a gas syringe to measure the volume of gas given off.
2) The more gas given off during a given time interval, the faster the reaction.
3) A graph of gas volume against time could be plotted to give a rate of reaction graph.

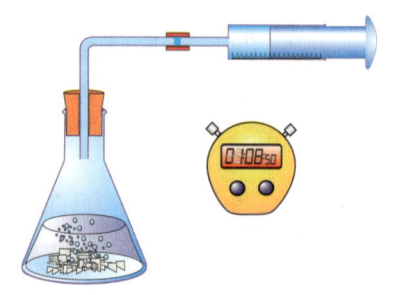

OK have you got your stopwatch ready *BANG!* — oh...

Each method has its pros and cons. The mass balance method is only accurate as long as the flask isn't too hot, otherwise you lose mass by evaporation as well as by the reaction. The first method isn't very accurate, but if you're not producing a gas you can't use either of the other two. Ah well.

Module 4 — Harnessing Chemicals

Rates of Reaction

As well as being able to measure the rate of a reaction, scientists in the chemical industry also need to know the things that affect the rate. This helps them get the optimum conditions for a reaction.

The Rate of a Reaction Depends on Four Things

1) **TEMPERATURE** — As the temperature increases, the rate of reaction increases.
2) **CONCENTRATION** — Increasing the concentration of the reactants increases the rate of reaction.
3) **SIZE OF PARTICLES** — The smaller the particles the faster the rate of reaction.
4) **CATALYST** — Using a catalyst increases the rate of reaction. A catalyst is a substance that changes the speed of a reaction, without being changed or used up in the reaction.

That's all very nice. But in the exam they might ask you to interpret rate-of-reaction data. Read on...

Changing Any of These Factors Alters the Reaction Rate Graph

The graph opposite shows how the speed of a particular reaction varies under different conditions. The quickest reaction is shown by the line that becomes flat in the least time.

1) Graph 1 represents the original reaction.
2) Graphs 2 and 3 represent the reaction taking place quicker, but with the same initial amounts. The same amount of product is produced overall — just at a quicker rate.
3) The increased rate could be due to any of these:

   a) increase in temperature
   b) increase in concentration
   c) solid reactant crushed up into smaller bits.
   d) catalyst added

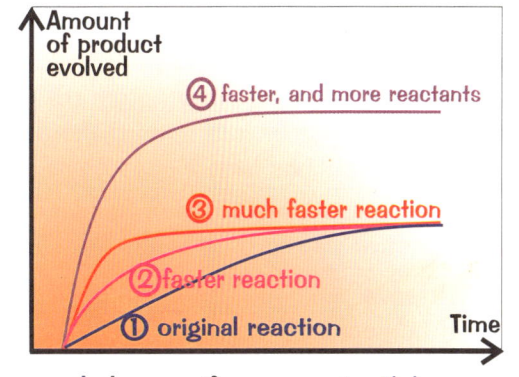

4) Graph 4 produces more product as well as going faster. This can only happen if more reactant(s) are added at the start. Graphs 1, 2 and 3 all converge at the same level, showing that they all produce the same amount of product, although they take different times to get there.

You've Got to be Able to Read Rate of Reaction Graphs

In this experiment, some marble chips were added to a solution of hydrochloric acid. Any gases released were collected using a gas syringe (see p.68) — the volume was recorded every 10 s.

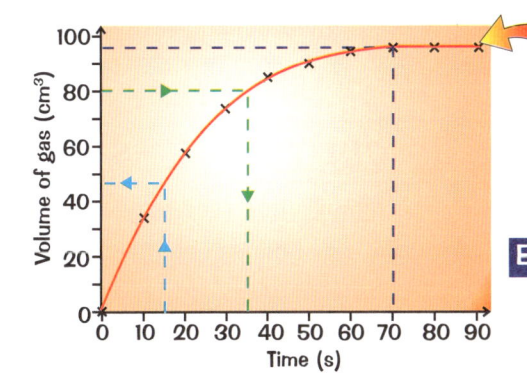

The results are shown on this graph.

1) The total volume of gas produced is 96 cm³.
2) The reaction had stopped after about 70 s — no more gas was produced (so the line on the graph was horizontal).

Examples: How much gas was produced after 15 s? 47 cm³
How long did it take to produce 80 cm³ of gas? 35 s
Easy.

My reactions slow down when it gets hot — I get sleepy...

Reaction rate depends on four factors. See if you can list them without looking — they're all on this page. These are really important to scientists planning an industrial process.

Module 4 — Harnessing Chemicals

Sustainable Chemical Production

Sustainability is about making the most of the Earth's natural resources.

There are Many Ways to Make a Process More Sustainable

All industrial chemical processes require raw materials and a source of energy. For example, glass is produced from limestone, sand and soda by heating them in a furnace. If any of the raw materials, or the fuel for the furnace, were to run out, then glass could no longer be made this way.

Processes can be made more sustainable by:

1) Reducing waste — if raw materials are used more efficiently they will last longer (see below).
2) Using less energy — so that less fuel is needed.
3) Using raw materials or fuels from renewable (won't run out) sources — e.g. plants.

> **Example:**
> Most plastics are currently manufactured using crude oil. But there is a limited supply of oil in the Earth, so new plastics are being made from renewable crops such as corn.

Atom Economy and Yield Affect Sustainability

1) In some reactions, every atom (or nearly every atom) of reactant goes into forming the useful product. These reactions have a good atom economy.
2) This means there's little or no waste, and it's a really effective way to use the Earth's resources. 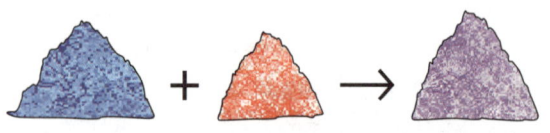
3) However, some processes form a useful product along with some not-so-useful by-products. If you can't use the by-products, they're waste. These reactions have a bad atom economy. 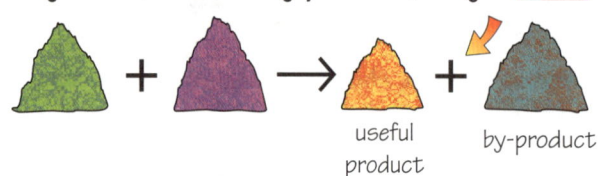
4) Reactions with a bad atom economy are bad for industry — all that waste needs to be dealt with. And they're bad in terms of sustainability — a lot of raw materials are being used to make rubbish.
5) There's also another issue... In a lot of reactions, not all the reactants actually react, or some of the product is lost along the way. Usually, the yield (actual mass of product formed) is less than the theoretical yield (what you'd expect to get).
Percentage yield can be calculated using this formula:

$$\text{percentage yield} = \frac{\text{yield}}{\text{theoretical yield}} \times 100$$

Catalysts Can be Used to Save Money and Resources

1) One way of making a reaction happen more quickly is by increasing the temperature (see page 69).
2) But this requires energy, meaning you have to burn more fuel, making the reaction less sustainable.
3) But catalysts also speed up reactions. So if you can find a catalyst for your reaction, you can use a lower temperature — saving all those fuel costs and Earth's resources.

Efficiency — covering sustainability in just one page...

A low yield can be a problem — but sometimes it's possible to reuse your raw materials, making it less of an issue. However, atom economy is always important. Bad atom economy means more waste.

Module 4 — Harnessing Chemicals

Chemical Purity

Chemical suppliers often sell several varieties of a chemical, each with a different degree of purity. Because the purification process is expensive, very pure chemicals cost more than ones with impurities.

There are Three Main Degrees of Purity

1) Technical grade — the cheapest and least pure of the three. Chemicals of technical grade purity are widely used in many industrial-scale processes in order to save money.
2) Laboratory grade — purer, but more expensive than technical grade. Most small-scale reactions performed in school or research laboratories use chemicals at this grade of purity.
3) Analytical grade — the purest of the three. Since it is the most expensive, it is only used when very high purity is essential.

Some Industries Need to Use Purer Chemicals Than Others

An industrial chemical company may buy thousands of tonnes of a chemical every month. It couldn't sell its product at a competitive price and still make a profit if it was paying extra for a higher degree of purity than was necessary.

A company that manufactures chemicals such as fertilizers, pesticides, and weedkillers can use cheaper, lower-purity chemicals. Very small quantities of impurities won't cause them to work less well, or be harmful to people.

Some chemical products have to be very pure for safety reasons. Pharmaceutical companies buy high-purity chemicals to make their drugs. It wouldn't be safe for people to take the drugs unless they know exactly what chemicals are present. It's cheaper for a company to buy very pure chemicals as reactants than to perform expensive purification processes on their product.

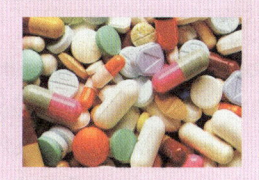

Some products won't work properly unless they're very pure. Chemicals used in the microelectronics industry have to be of the highest purity grade possible. Even very tiny amounts of an impurity can cause products such as computer processors and memory chips to fail.

It's Important to Choose the Right Grade of Purity

Example: Benzoic acid is used to make a preservative added to food and drink products to extend their shelf life. It's also used to make an ester to provide the fragrance for air fresheners. It's available as technical grade for £14 per kilogram and analytical grade for £71 per kilogram. Which grade do you think is used to manufacture the food preservative? Which would be used to make the air freshener?

Answer: The air freshener is made from the cheaper chemical to keep down the cost of production. The preservative uses the more expensive chemical to ensure that the product is safe for consumption.

Technical grade — really difficult revision...

The purer a substance, the more it costs. This means that companies usually have to weigh up things like cost, safety and effectiveness with the profit that they'll make when choosing which grade of chemical to use. There'd be no point buying the purest chemical when a cheaper one would do the job.

Module 4 — Harnessing Chemicals

Industrial Production of Chemicals

We use loads of chemicals like fertilizers every year — and they don't just fall off the back of a wagon (unless you're following a horse box). No, they have to be made — often on a massive scale.

Some Chemicals are Produced on a Large Scale...

There are certain chemicals that we produce thousands and thousands of tonnes of every year. Chemicals that are produced on a large scale are called bulk chemicals — ammonia, sulfuric acid and sodium hydroxide are three examples.

1) The chemical industry needs to make a fair bit of ammonia to meet the demand. It is used in many industrial processes, including the production of fertilizer and nitric acid.

2) You may have come across sulfuric acid in the lab at school. You might not think it, but sulfuric acid also has to be produced on a very large scale. As well as being a lab chemical, it has many other uses.

3) Another chemical produced on a very large scale is sodium hydroxide — again you may have come across this in the lab, but it's also used to make things like soap and ceramics.

4) Phosphoric acid is also a bulk chemical. Its uses include making detergents and fertilizers.

...And Some are Produced on a Smaller Scale

Some chemicals aren't needed in such large amounts — but that doesn't mean they're any less important.

1) Chemicals produced on a smaller scale are called fine chemicals. Examples of these include drugs, food additives and fragrances.
2) Many fine chemicals require several different production stages.

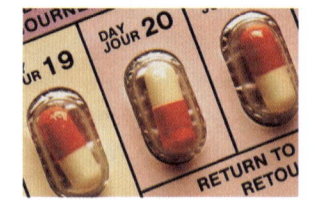

There are Lots of Different Jobs in the Chemical Industry

There are hundreds of different job opportunities in the chemical industry, because of the wide range of different chemicals that are produced. Some examples of jobs include:

1) Research and development — somebody has to come up with ideas for new products. Chemical products are the result of an extensive programme of research and development. Research scientists figure out what to make and how to make it, and they also make sure the product is safe. Some also work on making existing products better.

2) Designing or refining the manufacturing process — making several tonnes of a chemical on an industrial scale is quite different from making a small sample in a lab. Scientists are employed to make sure that large scale processes are safe, efficient and actually make money.

3) Quality control — most companies employ scientists to ensure that the quality of the product is consistent and up to scratch.

4) Environmental science — processes and products could potentially damage the environment. Many companies employ scientists to minimise this risk.

Fine chemicals — by appointment to Her Majesty, The Queen...

The chemical industry is a pretty complex thing. It's all well and good to have all the bits of equipment that are needed, but you wouldn't get very far without also having all the different people in their jobs. Many scientists, researchers and developers are there to make the whole process work smoothly.

Module 4 — Harnessing Chemicals

Scaling Up

Large-scale industrial processes are based on methods developed on a small scale in labs.

Industrial Scale Reactions Require Special Equipment

In a laboratory there's a limited set of equipment to choose from. Much more thought has to go into the choice of equipment when designing an industrial plant. Much of the equipment is specially built.

When planning large-scale reactions, chemical engineers have to consider:

1) The container to use for the reaction. Laboratory scale reactions are usually done in glass flasks. Industrial-scale reactions need large, strong vessels, so they often use metal containers.

2) How to get the chemicals in and out of the reaction vessel. When you're working in a lab you can pour liquids from one flask to another. In a large industrial plant this can't be done. Chemicals are transferred between containers through pipes.

3) The methods of heating or cooling. Many reactions need to be kept at a high temperature to speed them up. The reaction vessel will be fitted with a heater and a thermostat to control the temperature. Water flowing around the outside of a vessel will carry heat away and cool it, but to get things even colder, a refrigeration system has to be fitted.

4) How to mix the chemicals. When large volumes of liquids are being reacted together it's important to make sure that they're well mixed. Any chemicals that don't mix won't be able to react. Blades or paddles can be fitted inside the reaction vessel and are turned by a motor.

After a Reaction has Finished the Product has to be Purified

An industrial plant will contain some equipment for separating the product from any unreacted chemicals and unwanted products. Common separation techniques include:

1) Filtration — to remove a solid from a liquid.

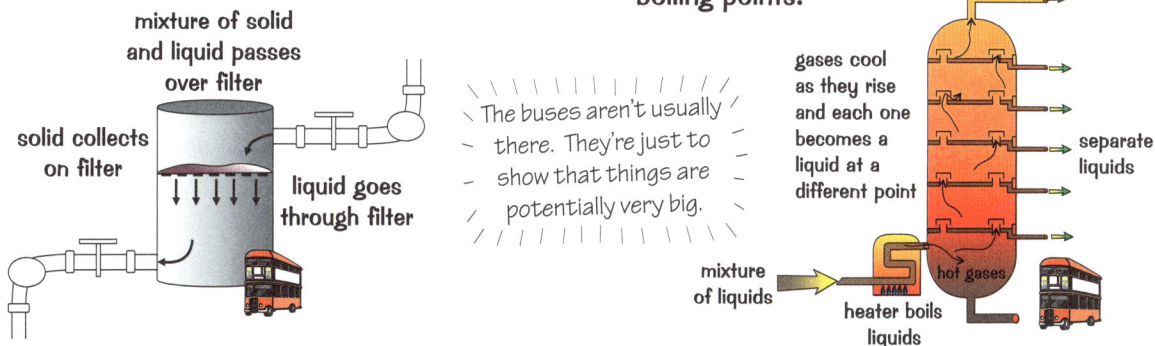

2) Distillation — to separate liquids with different boiling points.

The buses aren't usually there. They're just to show that things are potentially very big.

Scaling up — isn't that what kettles do...

Aye, chemical companies often make things on an absolutely massive scale. They might well carry out the same reactions as you'd do in a chemistry lesson, only with tonnes of reactants rather than grams.

Module 4 — Harnessing Chemicals

Planning Chemical Synthesis

Before a company begins building a plant to produce a chemical, a lot of research has to be done to find the best way of making the product. There are many factors that need to be considered.

There's Usually More Than One Method to Make a Chemical

To make a particular chemical, scientists have to decide which reaction (or sequence of reactions) to use. Often there are several methods that can be used to make the same product. Before deciding which to use, scientists will want to know many things, such as...

1) The yield and atom economy — if these are low the reaction will be wasteful and expensive.

2) The cost of materials — some reactions may require more expensive chemicals or equipment than others.

3) How much energy will be needed — maintaining high temperatures can burn a lot of fuel, which is expensive and creates pollution.

4) What the waste products are — if a reaction produces dangerous waste it can be very expensive to dispose of or to recycle.

Ethanol is an important industrial chemical used as a fuel, a solvent, an antiseptic, and in the production of many other substances. It's currently produced either from plant sugars (using crops such as corn or sugar cane) or from ethene (which comes from crude oil). Chemical industries prefer the second method because it gives a higher yield and generates no waste products. However, in the future, as crude oil gets more expensive, the cost of ethene may make it unprofitable to use this method.

Cost and Environmental Impact are Important

When chemical engineers are designing an industrial plant to manufacture a chemical they will look for ways to reduce the energy needed to run the process. This is important for two reasons:

1) Using less energy means the company's fuel bills are reduced.
2) Burning less fuel creates less pollution and makes the process more sustainable.

The energy efficiency of a process can be improved by recycling waste heat.

Example:

1) In the Contact process, sulfur dioxide and oxygen are reacted together to produce sulfur trioxide.
2) The reaction is exothermic — meaning that heat energy is given out, so the temperature rises.
3) This heat can be captured by heat exchangers and then used to heat other reactions — instead of burning extra fuel. Cunning.
4) The opposite of an exothermic reaction is an endothermic reaction. These take in heat energy from the surroundings and are shown by a fall in temperature.

Industrial plants — mechanical trees...

There are loads of factors that influence a company's choice of method when producing chemicals. Even though you produce the same thing, different methods use different amounts of energy, produce different waste products, cost different amounts and give different yields. Plenty to be weighed up.

Module 4 — Harnessing Chemicals

Testing Formulations

Companies are constantly testing their products in quality control procedures to make sure that they're performing as they should and are safe for customers to use.

Testing is an Important Part of Quality Assurance

To make sure that a product is always of the same quality, regular reports about its purity, chemical composition and physical properties will be written based on the results of tests. If the properties of a substance are not the same each time the tests are done, engineers will investigate why this is, and may make changes to the way in which the product is made. This process of checking and improving the manufacturing process is called quality assurance.

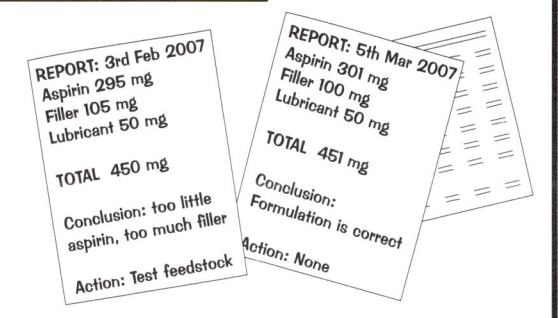

REPORT: 3rd Feb 2007
Aspirin 295 mg
Filler 105 mg
Lubricant 50 mg
TOTAL 450 mg
Conclusion: too little aspirin, too much filler
Action: Test feedstock

REPORT: 5th Mar 2007
Aspirin 301 mg
Filler 100 mg
Lubricant 50 mg
TOTAL 451 mg
Conclusion: Formulation is correct
Action: None

Testing is Necessary for Consumer Protection

There are laws in nearly all countries to ensure that when you buy a chemical product you're getting what you pay for. Companies must test their products to make sure they do the job they're meant to do and are not going to harm consumers. For example, washing powders will be tested to see if they clean clothes properly and also to make sure that they do not cause any skin reactions.

Example: Two new chemicals, A and B, designed to be stain removers are put through a series of tests.

	chemical A	chemical B
stains removed (out of 100)	98	43
skin reactions in patch tests	some irritation	no reactions

Neither of the chemicals is very suitable. A isn't safe (it causes skin irritation) and B isn't very effective (it removes less than half of the 100 different stains). However, chemical A could be used in industrial cleaners that are used by trained staff wearing protective gloves.

Products Must Meet National and International Standards

1) As well as companies testing their own products, there are national laboratories whose job it is to check that chemical products meet certain standards set by governments.

2) National laboratories randomly test chemical products that are on sale, and if they find a company is not meeting standards then that company will have to stop selling its product and can be fined a lot of money. To make sure this doesn't happen, companies do their own testing to prevent any of their products that don't comply with the standards from going on sale.

3) Cadmium compounds were widely used in red and yellow paints. In 1998 the United Nations began setting limits on how much cadmium was allowed.

4) Some of these standards are enforced within one country, and some are international standards that all companies must comply with. For instance, different countries around the world allow different levels of lead additive in petrol. Many countries have banned lead altogether. So some petrol formulations are illegal to sell in one country but not in another.

Checking and improving — sounds like revision to me...

It might seem like a lot of time and effort, but it's really important that products are regularly checked and tested, especially if they contain chemicals that could be harmful in the wrong amounts.

Module 4 — Harnessing Chemicals

Regulating the Chemical Industry

Some chemicals are harmful to people, animals or plants — and so care must be taken when working with them. People who work with chemicals have to be aware of lots of rules about how to handle them.

Governments Regulate Use, Storage and Transportation

To protect us and the world around us, governments create laws and guidelines for people working with chemicals. These are designed to:

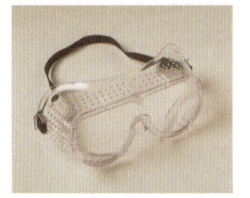

1) Limit our exposure to dangerous chemicals.
2) Prevent dangerous chemicals from getting into the environment.
3) Reduce the chance of accidents happening.
4) Minimise the damage caused if an accident does happen.

The Health and Safety Executive Regulates Chemical Industries

The Health and Safety Executive (HSE) is an organisation set up by the UK government to protect people's health at their school or workplace. One of its jobs is to make sure that when people work with chemicals, they protect themselves and the public from any danger. The HSE checks that safety rules are being followed by any company that works with chemicals. For example:

1) Companies producing agrochemicals (fertilizers and pesticides for farms).
2) Pharmaceutical companies producing medicines.
3) Oil refineries making petrol, diesel and other chemicals from crude oil. 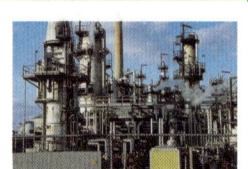
4) Companies producing household chemicals such as cleaning products.
5) Laboratories in schools, colleges and universities.

Laws Require People to Work Safely with Chemicals

Inspectors from the HSE visit places where chemicals are used. They check that chemicals are being handled and stored properly. During a visit an inspector may do several things.

1) If there are any minor safety problems, an inspector can give advice on how to work even more safely.

2) If an accident has been reported, an inspector can carry out an investigation to find out what caused the accident and what needs to be done to stop the same accident happening again in the future.

3) If there are serious safety problems, or laws about how to use or store certain chemicals are being broken, an inspector can force the company to stop working straight away. They will only be allowed to start work again when the inspector has seen that all of the safety problems have been solved.

Skiving chemistry — reducing the danger of chemicals...

...but it's not advisable though. You'll just be increasing the danger of not doing too great in your exam. Now, on to the important stuff — you won't be expected to remember any particular rules and regulations — just be aware that they exist and understand why it's important to follow them carefully.

Module 4 — Harnessing Chemicals

Revision Summary for Module 4

You've covered quite a lot in this section. So here are some questions to test yourself with. I know — just what you always wanted... If you can't remember something, it's really important that you check back through the section. Don't just ignore it — it could be something that comes up in the exam.

1) Give the chemical symbols for: a) magnesium   b) sodium.
2) Give the chemical formulas for: a) sulfuric acid   b) nitric acid.
3) What is a burette used for?
4) What is a heating mantle used for?
5) Describe how you could transfer a liquid from one container to another without spilling any.
6)* Write a word equation to show the reaction between sodium hydroxide and nitric acid.
7)* Write a word equation to show the reaction between calcium carbonate and hydrochloric acid.
8)* How many grams of sodium chloride are in 600 cm³ of a 0.5 g/cm³ solution?
9)* Write a word equation to show the precipitation reaction between lead nitrate and sodium sulfate.
10) You're mixing two solutions to form a precipitate of lead iodide. Explain how you would separate and dry the precipitate.
11) When making a soluble salt from an insoluble chemical and an acid, why is it important that the insoluble solid is added until no more will react?
12) Explain how you'd produce a solid salt from a solution using evaporation and crystallisation.
13) If you were producing a pure salt by the neutralisation of two soluble chemicals, how would you ensure that the final solution only contained the salt?
14) Give an example of an organic chemical.
15) A chemical has the formula C_2H_5OH.
    a) Give the functional group of this compound.
    b) Is it an organic or an inorganic compound?
16) Which two types of chemical are required to make an ester?
17) Why do esters need to be purified after refluxing?
18) What is an emulsion? Give an example of an emulsion found in the home.
19) What is a suspension?
20) Give one method for measuring the rate of a reaction.
21) What four things does the rate of a reaction depend on?
22)* Look at this rate of reaction graph. How long did it take for the reaction to complete?
23) Give three ways in which the chemical industry can make their processes more sustainable.
24)* A reaction's yield is 40 tonnes and its theoretical yield is 52 tonnes. Calculate the percentage yield.
25) A pharmaceutical company is choosing which grade of chemical to use in its products. Would you recommend technical grade or analytical grade? Explain your answer.
26) Give two examples of bulk chemicals.
27) Give two examples of fine chemicals.
28) Give two things that chemical engineers have to consider when a laboratory reaction is scaled up to an industrial process.
29) Give three factors that might influence the choice of method for making a chemical in industry.
30) Explain what the term 'exothermic' means.
31) Explain why products must be routinely checked.
32) Give two reasons why governments regulate the use, storage and transportation of chemicals.
33) What is the Health and Safety Executive responsible for?

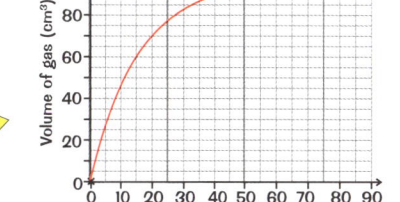

* Answers on p.132

Module 4 — Harnessing Chemicals

Communicating Information

Communication involves transferring information between people or electronic devices. There are loads of ways of doing this, and the best one depends on the situation you're in.

Communication Can Involve Visual Symbols

1) Visual symbols can communicate important information quickly and clearly.
2) They're also handy because they can be understood whatever language you speak — you can use them all over the world.
3) E.g. hazard symbols and road signs.

Communication Can Involve Sounds

1) Alarms are a very simple example — they make a noise to tell you something or warn you about something, whether it's a fire, a burglary or, even worse, time to get up.
2) Telephones use several sounds (no, really) — they ring when someone calls, there's a dial tone when the line's open, and there's an engaged tone if the person you're calling is already talking to someone.
3) The most complex example of communicating using sound is probably language — lots of complicated sounds strung together to make words and sentences.

Communication Can Involve Codes

1) Morse code uses sequences of 'dots' and 'dashes' — short and long noises, electrical pulses or flashes that represent letters, numbers and punctuation.
2) Binary code uses binary numbers (usually 0s and 1s) to represent letters, numbers and symbols — for example 'R' is 01010010 and 'b' is 01100010.

Using codes to send information means that there has to be an encoding process (where information is put into a code), and a decoding process (where it's converted back again).

> When you use a code, it's important to think about the transmission rate and the error rate:
> 1) Transmission rate is how fast information can be communicated — it could be measured in characters per second or bits per second (see p.96).
> 2) Error rate is the number of mistakes during transmission — e.g. the percentage of characters that are incorrectly received.

Different Methods Have Different Uses

To choose the best communication method, you need to think about three things:

1) Ease of use — e.g. simple visual symbols are easy to identify and need little or no training, whereas you'd need training (or a computer program) to decode something like Morse code.
2) Speed — e.g. using a telephone would be much faster than writing and posting a letter.
3) Range — this is how far you can communicate using a particular method. It could be a few metres for talking, or thousands of kilometres for e-mail.

Visual symbols involving 2 fingers don't count in exams...

Samuel Morse invented his code in the late 1830s, and it's really similar to the codes used in computers today. That's, like, 170 years ago... Pretty good going for an old-timer.

The Communications Industry

The communications industry uses electronic technology to improve communications between people.

Microphones and Hearing Aids Increase the Quality of Communication

1) Microphones convert sound into electrical signals. When they're used with a loudspeaker (which turns the electrical signals back into sound waves), you can increase the volume of sounds. They've made talking to large groups of people much easier — you don't have to shout any more...

2) Hearing aids contain a microphone that picks up sounds and a tiny loudspeaker that makes them louder. They can make a huge difference to the quality of life of people with hearing difficulties.

Mobile Phones and E-mail Increase the Quantity of Communication

Before the mid-1990s, very few people had mobile phones or e-mail. Today, millions of people use these technologies every day.

1) Mobile phones make it possible for people to keep in touch while they're on the move, talking to each other at any time from almost anywhere.

2) E-mail has made it possible to send written messages, files and photos almost instantly. It's become really important in the workplace, and allows people separated by huge distances to communicate easily. It's faster than the postal service, and if you've got an internet connection, it's free too...

TVs and Radios Increase the Distance of Communication

1) Television and radio programmes are broadcast locally, nationally and internationally.
2) They educate and entertain us, inform us of news from all over the world, and help to shape politics and culture.
3) In the old days people didn't know what was happening on the other side of the world, but today you can turn on a TV or radio and find out just about anything about people anywhere.

The Government Regulates the Communications Industry

The government acts as a 'watchdog' of the communications industry. They regulate it in three ways:

1) They license the use of different frequencies of the electromagnetic spectrum (radio, etc.). FM radio stations broadcast at around 100 MHz, and your mobile phone probably uses either 900 MHz or 1800 MHz. If two things use the same frequency, they interfere, so regulating which frequencies are used is really important.

2) They agree on standard protocols for messages.
Messages sent between different devices need to be in the same 'language'. The government helps to decide what languages are used, and these are called standard protocols. For example, mobile phones use 'GSM' — a digital system for putting speech onto radio channels.

3) They create markets for competing telecommunications firms.
The government encourages competition because it helps to get customers the best possible deal. Markets are reviewed regularly, and if one company is dominating an area they improve competition (e.g. by helping new companies enter the market).

It's a nation of information communication stations...

The development of all this new technology has made the communications industry explode over the last couple of decades. And it keeps on going — video calling, digital radio, HD TV, email on mobiles...

Module 5 — Communications

Designing Communication Systems

New and improved communications systems are always being developed, but designers are _limited_ by practical considerations like _cost_ and _available technology_.

Product Specifications Describe the Important Features

A product specification is used to _describe_ the _key features_ of a product.
It normally includes information about all or some of the following things:

the range of functions   *weight*   *image or sound quality*   *cost*   *size*

network coverage   *power output*   *the range of controls*   *type of power source*   *recyclable components*

EXAMPLE: Here's the product specification for the new Spamsung CGP-320.

- Touch screen controls
- High resolution screen
- 3.2 megapixel camera and video recorder
- Video calling and picture messaging
- 1 gigabyte memory
- MP3 player
- Games
- Battery with 5 hours' talk time and 300 hours' standby
- 90 x 50 x 18 mm, 80 g
- Can be used on any network
- 50% of components are recyclable
- £280

Lots of Factors Affect How a Product Specification is Decided

When manufacturers are deciding on the _specification_ of a _new product_, they have to think about _several things_, like...

1) The _COST_ of making the product — this has to be _reasonable_ or the company might go _bust_.
2) The product's likely _CUSTOMERS_ — there needs to be a _market_ for the new product.
3) Available _TECHNOLOGY_ — designers have to base their ideas on what's possible with _current technology_.
4) Current _FASHION_ — the product has to be _desirable_.
5) Expected _LIFETIME_ — the product has to _last_ a reasonable length of time.
6) The _PROFIT MARGIN_ — the company will need to _charge enough_ for the product but not so much that nobody will buy it.

A _combination_ of these factors affects what features manufacturers include with new products.

For example, '_video calling_' on mobile phones requires a lot of _memory_ (which makes phones larger and more expensive), a lot of _power_ (which means the battery needs to be bigger) and a _high speed network connection_ (using technology that's new and still developing).

On top of all this, video calling isn't really _in demand_ — the majority of customers _aren't interested_ in it yet, partly because you need to know someone else with a video phone to use it.
As a result, lots of phones on the market _don't offer_ this feature.

I think there's a demand for free mobile phones...

For a big company, it's normally the _market_ and current _fashion_ that decide a product's specifications.
If enough people want a certain _feature_, they can normally be sure to make _money_ if they provide it.

Module 5 — Communications

Designing Communication Systems

If you're thinking about buying a communications product, you'll probably <u>compare</u> different product specifications with each other, and with your <u>own needs</u>, to help you decide on the <u>right</u> product.

Product Specifications Can be Used to Compare Similar Systems

<u>Mobile phones</u>, <u>intercoms</u> and <u>radio receivers</u> are all used to communicate, but they have <u>very different features</u>. If you get a table like this in the exam, you'll need to compare the different products...

	Mobile phone	Intercom	Two-way radio
Functions	telephone, phone book, text messages	communication between intercom units wired together	communication between people with radio handsets
Controls	buttons control dialling, volume and text	buttons dial different units	switches select the radio channel, button allows user to talk
Sound quality	variable	good	variable
Power source	battery	mains	battery
Size	100 × 40 × 20 mm	200 × 150 × 60 mm	100 × 60 × 50 mm
Mass	100 g	600 g	300 g
Reliability	depends on network coverage	excellent	good
Cost	£60 plus call charges	£25 (no call charges)	£80 (no call charges)

1) So if someone wanted a device for calling their friends and family while they're <u>away from home</u>, they'd choose a <u>mobile phone</u> — it's the only device they could use to dial any telephone number they wanted.

2) If the owner of a <u>taxi company</u> wants something that allows drivers to <u>keep in touch</u> with each other and the base, they'll choose <u>radio receivers</u> — they're reliable and have no call charges.

3) A <u>hospital</u> that wants to install a system to allow staff in <u>different departments</u> to talk to each other would choose <u>intercoms</u> — they're very reliable, have good sound quality and no call charges.

Battery Power is Portable but Mains Power is More Reliable

Product designers need to think about whether their communications devices should be <u>battery powered</u> or <u>mains powered</u>.

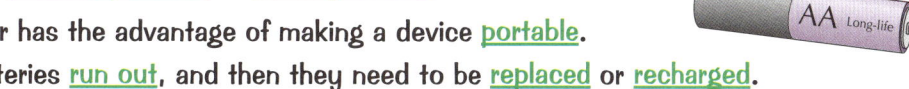

1) <u>Battery</u> power has the advantage of making a device <u>portable</u>.
2) However, batteries <u>run out</u>, and then they need to be <u>replaced</u> or <u>recharged</u>.
3) <u>Mains</u> power has the advantage of being more <u>reliable</u>. It won't run out, but it does mean a device has to be attached to a <u>mains supply</u>.
4) Lots of products end up having <u>both types</u> of power — they can run off either batteries or mains. Laptop computers, for example.

My phone runs off a car battery. It's not very portable...

If you've ever seen a picture of a mobile phone from the 1980s, you'll know that they were the size of a <u>small continent</u>. That's old-fashioned <u>batteries</u> for you — modern <u>lithium-ion</u> ones are much smaller and last much longer. You can't keep recharging them forever though — they <u>pack up</u> after two or three years.

Module 5 — Communications

Jobs in the Communications Industry

All sorts of jobs are available in the communications industry, and many of them require technical skills like electronics or computing. Lots of workers get training in specialist areas, like broadcasting engineering or wireless network operation.

Telecommunications Engineers Need the Right Skills

1) Telecommunications engineers develop, install, maintain and repair telecommunications equipment.
2) This can include telephones, mobile phones, fax machines, satellite systems and computer networks.
3) Telecommunications engineers need an understanding of electronics (circuits and microchips) and electrical engineering (wiring etc.).
4) They need to understand and use technical drawings (like circuit diagrams).
5) They also need to have computer software skills because computers often control the systems they're working with.

Sound Technicians Need Electronics Skills

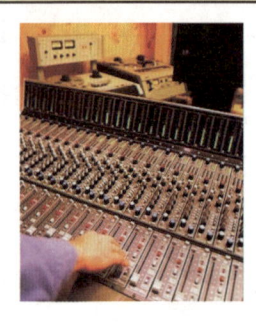

1) Sound technicians set up, use and look after technical sound equipment like microphones and mixing desks. They aim to record the best possible sound, whether it's in a studio or on the set of a film or television programme.
2) They also alter sounds after they've been recorded — balancing, mixing, editing, sampling, adding beats and sound effects and all that other fancy stuff.
3) Sound technicians need to have an understanding of the physics of sound and electronics. They also need to have good hearing, some musical ability and a fairly creative mind.

'Live' Outside Broadcast Systems Transmit from Anywhere

Live outside broadcast systems are used to film events and transmit the images and sounds to people's TVs as they happen. This can be done from almost anywhere in the world.

The major parts of a live outside broadcast system are:
1) Cameras — to record the action.
2) Microphones — to record the sound.
3) Transmitter — to send footage to the broadcaster's control room.
4) Editing suite — to add in any pre-recorded bits from the control room, and sometimes to remove anything unwanted (like swearing).
5) Satellite — to broadcast live footage by satellite.
6) Ground-based TV transmitter — to broadcast live footage from the control room to homes.
7) Domestic TV receiver — to receive footage from the control room.

The recording equipment and the transmitter will all be transported in a large vehicle, like a van or truck. There'll be work space for all the crew, with areas for sound, video and production.

If the editors want to check for things like swearing, there'll be a delay of a few seconds before they broadcast the footage. In which case it's not quite 'live', but I guess it's close enough...

Good evening — we're coming to you live from page 82...

Three things to remember from this page: 1) what telecommunications engineers and sound technicians do, 2) what skills they need and 3) how a live broadcast system works... Actually, that's the whole page...

Module 5 — Communications

Health and Safety

Health and safety regulations protect people who make, install, service and use electrical equipment.

Safety Symbols Help You Recognise Hazards

Some safety symbols are often found in factories and workplaces. And you need to know four of them...

Emergency stop	Emergency stop symbol. This indicates the, err.. emergency stop button. It stops all the machinery in the area.	 First aid post	First aid point symbol. This shows where you can find a first aid kit.
 DANGER 230 volts	Electrical shock hazard symbol. Found on any equipment operating on a high voltage or current.	!	Danger symbol. This is used for other dangers. There's normally a sign underneath that explains what the danger is.

And then there are symbols that you'll see on electrical products you can buy in the shops. You need to know four of these too...

♡	BSI Kitemark symbol. This shows that a piece of equipment has met British Standards — a set of guidelines meant to improve production quality.	☀	Laser symbol. Lasers can damage the eyes, so anything containing one has to have this symbol.
▣	Double insulated symbol. Found on equipment that's double insulated (see below).	⏚	Earth symbol. Indicates that a piece of equipment has an earth wire (see below).

Earths, Fuses and Double Insulation Make Equipment Safer

1) Equipment with a metal casing should have an earth wire — a wire that connects it to the ground. If a live wire touches part of the metal casing, all the current flows down the earth wire. When this happens, a fuse blows, which breaks the circuit so that nobody gets electrocuted.
2) Over-current devices include fuses and trip switches. Too much current flowing through a piece of equipment often means that it's developed a fault. This could be dangerous, so over-current devices are designed to cut the power supply when the current exceeds a set limit.
3) Double insulated devices have two layers of insulating material (e.g. plastic) around the live parts, which helps prevent the equipment becoming dangerous if a fault develops.

Risk Assessment Identifies Hazards and Reduces Risks

1) A hazard is something that could cause harm (e.g. an exposed electrical cable).
2) A risk is the harm that could be caused (e.g. an electric shock).
3) Risk Assessment involves identifying hazards, assessing how likely and how severe the risks are, and suggesting ways of avoiding or reducing those risks.
4) Electrical hazards include damaged equipment or plug sockets, damaged or exposed cables, cables touching something wet or hot, overloaded sockets and machines without covers.
5) Electric shocks can cause burns or death. You can reduce the risk of electric shocks by checking that equipment meets safety standards, is in good working order and is kept away from heat and water.
6) Damaged equipment needs to be repaired by a professional or thrown away or recycled.

Module 5 — Communications

Flowcharts and Datasheets

Electronic systems are made by connecting together electronic <u>units</u>.
Flowcharts and datasheets can help you <u>pick</u> the units you need.

Flowcharts are Like Sketches of the System's Parts

1) Flowcharts can be used to represent <u>processes</u>, find <u>faults</u>, and help find answers to <u>questions</u>.
2) They are a good way of sketching the things that a system has to <u>do</u>, so they're really helpful when you're <u>designing</u> and <u>developing</u> equipment.
3) They use <u>different shapes</u> for different parts of a system:

EXAMPLE: This flowchart describes the basics of what happens when you <u>dial a number</u> on a house phone.

- User picks up the phone.
- User dials phone number.
- Telephone exchange processes number.
- Is the number recognised?
  - yes → Telephone exchange connects call.
  - no → 'Number not recognised' message played back to user.

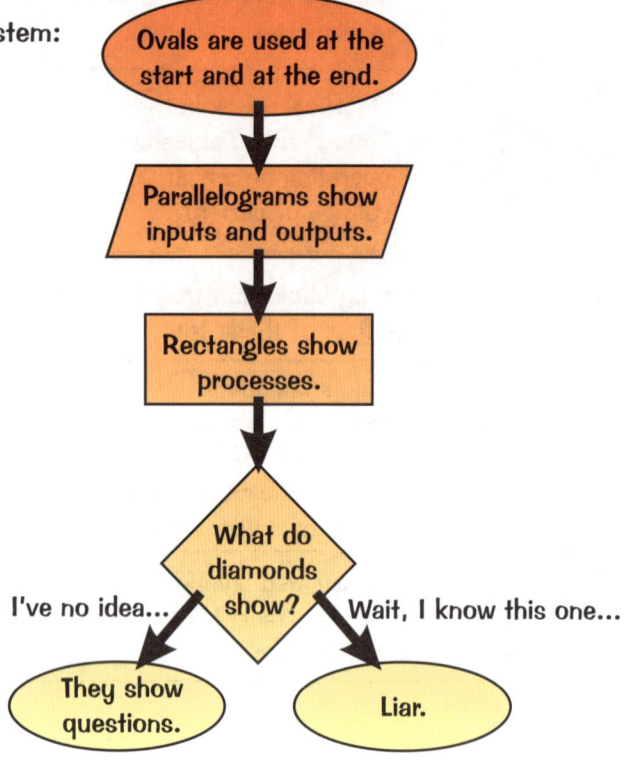

- Ovals are used at the start and at the end.
- Parallelograms show inputs and outputs.
- Rectangles show processes.
- What do diamonds show?
  - I've no idea... → They show questions.
  - Wait, I know this one... → Liar.

Datasheets List Information

Datasheets contain important information about electronic devices — like their <u>properties</u>, <u>power consumption</u> and <u>operating conditions</u>. Manufacturers use this information to pick the <u>best device</u> for their system.

Model number	M674	M521
sensitivity	1.4 mV/Pa	0.8 mV/Pa
frequency range	5 – 20 000 Hz	1 – 10 000 Hz
dynamic range	75 dB	45 dB
operating temperature	–55 – 100 °C	–3 – 70 °C

If a manufacturer needs a microphone for a device with a dynamic range of at least <u>60 dB</u>, they could compare data sheets like this to pick a suitable one. Out of the two, they would choose <u>Model M674</u>, because it's the only one that can do what they want.

Check ma flow. Actually don't, it's pretty boring. Fo' sho.

Flowcharts are really <u>handy</u>, but you need to memorise the meaning of the different <u>shapes</u>...
It's easy enough to remember that you start and end with <u>ovals</u>, but the bit in between's a bit <u>trickier</u>.
Try drawing <u>your own</u> flowchart on a piece of paper, then check whether you've used the right shapes.

Module 5 — Communications

Block Diagrams

Block diagrams break complex electronic systems into <u>simple units</u> — blocks.
You can represent some straightforward systems with just <u>three blocks</u>.

Blocks Represent the Different Processes in a System

1) Each block represents a <u>device</u> that performs a <u>process</u>.
2) The arrows joining the blocks show the <u>flow of information</u>.

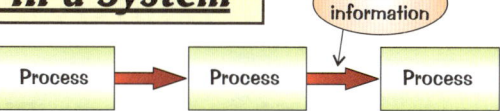

Input Devices Send Info In, Output Devices Send It Out...

1) <u>Input</u> devices convert information into a form that can be <u>transported</u> — e.g. into <u>electrical signals</u> or <u>radio waves</u>.
2) <u>Output</u> devices convert information back into a form that's <u>more useful</u> to the person using the system, e.g. <u>sound</u> or <u>pictures</u>.

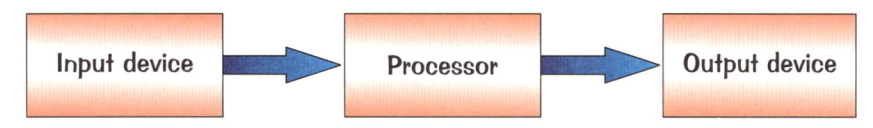

Telephones Convert Sound into Electricity and Back Again...

If the person with the handset at point 5 talks, the exact same process happens, but in reverse.

1) The <u>input</u> device is a <u>telephone handset</u> — when someone talks into it, it converts the <u>sound</u> of their voice into <u>electrical signals</u>.
2) The electrical signals travel along a <u>telephone cable</u>.
3) The telephone exchange <u>processes</u> the electrical signal, recognising where to send it.
4) The electrical signals travel along <u>another</u> telephone cable.
5) The <u>output</u> device is another telephone handset — which converts the <u>electrical signals</u> back into <u>sound</u>, so that whoever's holding this handset can hear what the first person said.

Televisions Convert Radio Waves into Sounds and Images...

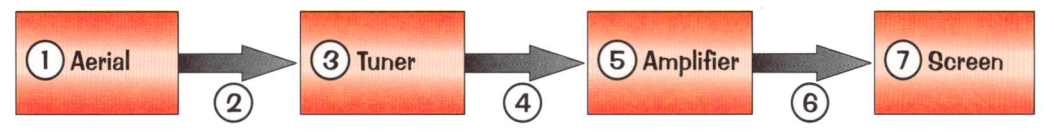

1) The <u>input</u> device is an <u>aerial</u> — which converts <u>radio waves</u> into <u>electrical signals</u>.
2) The electrical signals travel along a <u>cable</u>.
3) The <u>tuner</u> selects an electrical signal from the available channels.
4) The electrical signal travels along another cable.
5) The <u>amplifier</u> increases the <u>size</u> of the signal.
6) The electrical signals travel along <u>another</u> cable.
7) The <u>output</u> devices are a <u>screen</u> and a <u>speaker</u> — which convert <u>electrical signals</u> into <u>images</u> and <u>sounds</u>.

Woo! A page full of rectangles! I love shapes! (Ahem...)

Block diagrams are basically well easy (as long as you understand the system you're describing...).

Module 5 — Communications

Block Diagrams

Here are some more block diagrams for your enjoyment... OK, so that first one's got a whole five blocks, but power through and you're back onto three...

Fax Machines Convert Images into Electricity and Back Again...

① Fax scanner → ② → ③ Modem → ④ → ⑤ Exchange → ⑥ → ⑦ Modem → ⑧ → ⑨ Fax printer

1) The input device is a fax scanner — which converts images into electrical signals.
2) The electrical signals travel along a wire.
3) The modem processes the electrical signals so they can be sent through the telephone system.
4) The signals travel along a telephone cable.
5) The telephone exchange processes the electrical signals, recognising where to send them.
6) The electrical signals travel along another telephone cable.
7) Another modem decodes the electrical signals.
8) The signals travel along another wire.
9) The output device is a fax printer — which converts the electrical signals back into an image.

Microphones and Loudspeakers Convert Sound and Electricity...

A P.A. (public address) system involves hooking up a microphone to an amplifier and some speakers.

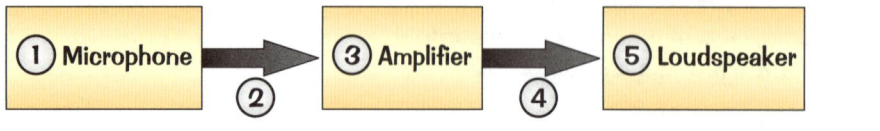

① Microphone → ② → ③ Amplifier → ④ → ⑤ Loudspeaker

1) The input device is a microphone — which converts sound into electrical signals.
2) The electrical signals travel along a cable.
3) The amplifier increases the size of the electrical signals.
4) The electrical signals travel along another cable.
5) The output device is a loudspeaker — which converts the electrical signals back into sound.

Scanners and Printers Convert Images and Electricity...

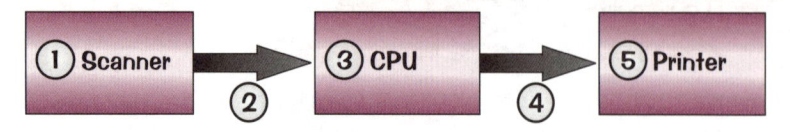

① Scanner → ② → ③ CPU → ④ → ⑤ Printer

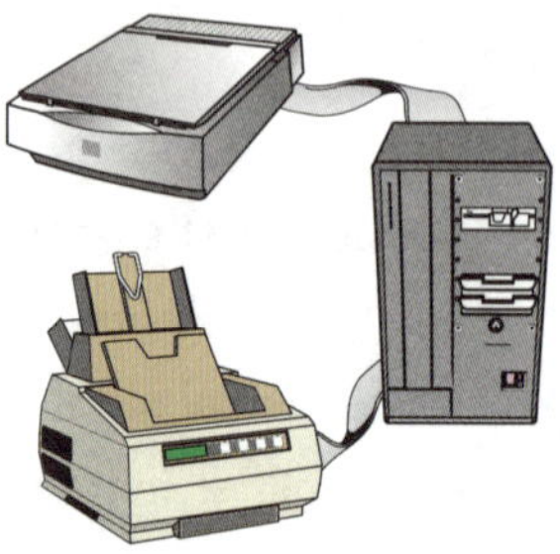

1) The input device is a scanner — which converts images into electrical signals.
2) The electrical signals travel along a cable.
3) The CPU processes the electrical signals, recognising where to send them.
4) The electrical signals travel along another cable.
5) The output device is a printer — which converts the electrical signals back into an image.

Since when is a fax more complicated than a TV?!
All you need to do here is identify the input, processor and output stages for each of these systems, then give a brief description of what they do. Once you've done a few of these, you've done 'em all...

Module 5 — Communications

Circuit Diagrams

Block diagrams are a great way of simplifying circuits, but you also need to have a go at the real deal... Welcome to a world of a billion circuit symbols.

Circuit Diagrams Show Lots of Detail

1) Block diagrams represent circuits by dividing them into chunks, each with its own purpose, but they avoid the details of a circuit.
2) Circuit diagrams, on the other hand, show every part of a circuit and how they're all linked together.
3) They use special symbols to represent electrical and electronic components.

You Need to Know the Basics of Circuits

You've probably covered this lot before, but it's pretty essential stuff if you want to understand circuits...

1) CURRENT is the flow of electrons round the circuit. Current will only flow through a component if there's a voltage across that component.   Unit: ampere, A.

2) VOLTAGE is the driving force that pushes the current round. Kind of like "electrical pressure".   Unit: volt, V.

3) RESISTANCE is anything in the circuit which slows the flow down.   Unit: ohm, Ω.

4) There's a BALANCE: the voltage is trying to push the current round the circuit, and the resistance is opposing it — the relative sizes of the voltage and resistance decide how big the current will be:

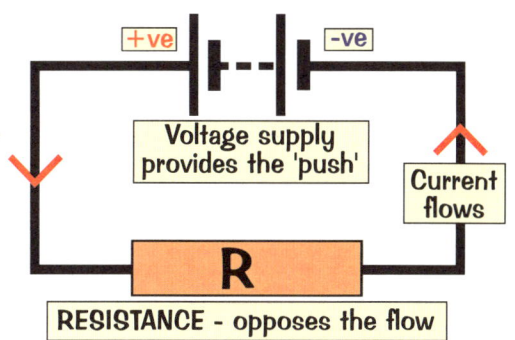

If you increase the voltage in a circuit, then more current will flow. But if you increase the resistance, then less current will flow (unless you increase the voltage again to keep the current the same...).

Have a Look at This Fairly Standard Circuit...

Here's a tasty example of how to draw a circuit:

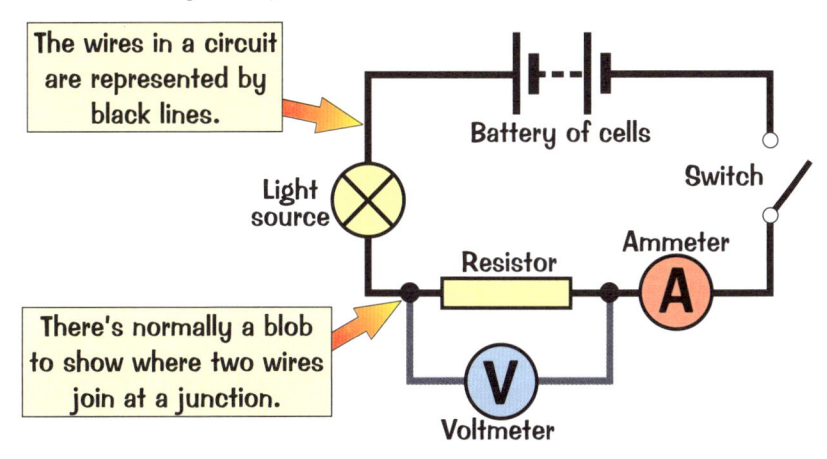

- The wires in a circuit are represented by black lines.
- There's normally a blob to show where two wires join at a junction.

1) An ammeter measures the current in a circuit. You can put it wherever you like, but it has to be in line with the other components (i.e. in series — see p.89).
2) A voltmeter measures the voltage across a component. You have to attach it on a different bit of wire (i.e. in parallel — see p.89) so that it just measures the voltage across the component you're interested in.
3) The proper name for voltage is potential difference (or P.D.).

The current will enslave all fruits. Resistance is futile...

Hopefully you'll have seen most of this stuff before, even if your memory's a bit hazy... It really is important stuff — if you don't understand it all, you'll probably find it pretty difficult to work out what's going on in a circuit. When you've got this page sorted though, the rest is fairly straightforward...

Module 5 — Communications

Circuit Diagrams

Here's a Load More Circuit Symbols for You to Remember...

1) You've already seen a few of the more common circuit symbols, like battery, resistor, switch, etc.
2) But luckily for you, there are absolutely loads more of them, and you have to remember a fair few for the exams. (It might be handy to remember what they do too...)

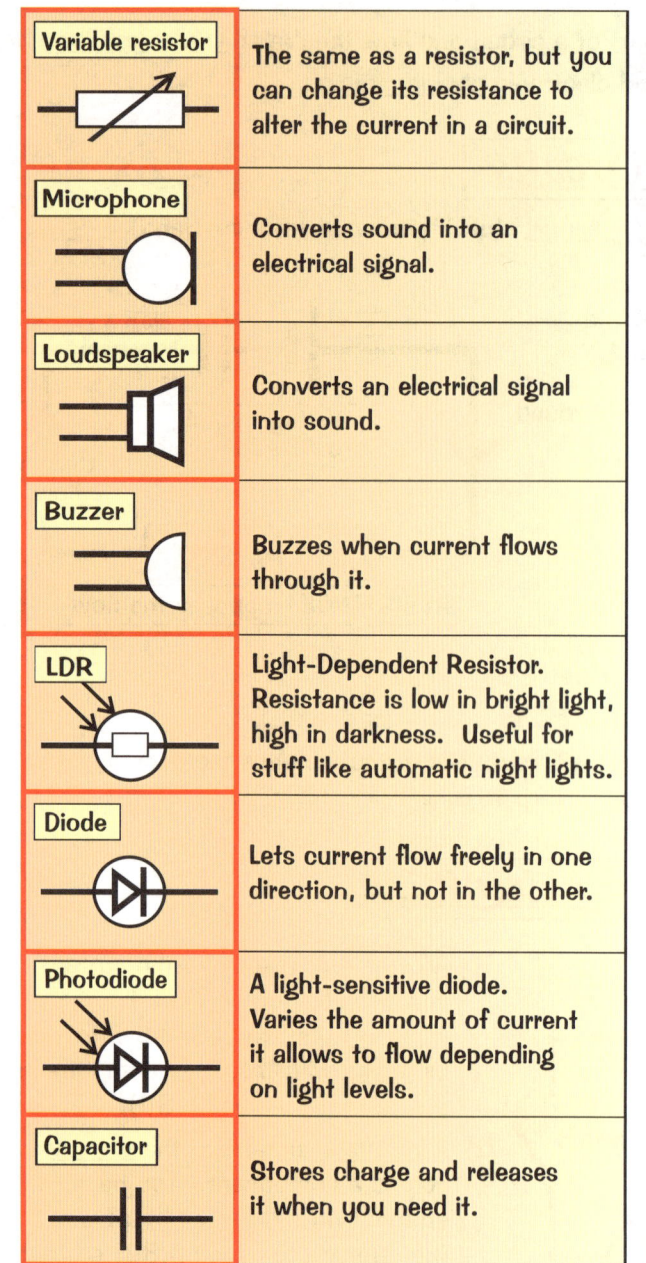

Component	Description	Component	Description
Variable resistor	The same as a resistor, but you can change its resistance to alter the current in a circuit.	**Integrated Circuit**	A chip. Basically a tiny little circuit in itself. The symbol's just a box, but the number of wires going into it varies.
Microphone	Converts sound into an electrical signal.	**Amplifier**	Boosts a signal's strength.
Loudspeaker	Converts an electrical signal into sound.	**Thermistor**	A temperature-dependent resistor. Resistance is low when it's warm, high when it's cold. Useful for temperature sensors.
Buzzer	Buzzes when current flows through it.	**Fuse**	If current gets too high, the fuse wire melts, breaking the circuit. It's a handy safety device.
LDR	Light-Dependent Resistor. Resistance is low in bright light, high in darkness. Useful for stuff like automatic night lights.	**Earth**	Connects a circuit to the earth.
Diode	Lets current flow freely in one direction, but not in the other.	**Transformer**	Changes the voltage of a power supply. (The two curved wires don't meet — charge is transferred between them by a magnetic field.)
Photodiode	A light-sensitive diode. Varies the amount of current it allows to flow depending on light levels.	**LED**	Light-Emitting Diode. It's a diode that, err.. emits light.
Capacitor	Stores charge and releases it when you need it.	**Motor**	It's a, erm.. motor. Converts electrical energy into movement.

3) Try not to get mixed up about how LDRs and thermistors work.
   Low light or heat = high resistance. And don't you forget it.

Light-Eating Donkeys: No mercy.

I heard that transformers were robots in disguise...

This lot might look pretty daunting, but it's not really too bad — most of the names are a bit of a give-away, so if you can remember the symbol it shouldn't be too hard to work out what it does. Write all the names of the components on a piece of paper, then draw the symbol for each one without looking at this page... It might be 95% boredom*, but it shouldn't take toooo long.

Module 5 — Communications   *CGP has predicted 5% unrestrained joy

Series and Parallel Circuits

There are two ways you can make a circuit — in series and in parallel. You need to know what they look like, and a few points about each. So get reading...

Series Circuits have Everything In Line

1) In series circuits, the different components are connected in a line, end to end, between the +ve and –ve of the power supply (except for voltmeters, which are always connected in parallel, but they don't count as part of the circuit).
2) If you remove or disconnect one component, the circuit is broken and everything stops.
3) This is generally not very handy, and in practice very few things are connected in series.

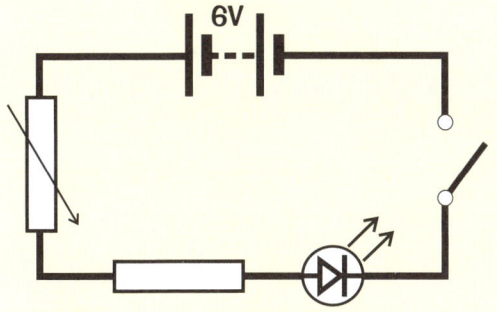

4) With this series circuit, altering the resistance of the variable resistor would change the current, which would change the brightness of the LED. The whole thing could be switched off with the switch.
5) In a series circuit the P.D. (or voltage) is shared between the components — the diagram shows that the battery's voltage is 6 V, so when it's switched on there might be 1 V across the LED, 2 V across the fixed resistor and 3 V across the variable resistor (1 + 2 + 3 = 6 V).
6) The current is the same at any point in a series circuit — if you were to measure it, it'd make no difference whether you put the ammeter next to the LED or between the two resistors.

Parallel Circuits have Everything Wired Separately

1) In parallel circuits, each component is separately connected to the +ve and –ve of the supply.
2) If you remove or disconnect one of them, it will hardly affect the others at all.
3) This is how most things have to be connected, for example in cars and in household electrics — you have to be able to switch everything on and off separately.

4) This parallel circuit has a motor and an LED, both of which can be controlled separately, since they each have their own switch. This wouldn't be possible in a series circuit because one switch switches off the whole circuit.
5) In parallel circuits the P.D. is the same across every component — there's 6 V across the motor, 6 V across the LED and 6 V across that rather pointless-looking resistor at the bottom.
6) The current is shared between the branches of the circuit. So if the total current coming from the power source is 8 A, there could be 1 A through the LED, 1.5 A through the resistor and 5.5 A through the motor (1 + 1.5 + 5.5 = 8 A).

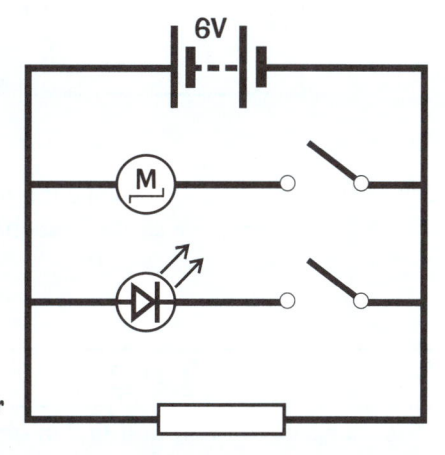

So there you go. When it comes to sharing voltage and current across their components, series and parallel circuits are exact opposites — series divides up the voltage, parallel divides up the current.

Series circuits — they're no laughing matter...

If you connect a lamp to a battery, it lights up with a certain brightness. If you then add more identical lamps in series with the first one, they'll all light up less brightly than before. That's because in a series circuit the voltage is shared out between all the components. That doesn't happen in parallel circuits...

Module 5 — Communications

Electric Current and Power

You've learnt all those symbols, and got parallel and series circuits covered, and now you get to do some calculations! It's a nonstop roller coaster ride to funville, and everyone's invited...

You Need to Know the Current Equation...

1) The current that flows through a component always depends on the resistance of the component and the voltage across it. There's a nice simple equation for it:

$$\text{Current (amps, A)} = \frac{\text{Voltage (volts, V)}}{\text{Resistance (ohms, } \Omega\text{)}}$$

V is Voltage, and R is Resistance, but, oddly, I is for Current.

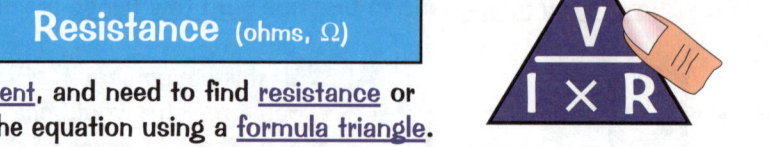

2) If you already know the current, and need to find resistance or voltage, you can rearrange the equation using a formula triangle.
(Cover up the thing you're trying to find, then what you can still see gives the formula to use.)

EXAMPLE:
a) The voltmeter reads 10 V. Calculate the current flowing through the resistor.
b) Using your answer to part a), find the resistance of the lamp.

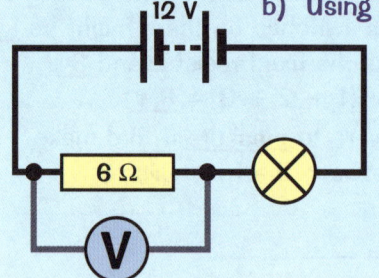

ANSWER:
a) $I = V \div R = 10 \div 6 = \underline{1.67 \text{ A}}$
b) $R = V \div I$, so you need the voltage and current. The voltage across the resistor was 10 V, so the remaining 2 V must be across the lamp. The current through the resistor was 1.67 A, and since it's a series circuit the current's the same everywhere. $R = 2 \div 1.67 = \underline{1.20 \text{ } \Omega}$.

Power = Current × Voltage

Electrical power is a measure of how quickly a component converts electrical energy into other, useful, forms of energy. There's another nice easy equation:

$$\text{Power} = \text{Current} \times \text{Voltage}$$
(watts, W)   (amps, A)   (volts, V)

EXAMPLE: The ammeter reads 1.2 A. What is the power of the motor?
ANSWER: $P = I \times V$. Since it's a parallel circuit, the voltage is the same for all the branches — it's 6 V.
So $P = 1.2 \times 6 = \underline{7.2 \text{ W}}$.

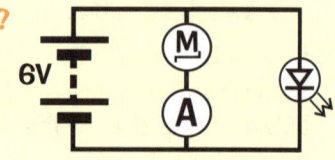

Components have Maximum Ratings

1) The components that you find in circuits all have maximum ratings for power, voltage and current. These are limits to how much current the component can handle — if you go past the limit, they'll give up, which could be dangerous.
2) That's why it's important to consider the power source of a circuit — if its voltage is too high, your components will pack up...

Watt's the answer — well part of it...

These equations are pretty easy as long as you can remember which bit goes where in the triangles... Once you've remembered them, you can use them for any component you can think of. Result.

Module 5 — Communications

Wireless Communication

Right, now you've got your circuits sorted, you can build systems for things like wireless communication. It's communicating, without, err... wires. Oh, and it normally uses microwaves or radio waves.

A Radio Communications System Can be Shown as Blocks

Remember page 85 — the one with loads of block diagrams on it?
Well, radio communications systems let you relive all that fun...

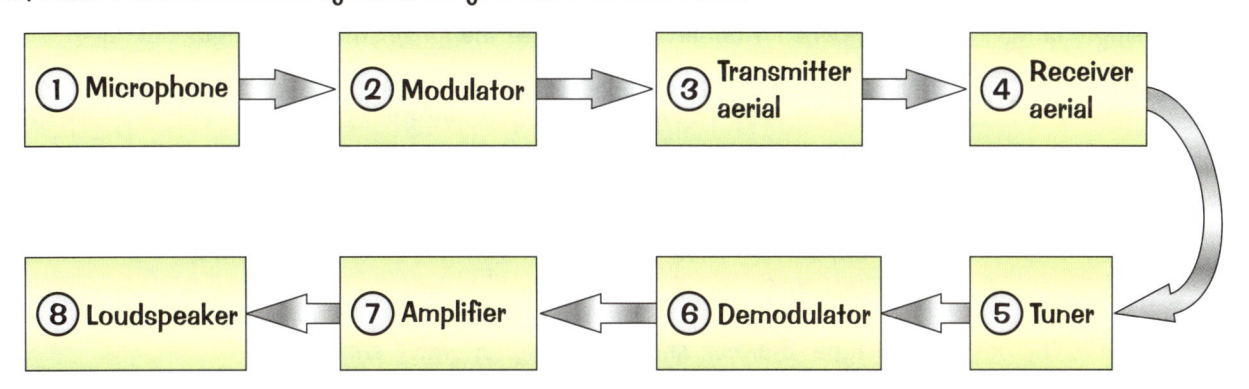

① Microphone → ② Modulator → ③ Transmitter aerial → ④ Receiver aerial → ⑤ Tuner → ⑥ Demodulator → ⑦ Amplifier → ⑧ Loudspeaker

1) The microphone converts the sound (of Terry Wogan's ramblings, say) into an electrical signal.
2) The modulator converts the electrical signal into a radio wave.
3) The transmitter aerial (fairly obviously...) transmits the radio waves. Away they go...
4) ...and then the receiver aerial receives them.
5) The tuner picks out the specific frequency of radio wave so that you get the right one.
6) The demodulator is the opposite of the modulator — it changes the radio wave back into the electrical signal created by the microphone.
7) The amplifier increases the size (amplitude) of the electrical signal.
8) The loudspeaker converts the electrical signal back into sound.

'Carrier' Radio Waves Carry a Signal

1) You can use a radio wave to carry information — like sounds, pictures or data — by varying the shape or size of the wave.
2) The information you're sending is called the signal, and the radio wave that transports the signal is called the carrier.
3) The process of putting signals onto carrier waves is called modulation.

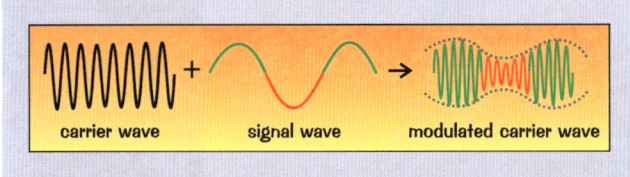

carrier wave + signal wave → modulated carrier wave

A signal is just an alternating electrical current. Modulation changes the size or shape of the carrier wave according to the variations in the electrical current (the signal). It's like putting a code onto the wave to represent the signal.

4) Once the carrier wave has been modulated to carry the signal, it's transmitted from an aerial.
5) When the modulated radio waves are received, the signal is converted back to its original form (an electrical current) using a demodulator.

If carriers carry things, maybe couriers make curry...

Modulation can be a fairly tricky thing to get your head around, but you need to be able to describe it...

Module 5 — Communications

Wireless Communication

Time for some aerials — you'll find these everywhere, receiving and transmitting radio waves. On your roof, on the hilltops, out in space, up your nose... OK, sorry, I got carried away, but you get the idea.

Aerials are Used to Transmit or Receive Radio Waves

1) Transmitting aerials convert electrical signals into radio waves.
2) Receiving aerials convert radio waves into electrical signals.
3) Wavelength is really important when it comes to aerials — the longer the wavelength, the bigger the transmitter aerial you'll need.
4) There are lots of different types of aerial — different shapes, different structures, different uses...

A Simple Dipole Aerial Has 360° Reception

A simple dipole aerial is made up of just two wires pointing in opposite directions.

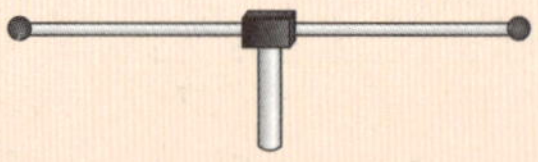

1) They're the commonest type of aerial, and are simple, effective and cheap.
2) Television and radio signals are normally received through dipole aerials. 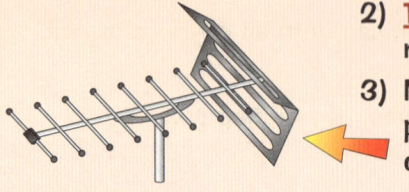
3) More complicated aerials (like the one that's probably on your roof) are normally just a dipole aerial with extra branches or loops.

Dish-Shaped Aerials Get Signals from a Particular Direction

Dish-shaped aerials have a dish-shaped reflector (surprise, surprise...).

1) The dish is pointed at a satellite, and its shape focuses the signal onto a receiver at the centre of the dish.
2) They're used for things like satellite TV reception and deep space radio communication.

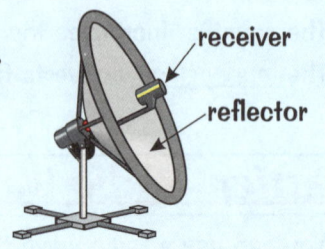

Ferrite Rods are Useful Internal Aerials

Ferrite rod aerials consist of a coil of wire wrapped around a ferrite (iron-rich) material.

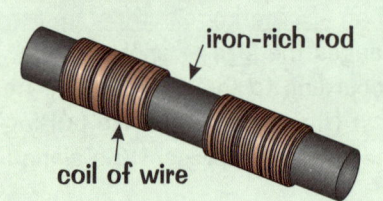

1) Because they are compact they're useful to use as internal aerials.
2) You'll find them inside portable radios and mobile phones.

Ferret Rods — a coil of ferrets wrapped around Rod Stewart.

Using the right sort of aerial is pretty important. If you tried picking up a TV signal with a simple dipole you probably wouldn't get very far... Which is why most TV aerials are those complicated looking branched things. The only problem with those is that you have to be pretty careful about the direction you point them in (unlike a simple dipole). Make sure you learn two things each aerial is used for...

Module 5 — Communications

Wireless Communication

Thought choosing an aerial was the end of this wireless communication malarkey? No such luck matey...

Waves Have Wavelength, Amplitude and Frequency

Radio waves (like all waves) have a wavelength, frequency and amplitude.

1) Wavelength is the distance from one peak to the next. The wave in diagram A has a longer wavelength than the wave in diagram B.
2) Amplitude is the height from the mid-line to the peak. Wave B has a greater amplitude than wave A.
3) Frequency is the number of complete waves there are per second. So 1 kHz is 1000 waves a second, and 1 MHz is 1 000 000 waves a second.
4) You can use oscilloscopes to 'see' and measure waves and the signals they carry.

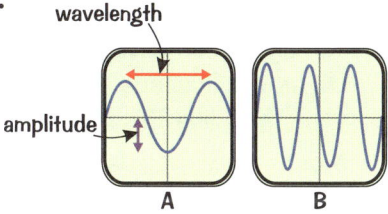

Different Signals are Broadcast on Different Frequencies

Different signals are broadcast on waves with different frequencies, so that they don't interfere with each other. That's why you have to tune a radio receiver to the broadcast frequency to pick up the signal you're after.

1) Radio waves include MW (Medium Waves) with a frequency of about 500 kHz to 1.5 MHz, and LW (Long Waves) with a frequency of about 150 to 300 kHz.
2) VHF (Very High Frequency) waves have a frequency of 90 to 110 MHz.
3) Terrestrial television uses a frequency of about 600 MHz.
4) Wi-Fi / Bluetooth uses a frequency of about 2.4 GHz.
5) Mobile phones use frequencies of about 0.9 to 2.5 GHz.
6) Satellite communications normally have a frequency between 3.7 and 31 GHz.

1 GHz = a billion waves per second

100 kHz	1 MHz	10 MHz	100 MHz	1 GHz	10 GHz
LW	MW		VHF TV	Wi-Fi	Satellites

Radio Waves Can be Absorbed or Reflected...

Radio waves can travel through solid objects, but they can also be absorbed or reflected by them.

1) Absorption is when the radio wave passes into an object, but doesn't make it to the other side.
2) Reflection is when the radio wave bounces back off an object.

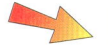

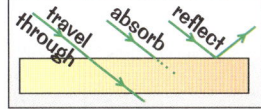

...or Interfered With

When radio waves with similar frequencies overlap, they distort each other. This is called interference, and is what causes 'fuzziness' when you listen to the radio. There are two main types of interference:

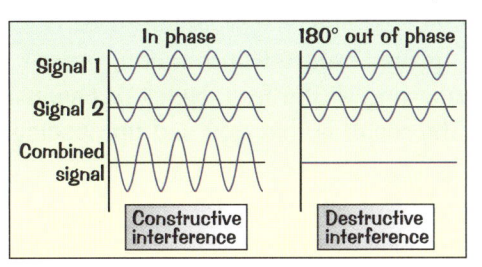

1) CONSTRUCTIVE INTERFERENCE happens when two waves are 'in phase' (peaks together and troughs together) — their amplitudes combine.
2) DESTRUCTIVE INTERFERENCE happens when two waves are 'out of phase' (peaks with troughs). This decreases the amplitude of the wave. In fact, if identical waves are exactly 180° out of phase, they cancel out completely.

Waves travelling from the same point (like a transmitter aerial) can take different paths — some might travel in a straight line, and others might bounce off a few surfaces. This means that some of the waves are out of phase when they arrive at a receiver, and you get destructive interference.

Module 5 — Communications

Analogue and Digital Signals

So you know about sending a signal, but what about the signal itself? It's either analogue or digital...

Analogue Signals Can Have Any Value

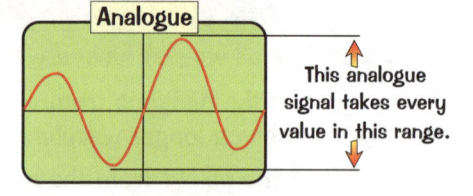

1) Analogue signals are continuous, variable signals.
2) The signal can have any value (within a certain range). On an oscilloscope (see previous page), it'd look something like this nice diagram right here...
3) Most natural data is analogue — speech, music, light intensity, that kind of stuff.

Analogue — This analogue signal takes every value in this range.

Digital Signals Have Fixed Values

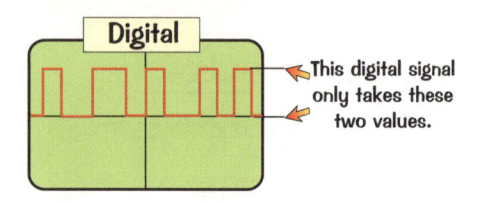

Digital — This digital signal only takes these two values.

1) Digital signals are non-continuous.
2) The signal is sent in pulses which have discrete, fixed values — it's a series of 0s and 1s (or ONs and OFFs) like this: 01100101011100101010011011010
3) All the electronic equipment you use (computers, CD players, etc.) uses digital signals.

Analogue's More Accurate, but It's Normally Distorted

1) The main advantage of analogue signals is that they're a true representation of the original 'natural' signal (speech, etc.).
2) You can send analogue signals using simple transmitters and receivers.
3) The main problem is that signals get degraded as they travel along (i.e. they get weaker), so you have to amplify them at the receiving end. If they've picked up noise (fuzziness and inaccuracy) along the way, then you'll amplify that too — the signal gets distorted.
4) Analogue signals are also difficult to compress or encrypt, so they're trickier to store and less secure.

"How's things Doris?" "Not bad cheers Anna."

Digital Signals are Normally Better Quality

1) The main advantage of digital signals over analogue ones is that they can be transmitted without losing much quality. They pick up noise just like analogue signals, but it's easy to work out what the original signal looked like if it's digital, so noise isn't a problem — and doesn't get amplified.

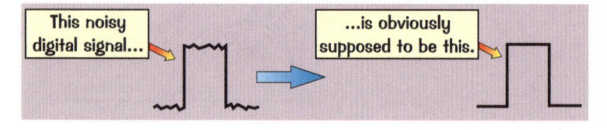

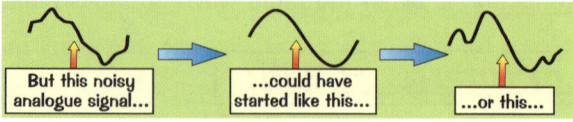

This noisy digital signal... ...is obviously supposed to be this.
But this noisy analogue signal... ...could have started like this... ...or this...

2) They can also be manipulated easily (compressed or encrypted — see next page).
3) Multimedia uses digital signals because digital devices can all be compatible with each other.
4) The main problem is that digital signals often need to be compressed before transmission, and uncompressed when they're received. For example, transmitting all the free digital TV channels in the UK would be impractical if they weren't compressed. The result is that you end up needing more complex equipment than for analogue signals.
5) They're also a less accurate representation of the original signal. Not all values are possible, so there's a certain level of distortion (depending on the bit rate — see next page).

I've heard that digital signals are made of fingers...

Make sure you understand the difference between analogue and digital signals — it's easy marks...

Module 5 — Communications

Converting Analogue to Digital

Right then, if digital's so good, you'd better learn how to convert analogue signals to digital ones... And while you're at it, why not find out about encryption and costs. It'll be great fun. Honest.

Digital Signals are Created by Sampling

1) Analogue signals are continuous in time. An analogue-to-digital converter reads the analogue signal at regular points in time and turns it into a digital number. This process is called sampling.

2) The sampling rate is the rate at which the converter samples the analogue signal. For example, telephones take a reading from the analogue signal of your voice 8000 times every second (8 kHz), so they're not as good quality as CD audio, which has a sample rate of 44.1 kHz.

3) The digital numbers obtained by sampling are changed into binary code to form a digital signal.

Number	0	1	2	3	4	5	6	7	8	9
Binary Code	0	1	10	11	100	101	110	111	1000	1001

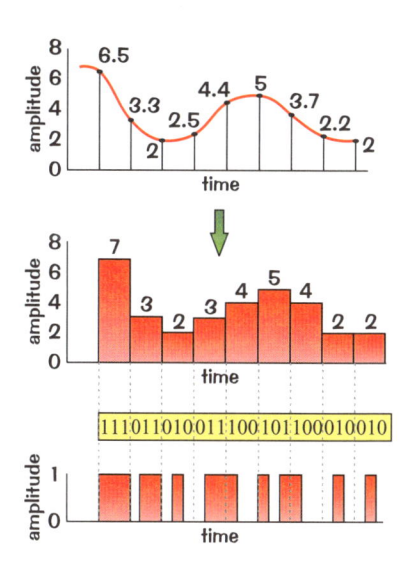

Digital Signals are Made Up of Bits and Bytes

Digital signals usually consist of binary data, which is a sequence of bits.

1) A bit is a binary digit (usually 0 or 1). It is the basic unit of information storage and communication.
2) A byte is a group of 8 bits.
3) Bit rate is just the number of bits processed per second. It affects the connection speed and transfer rate in communication systems (higher bit rate = faster system...).

Digital Signals Can be Encrypted for Security

Digital signals can be encrypted and sent in code to keep them private.

1) Encryption is used for internet shopping. Customers' personal details and credit card details are encrypted before transfer so they can't be read by anyone else. This is really important — if other people could read the details they could go off shopping with your credit card.

2) It's also used to encode some cable and satellite TV channels. This way broadcasters can charge money for particular channels — if you don't pay the fee you can't decode the channel.

3) Spies love a bit of encryption too, when they're sending top secret information to each other.

The More We Use Digital the Cheaper It Becomes

Converting analogue systems to digital systems involves lots of different costs — developing new technology, building and installing devices to convert analogue to digital, adapting existing communications networks to carry digital signals, maintaining digital networks...

However, the more digital communication is used, the more cost-effective it becomes. Digital communications networks can be used by a large number of customers at once. So if more people use a network, the costs involved in running it are spread out, making it cheaper for each individual.

So if everyone buys new phones, I can get one for free, right?
That whole sampling thing is a bit tricky. Make sure you've understood the diagrams...

Module 5 — Communications

Communication Links

There are lots of ways to send both analogue and digital signals, whether it's with waves or wires...

Copper Wires Use Electric Current to Carry Signals

Copper wiring is a cheap and cheerful way of carrying signals as varying electrical currents. A lot of copper wire networks have been replaced by optical fibres now, but it's still handy for sending information over short distances — e.g. from a radio aerial to a receiver, or between intercoms.

Optical Fibres Use Light or Infrared to Carry Signals

Optical fibres are much better for transmitting digital data over long distances, and for transmitting large amounts of data.

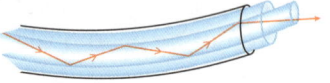

1) The signals are carried as waves of light or infrared radiation (like radio waves but with a shorter wavelength).
2) Most telephone networks now use optical fibres. They're better than copper wires because you can use them for telephone signals, the internet and cable TV signals, often all on the same line.
3) Optical fibres are also used to link computers in a network because they can transmit loads of data.

Radio Waves Carry Signals Without Using Wires

1) Radio waves are used in wireless communications systems like radio, TV and mobile phones.
2) Radio signals are broadcast on a range of different frequencies (see p.93).
3) They're really useful if you want to transmit information across an area where you can't install wires.

Communication Links Can Use Analogue and Digital Signals

Analogue signals are often converted to digital signals (see p.95) before being broadcast or sent down wires.

EXAMPLE: TELEPHONE LINKS — the phone converts your voice into electrical analogue signals (1), which are carried down copper wires (2) to a local exchange (3). The exchange converts them to digital signals to be sent over long distances down optical fibres (4). At the other end, they're converted back into analogue signals (5) and sent down copper wires (6) to someone's phone (7).

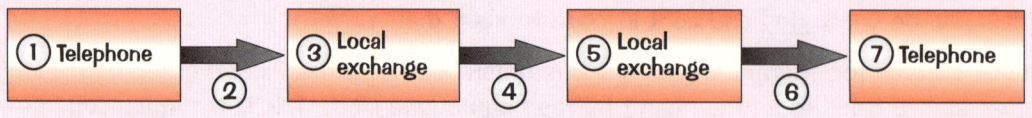

① Telephone → ② → ③ Local exchange → ④ → ⑤ Local exchange → ⑥ → ⑦ Telephone

EXAMPLE 2: EMAILS mainly involve digital signals. When you type words into a keyboard, you're creating a digital signal, but it's converted to analogue by the modem to be sent down your copper telephone wires. A modem at the other end converts it back to computer-friendly digital.

Computer → Modem → Telephone network → Modem → Computer

Digital Data Can be Stored Easily

There are loads of devices around that store digital data, and you probably use a fair few of them every day: CD-ROMs, memory sticks, hard disk drives, 'flash' memory cards... I could carry on listing them, but in the exam they'll expect you to know no more than two examples.

No optical fibres? Say goodbye to broadband...

Optical fibres have revolutionised communication links — without them, your computer network would be unbelievably slow, there'd be no cable TV and surfing the net would be more like running through custard.

Module 5 — Communications

Pictures and Video

The transmission of good quality pictures and videos is becoming more and more important, and if you want good quality you need a system that can handle lots of data at high speed...

Pictures Can be Represented by Rows of Pixels

1) Digital cameras contain millions of tiny sensors that measure the light at millions of single points to form an image.
2) These single points are called pixels, and they're given a value that represents their colour.
3) The value's usually a binary word — a series of binary numbers called bits (see p.95).

   - '1 bit colour' pixels are represented by 0 or 1. They're black or white.
   - '2 bit colour' pixels use a 2 bit binary word (2 numbers long). The word can be 11, 00, 10 or 01, so they're one of four different colours.
   - '4 bit colour' pixels use a 4 bit binary word — they're one of 16 different colours.
   - '8 bit colour' pixels use an 8 bit binary word — they're one of 256 different colours.

   a 4 bit fish

4) So, if more bits are used for each pixel, there can be more colours on the final image, making it a closer representation of the original scene.
5) Also, the greater the total number of pixels in a given area, the more detailed the image can be:

   The array in a 3.1 megapixel camera is normally 2048 sensors wide by 1536 sensors high — it records an image as 3.1 million pixels. A 6 megapixel camera has lots more sensors, and records an image as 6 million pixels. The 6 megapixel camera would be able to take more detailed pictures than the 3.1 megapixel camera.

Videos Can be Represented by Frames

Videos are made up of lots of frames. Each frame is a picture made up of pixels.

1) A video camera records a certain number of frames per second — normally about 30.
2) There can be thousands of frames in a movie, hundreds of thousands of pixels on each frame, and a few bits to every pixel — that's billions of bits per movie... Which is why video uses so much data.

Video Bit Rate is the Amount of Data Transferred per Second

To work out how much data is transferred every second, you need this formula:

video bit rate = pixel word size × no. of pixels per frame × refresh rate

- in bits per second
- the number of bits per pixel (e.g. 4 bit colour)
- this one sort of speaks for itself... (e.g. 3.1 million pixels)
- the number of frames per second (e.g. films are 24 frames per second)

Don't be fooled by cameras with 76 gazillion pixels...

In theory, a 1.3 MP camera should be able to make standard sized photos (6 × 4 inches). OK, so you'll need a fair few more than 1.3 MP to be on the safe side, but once you get past 4 or 5 MP, it's really just about how good the lens is, not how many pixels you've got. Unless your prints are 10 miles wide...

Module 5 — Communications

Revision Summary for Module 5

Well here's the end of module 5, and what a crazy module it was. Some bits were really easy (like product specifications and basic block diagrams) and other bits could've been brain-implodingly difficult (like sampling and bit rates). Oh... but... hang on a minute... what's this? A page full of questions to work through so that you can cover the whole thing in one graceful move? Hazaah! The Sun is shining on you today, my friend.

1) What's the 'error rate' of a coding system?
2) How has email affected people's lives?
3) Give three ways in which the Government regulates the communications industry.
4) List seven things that you would expect to find on a product specification.
5) What six things do companies need to consider before creating a new product?
6) List the advantages and disadvantages of mains power and battery power.
7) What do sound technicians do?
8) Describe the main parts of a live outside broadcast system.
9) Draw the hazard symbols for the following:
   a) a laser   b) an electric shock hazard   c) double insulation
10) What's involved in risk assessment?
11) In a flowchart, when would you use ovals, parallelograms and diamonds?
12) Draw a block diagram for a television.
13) Describe the flow of information that occurs when you scan an image into a computer then print it off.
14) Label all six components in this circuit.
15) What does 'LDR' stand for? What does an LDR do?
16) Is the circuit in question 14 series or parallel?
17) Draw the formula triangle relating current to voltage and resistance.
18)* The voltage across a component is 6 V and the current passing through it is 1.2 A. What is its resistance?
19) What equation can you use to calculate power from current and voltage?
20) Draw a block diagram of a radio communication system.
21) What does 'modulation' mean?
22) What are the advantages of a simple dipole aerial over a dish-shaped aerial?
23) State two common uses of ferrite rod aerials.
24) How are radio signals prevented from interfering with each other?
25) Draw a diagram to show constructive interference of radio waves.
26) Describe the difference between analogue and digital signals.
27) What are the advantages of digital signals over analogue signals?
28) What is meant by 'sampling'?
29) How many bits are there in a byte?
30) Give two examples of copper wire being used in a communication link.
31) How do optical fibres carry signals? What are they used for?
32) Name two devices that store digital data.
33) What information do you need to calculate the bit rate of a video?

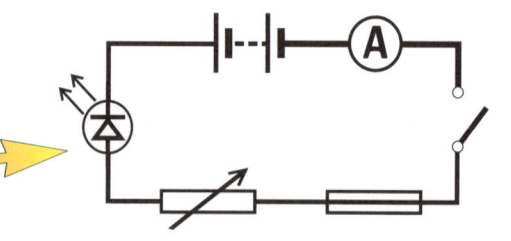

* Answers on p.132

Module 5 — Communications

Module 6 — Materials and Performance

Selecting Materials

When you buy stuff, you can usually assume that it'll work and that it won't fall apart straight away. That's because the people who made the things you buy have (hopefully) thought a lot about what materials to use and how those materials are put together.

In Some Jobs You Need to Know About Materials

There are loads of people who need to know a lot about materials to be able to do their jobs. Here are some examples:

1) A researcher who develops artificial hip joints.
2) A toy designer who makes toys for young children.
3) A designer of sports equipment.
4) A stage designer who has been asked to create a new film set.

Designers Need To Use Criteria to Select the Right Materials

1) Designers need to think carefully about what materials they could use.
2) They need to consider the main criteria for a particular material, e.g. durability (how hard-wearing the material is), cost, environmental impact and aesthetic appeal (how attractive the material is). Here are three examples:

HIP JOINTS

Hip joints need to be durable — you wouldn't really want to keep having new operations to replace them. However they don't need to be aesthetically appealing since they're inside the body.

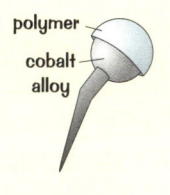

polymer, cobalt alloy

CHILDREN'S TOYS

Young children's toys have to be tough so they don't break up into small parts if they're chewed.

They also need to be aesthetically appealing and fairly cheap so that people will want to buy them.

RACING BIKES

Racing bikes need to be light and strong. The best materials tend to be very expensive, so manufacturers need to choose the material very carefully if they want to sell the bikes in any great quantity.

Materials Can Be Shaped and Joined in Different Ways

1) When you're deciding which materials to use, you also need to think about how they can be shaped, and how different bits can be joined together.
2) Metals can be shaped using plastic deformation (see page 104) or by casting (pouring molten material into a mould).
3) Wood can be carved, and plastic can be moulded in lots of different ways.
4) Materials can be joined by, e.g. gluing, soldering, crimping (bending together) and riveting.

Crimping — I thought that was just for 80s hairstyles...

A lot of thought and planning goes into creating new products. The right materials need to be chosen so that the product has suitable properties. It'd be no good riding along on a racing bike made from lead or having a replacement hip joint made of jelly. You wouldn't be going far on either...

Health and Safety

OK, it's not the job that dreams are made of, but the people who work in standards organisations are unsung heroes. They're the people who make sure stuff does what it's supposed to and does it safely.

Products Need to be Safe — and Work Properly Too

1) You'd be cross if a product didn't do its job properly, or broke after only a few days.
2) A badly made product might also be dangerous.
3) That's why it's important for products to meet certain basic standards.

Some Organisations Help to Promote Good Standards

There are three main organisations that help to ensure good standards.

1) The British Standards Institution (BSI) produces standards labelled with 'BS' and a number. Each standard is a document describing how well a product should do its job, how safe it should be, etc.

    This is the BSI Kitemark. If a product displays this logo, then it has been tested by the BSI to make sure it conforms to the BSI standards the manufacturer says it does.

2) The European Committee for Standardisation. A product marked 'CE' means that it meets European legal requirements, which include some basic European standards.
3) The International Organisation for Standards (ISO). These standards can be used throughout the world.

Products Must Remain Safe Even in Exceptional Circumstances

Although you can't guarantee that something could never be dangerous, you can build in a safety margin. This means that the product is safe even in conditions much more extreme than normal use. Here are two examples:

1) Bridges are built to withstand a larger weight than the greatest possible weight of traffic on them. They also need to be strong enough to cope with high winds and earthquakes.
2) Food manufacturers mustn't exceed tolerable daily intakes for any of their ingredients. These tolerable daily intakes are calculated with a wide safety margin to reduce the chances of making anyone ill.

Some People's Jobs Involve Enforcing Standards

1) A Trading Standards officer makes sure that products are consistently of a sufficient quality and that they're safe to use.
2) An Environmental Health practitioner makes sure that workplaces are healthy and safe.
3) A building control surveyor checks that all of the relevant regulations are being observed during the construction of new buildings.

It's your job to enforce good standards — of revision...

It makes sense to make sure that products are made to good standards — think about how dangerous it could be if they weren't. We get into cars fairly confidently knowing that they've been put through lots of different safety tests — but it'd be a very different matter without these standards.

Module 6 — Materials and Performance

Mechanical Properties

To help you choose between different materials for a job, you can look up their properties in reference books or on the Internet. But to make any sense of them, you've got to understand what the technical terms actually mean.

Compression and Tension — Squashing and Stretching

1) Objects can be loaded under compression or tension.

COMPRESSION
- Compression means that the object is being squashed.
- This bottle is under compression.

TENSION
- Tension means it's being stretched.
- This rope is under tension.

3) The maximum load that an object can withstand under tension (or compression) is called the tensile (or compressive) strength. If the load is bigger than this value, the object will break.

To Describe Materials Usefully You Need to Use the Right Words

STIFFNESS / FLEXIBILITY

If a material doesn't deform (change shape) much under a large load then it's stiff. If it changes shape easily it's flexible. Something can be made more rigid (stiffer) by using a different, stiffer material or by changing its shape (making it thicker, say).

Using stiffer poles makes a tent more rigid.

TOUGHNESS / BRITTLENESS

A tough material can deform quite a lot without breaking. A brittle material breaks before it deforms very much at all.

If you sit on a pair of glasses made from a tough material, they can (in theory) be bent back into shape afterwards. If the material is brittle though, they'll just break. Oops.

HARDNESS

A hard material is resistant to scratching or indentation. A harder material will be able to cut through a softer one.

Chisels are made out of hard material so that they can cut easily through softer materials like wood.

DENSITY

A dense material has a large mass contained in a small volume. Most sports equipment is made from materials of low density, since you usually want it to be as light as possible.

You need a racing bike to be big enough for you but as light as possible (so you can go as fast as possible). Similarly, you'd want a lightweight tennis racket — it'd take a lot more effort to swing something really heavy.

Sometimes it's useful for materials to be stiff and hard...

It's really important that you use the right words to describe properties of materials. It's easy to get confused, so make sure you know what's meant by stiff, flexible, tough, brittle, hard and dense...

Module 6 — Materials and Performance

Measuring Properties

It's not enough to know the jargon — you have to know how to test various properties. Scientists will have used similar tests to the ones below to work out the data you can find in reference books.

You Can Use Force-Extension Graphs to Compare Stiffness

1) To compare the stiffness (see p.101) of different materials, this is what you'd do:

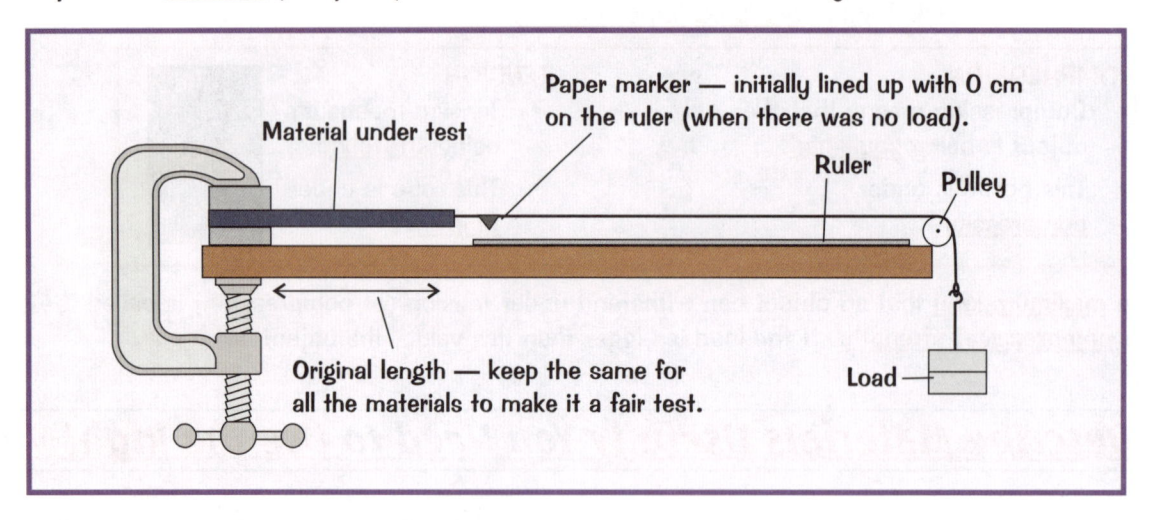

Diagram: Material under test clamped to a bench, with a paper marker initially lined up with 0 cm on the ruler (when there was no load). Ruler extends along the bench to a pulley at the edge, from which a load hangs. Original length — keep the same for all the materials to make it a fair test.

2) Remember to wear safety specs and to keep your feet well away from the hanging loads.
3) Gradually increase the load on the material by adding weights, and measure the extension (total length – original length) of the material each time using a ruler, as shown above.
4) Plot a force-extension graph for each different material.
5) This graph shows the results of testing three different materials with increasingly heavy loads. The stiffest material is shown by the shallowest gradient.

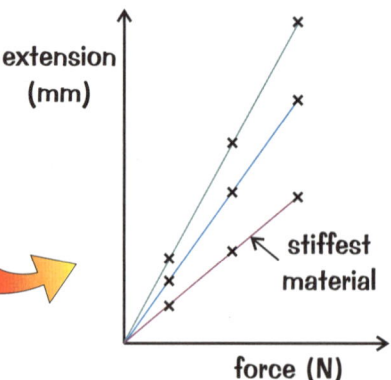

Graph: extension (mm) vs force (N), showing three lines with crosses; the shallowest line is labelled "stiffest material".

You Can Measure Tensile and Compressive Strength

1) To find a material's tensile strength you could use the apparatus shown in the diagram above for measuring stiffness. You'd just keep on adding the loads until the material broke.
2) The load at which an object breaks is its tensile strength.
3) To measure compressive strength you could use the apparatus in this diagram. You'd keep tightening the clamp until the object broke.
4) The load at which the object breaks is its compressive strength.

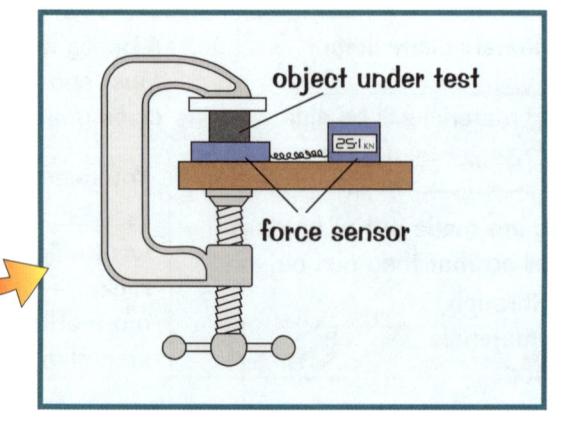

Diagram: object under test being compressed in a clamp with a force sensor reading 25.1 kN.

And the compressive strength of my finger is — ouch...

Make sure you know what experiment you'd do to compare the stiffness of materials in the lab, and also how to measure compressive and tensile strength. Cover up the page and see how much you can remember — get scribbling those diagrams down.

Module 6 — Materials and Performance

Interpreting Data

I hope you didn't think force-extension experiments were boring — because to make your results more reliable, you have to do the same experiment at least twice. Who said materials science wasn't fun...

Results Tables are Useful in Experiments

1) When you design a table, you need to put headings in the top row and include the units.
2) To make your data reliable you should repeat your readings, keeping all the conditions the same, and find the average. The more times you do your experiment, the more reliable your result will be.
3) To work out an average you need to use this formula:

> Average = total of the results ÷ number of results you added

temperature (°C)	length 1 (mm)	length 2 (mm)	average length (mm)
20.0	500.12	500.14	500.13
30.0	500.14	500.15	500.15
40.0	500.26	500.46	500.36
50.0	500.31	500.24	500.27
60.0	500.32	500.28	500.30
70.0	500.35	500.46	500.41
80.0	500.40	500.50	500.45
90.0	500.50	500.51	500.51

For example, you might investigate how the length of a steel rod depends on temperature (see page 109) and you'd make a table of results a bit like this. The experiment has been done twice, and the averages are in the last column.

This average was calculated by doing (500.40 + 500.50) ÷ 2 = 500.45

Draw a Graph to Spot a Trend...

1) When you draw a graph, always plot the independent variable (the one you change) on the x-axis, and the dependent variable (the one you measure) on the y-axis. Remember to include the units.
2) Then you can draw a line (or curve) of best fit.

... And Outliers...

1) An outlier in the data is a point that's a long way away from where you'd expect (from looking at the rest of the data points).
2) 'Dodgy' points like this are also called anomalous results. You should ignore them when you're drawing a line of best fit.
3) For example, in this data the 40 °C measurement is an outlier. A quick check of the table suggests that the second reading could be wrong. It might be because you misread the thermometer, or a squirrel armed with a blowtorch burst through the window and heated the rod just before you took a reading. You would need to go back and re-measure.

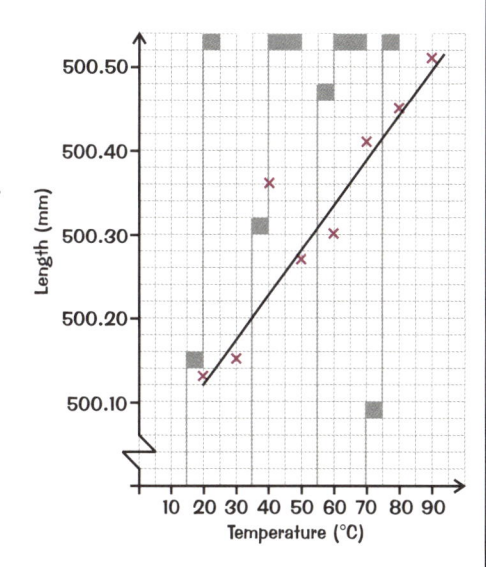

...And Draw Conclusions

1) From the graph above, you can see that as the temperature increases, the length of the steel rod increases. The trend is a straight line — there's a linear relationship.
2) BUT... there is quite a lot of scatter in the graph — maybe your results weren't very accurate.
3) Also, the range of temperatures tested is quite small. If you investigated a bigger range you might actually get a curved graph. When scientists are choosing materials to use, they have to test the materials in all the conditions they'll have to cope with... and then some (for safety — p. 100).

Module 6 — Materials and Performance

Elastic and Plastic Behaviour

Some clothes stretch slightly when you put them on — stretch jeans or a nice leotard, say. Then when you take them off they return to their original shape. Welcome to the world of elastic behaviour.

Materials Change Their Shape Under Tension and Compression

1) All materials change their shape (deform) when they're put under tension or compression (p.101).
2) If the material behaves elastically, it will return to its original shape when the force is removed.
3) If the material behaves plastically, it won't return to its original shape. It's permanently deformed.
4) Note — a material doesn't actually have to be made from plastic for it to 'behave plastically'. 'Plastic' and 'elastic' are ways of behaving.
5) Usually, materials behave elastically when experiencing small forces and plastically when experiencing large forces. The point at which a material stops being elastic and starts to behave plastically is called the elastic limit. Different materials have different elastic limits.
6) For example, seat belt material acts elastically when you pull gently to put the belt on. In a collision, when the force on a seat belt is large, it behaves plastically, reducing the chance of injury (p.108).

You Can Show Elastic and Plastic Behaviour on a Graph

1) You can predict the elastic and plastic behaviour of a material from a force–extension graph.
2) The straight-line part of the graph shows where the material will behave elastically.
3) The elastic limit is where the graph starts to curve. (These graphs usually start off as a straight line but become a curve as larger forces are added.)
4) With loads that are bigger than the elastic limit, the material will behave plastically.

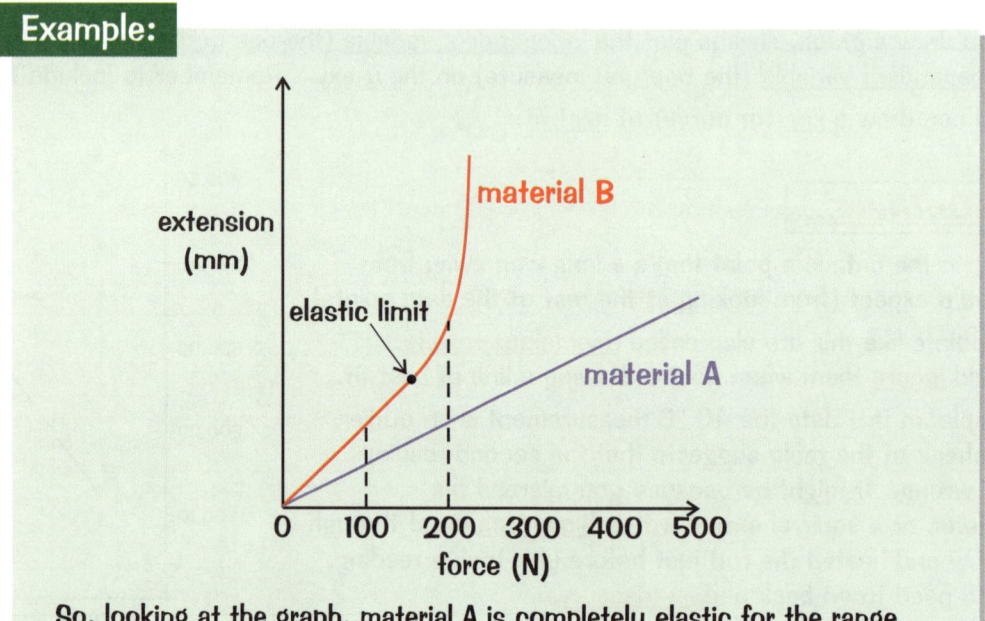

Example:

[Graph showing extension (mm) vs force (N) from 0 to 500. Material A is a straight line. Material B curves upward with elastic limit marked around 100-200 N.]

So, looking at the graph, material A is completely elastic for the range of values shown. However, a force of 100 N on material B will make it deform elastically but a force of 200 N will make it deform plastically.

I'm not flicking rubber bands — I'm studying elastics...

It's really important to know the difference between plastic and elastic behaviour — especially if you design cycling shorts for a living. Graphs are really useful for showing when a material will behave elastically or plastically — make sure you know how to spot when a material is behaving in which way.

Module 6 — Materials and Performance

Metals, Ceramics and Polymers

It's important that new products are made from suitable materials, and there's plenty of choice...

Different Materials are Suited to Different Jobs

There are loads of different materials out there. What they're used for depends on their properties.

Different Metals and Alloys Have Different Properties...

...but, generally speaking, most metals are:

1) MALLEABLE — they can be hammered or rolled into flat sheets or pipes.
2) GOOD CONDUCTORS of heat and electricity.
3) DUCTILE — they can be drawn into wires.
4) SHINY
5) STIFF

See the next page for more on the properties of alloys.

These properties make metals suitable for things like water pipes, saucepan bases, electrical wires, girders in buildings, car bodies... the list goes on.

Polymers Have Many Useful Properties

Polymers include nylon, polythene and PVC.

1) Polymers are INSULATORS of heat and electricity.
2) They're often FLEXIBLE — they can be bent without breaking.
3) They often behave PLASTICALLY.

Polymers are just plastics, made by joining loads of little molecules together in long chains.

These properties make polymers useful for drinks bottles, bags, electrical wire insulation and much much more.

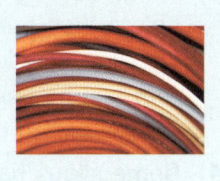

Ceramics are Stiff but Brittle

Ceramics include glass, porcelain and bone china (for posh tea cups). They are:

1) INSULATORS of heat and electricity.
2) BRITTLE — they aren't very flexible and break easily.
3) STIFF

Ceramics are made by 'baking' substances like clay.

Ceramics are used for cups and plates, windows, floor and wall tiles and parts of spark plugs (in cars) among other things.

Then There's Wood and Composites

Wood and wood products are used for doors, pencils, paper, cricket bats, ...

Composites (see page 106) are used for aeroplane bodies, bicycle frames and all sorts of other stuff.

My Mum keeps telling me to learn some uses of iron...

It's really important to take a material's properties into account when designing things — you wouldn't want to use a bendy polymer to make the beams of a house... Make sure you know the main properties and have a few examples of products up your sleeve (not literally, that would be uncomfortable).

Module 6 — Materials and Performance

Alloys and Composites

Sometimes no single material has all the properties you need. By mixing different materials together, you can combine their most useful properties to get the behaviour you want from your new material.

An Alloy is a Metal Mixed With Other Elements

1) A metal alloy is usually a mixture of two or more metals. Sometimes non-metals, such as carbon, are used in alloys too.
2) You can think of it as a solid 'solution' — the atoms of one metal fit into the gaps between the atoms of the other metal (or whatever) — a bit like what you get when sugar dissolves in a cup of tea, but solid.
3) E.g. bronze is a mixture of copper and tin (and is often used to make nice statues).

Alloys Can Improve the Overall Properties of Pure Metals

1) Pure metals can be quite soft.
2) Alloys tend to be a lot harder than pure metals, because the atoms of one metal get in the way of sliding layers of atoms in the other metal.
3) Alloys usually have lower melting points than pure metals. E.g. solder is an alloy of tin and lead that can be used to join ('solder') wires and pipes together — you can melt the solder (to make the join) without melting the wires or pipes themselves.
4) Some alloys have very high tensile strength. E.g. nickel steel (an alloy of iron, carbon and nickel) is used for building bridges.
5) Some alloys are corrosion-resistant, e.g. stainless steel (iron with chromium) is often used for kitchen equipment and cutlery because it doesn't rust.

The pins of a plug would bend too easily if they were made from pure copper. Instead, they are made from brass.

Brass is an alloy of 70% copper and 30% zinc. It's almost as good at conducting electricity as copper and is much harder.

Composite Materials Have One Material Embedded in Another

Composites use the best properties of two or more materials. You have to know a couple of examples:

1) Glass Reinforced Plastic (GRP) consists of fibres of glass embedded in a matrix of plastic. (That's why it's also rather inventively known as fibreglass.) The glass fibres have a high tensile strength but they're brittle. Embedding them in the plastic makes a material that's stronger overall, tougher and is also easily mouldable.

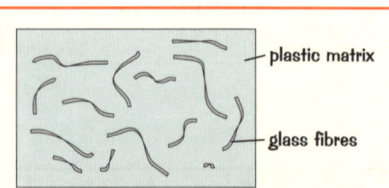

2) Medium Density Fibreboard (MDF) consists of particles of sawdust embedded in a paste of glue. It's nearly as strong and durable as pure wood but it's a lot cheaper.

GRP is used for skis, boats, surfboards...

Alloy Alloy, what have we here...

Alloys and composites are pretty important in the design world. Making them is almost like mixing and matching materials to get exactly the properties you want. Remember, an alloy is a 'solid solution' with at least one metal in it. A composite could be a combination of all sorts of materials.

Module 6 — Materials and Performance

Materials and Forces

Velocity — eh? What's that got to do with 'Materials and Performance'? Well, it's the performance bit that's coming up. So buckle your seat belts (see next page) and get your popcorn ready.

Velocity is How Fast You're Going in a Given Direction

1) To work out the velocity of an object, you need to know how far it travels in a certain time.
2) There's a nice easy formula:

$$\text{Velocity (m/s)} = \frac{\text{Distance (m)}}{\text{Time (s)}}$$

3) Velocity also depends on the direction something's travelling. For example, a car that's travelling eastwards at 30 m/s has a different velocity from one that's going westwards at 30 m/s.

Example:
A car travels 200 m due north in 10 s. What is its velocity?
Velocity = distance ÷ time = 200 ÷ 10 = **20 m/s due north**

Momentum = Mass × Velocity

The momentum of an object is about how much 'oomph' it has and affects how hard it would be to stop.

1) You need to be able to work out the momentum by using this formula.

$$\text{Momentum (kgm/s)} = \text{mass (kg)} \times \text{velocity (m/s)}$$

2) Momentum is proportional to mass and velocity — if you double something's mass or velocity, its momentum also doubles.
3) Like velocity, momentum has direction — it's the same as the direction of the velocity.

Example:
A 2000 kg car is travelling northwards at 20 m/s. Calculate its momentum.
Momentum = mass × velocity = 2000 kg × 20 m/s = **40 000 kgm/s due north**

A Resultant Force Produces a Change in Momentum

1) When you exert a resultant (unbalanced) force on an object, its momentum changes.
2) This momentum change is in the direction of the force. For example, take a supermarket trolley that's travelling at a constant velocity in a straight line. You apply a resultant force to it by pushing it:

Pushing in the same direction as the trolley is travelling increases its momentum in that direction (it speeds up).

Pushing in the opposite direction makes the trolley lose momentum in that direction (it slows down).

Hold on — just one momento...

There are some tricky bits on this page, but stick at it. Velocity, momentum, resultant forces... it all sounds a bit mind-boggling at first. Read the page through a couple of times and it should soon start to make sense. And make sure you work your way through the examples so you know what's going on.

Module 6 — Materials and Performance

Materials and Forces

To change an object's momentum, you need to exert a force on it. That's how kicking balls works.

Force × Time = Change in Momentum

The harder you push something, and the longer you keep pushing for, the more its momentum will change. Here's another lovely formula.

Force (N) × time (s) = change of momentum

Example:
A striker kicks a football with a force of 200 N for 0.1 s.
What is the change of momentum of the football?
Change of momentum = force × time = 200 × 0.1 = 20 kgm/s.

From the formula above you can see that a large force acting for a short time produces the same change of momentum as a small force acting for a long time.

For example, take a trapeze artist who's fallen off her perch. Her momentum will have to change from high (as she hurtles towards the ground at high speed) to zero (when she's stops moving). It's just a question of how quickly that change in momentum happens...

A safety net will stretch as she hits it and slow her down gradually — exerting a smallish force over a longish time. The fairly small forces mean she'd be unlikely to get hurt.

If she's been very daring and performed without a safety net, the solid ground will provide a large force over a short time to stop her. Ouch.

The Right Materials Can Improve Road Safety

Good design of vehicles and safety devices can reduce the risks of road travel — and good design includes choosing materials with suitable properties.

1) For example, you could choose ceramics (p.105) for car brakes. Ceramics provide a lot of friction, they are very hard and they have a high melting point (so won't melt if you brake very suddenly).

2) Materials, such as metal alloys (p.106), which will plastically deform are useful in crumple zones. Crumple zones are parts of the car that crumple on impact, increasing the time taken for the car to come to a complete stop. This makes the forces on the car and the people inside smaller and safer.

3) Crash helmets aren't just a pretty bowl that you strap to your head when you're on a bicycle or motor bike. Most of a helmet is made from a material that will compress or crush on impact, e.g. polystyrene foam. This means your head takes longer to slow down, making the force on it smaller. (Helmets also have a hard outer shell, usually made from some kind of plastic, to help prevent sharp things getting through to your head.)

4) Wearing a seat belt stops you being thrown through the windscreen in an accident — the seat belt snaps tight if there's a collision. But seat belts are made from slightly stretchy material to increase the time it takes for your body to stop moving.

May the force be with you...

Momentum and forces aren't just used in pointless equations. They're really important in safety devices such as bike helmets, and in crumple zones in cars. The aim is always to slow people (or bits of them) down gently — making the force of an impact as small as possible over the longest time possible.

Module 6 — Materials and Performance

Electrical and Thermal Properties

Of course. Electrickery. That's what instantly springs to mind after you've been doing stuff on momentum. What's going to be on the next page? Lion taming, maybe.

Electrical Conductance is the Ability to Conduct Electricity

1) Materials with a high electrical conductance conduct electricity very well — a large electrical current can flow through them for a given voltage.
2) For example, gold and copper have a very high conductance.
3) Materials with a low electrical conductance don't conduct electricity very well.
4) Materials with an electrical conductance that is nearly zero are called electrical insulators.
5) Glass and plastic are examples of good insulators.

Electrical Fittings Need Materials with Electrical Properties

1) The materials in electrical fittings need to have certain mechanical and electrical properties — so that your kettle can work but without giving you a shock, say.
2) For example, the pins on a plug are made from brass (see p.106). That's because it has a high electrical conductance and is very hard.
3) The casing of the plug is made from plastic. That's because plastic can be easily moulded into the right shape and is an electrical insulator.
4) Plastic is also used to insulate electrical wiring around the house. The wires themselves are made from copper because it has a high conductance and is flexible.

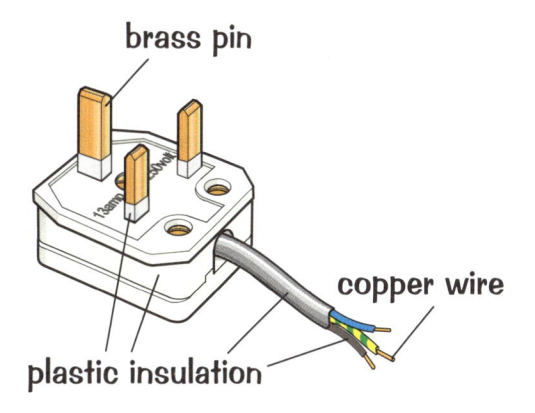

When Things Get Hotter Their Volume Increases

1) When a material gets hot, the atoms inside it vibrate more vigorously and take up more space — the material expands.
2) This is known as thermal expansion.
3) The same rise in temperature causes different materials to expand by different amounts.
4) You can see this effect in a bimetallic strip — a strip with two different metals that expand at different rates when heated.

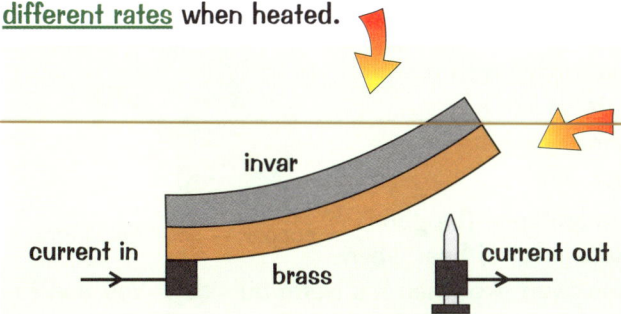

A bimetallic strip can be used to make an electrical switch that's controlled by temperature.
- Brass expands more than invar so the bimetallic strip bends as it gets hotter.
- If the temperature gets high enough the strip will bend far enough upwards and break the circuit.

Conducting electricity — I've never heard of that orchestra...

Materials with high electrical conductance are pretty useful when it comes to making electrical gizmos — it'd be no good having wires made out of string. But electrical insulators are just as important — plug casings are made from insulating material so that there's no risk you'll get zapped when you touch them.

Module 6 — Materials and Performance

Electrical and Thermal Properties

Thermal Expansion Can Be Measured

Different materials expand by different amounts when heated. You could measure how much a material expands using the apparatus below.

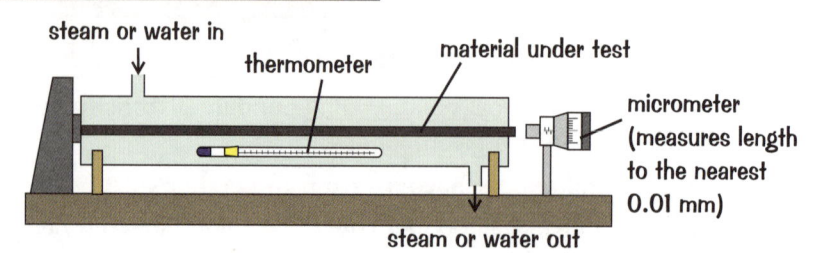

Thermal Conductance is the Ability to Conduct Heat Energy

1) In the same way that some materials conduct electricity better than others, certain materials also conduct heat better than others.
2) The ability to conduct heat energy is called thermal conductance.
3) Materials with a high thermal conductance (e.g. metals) conduct heat energy very quickly when there is a difference in temperature between one side of the material and the other.
4) Materials that have a very low thermal conductance (e.g. air) are called thermal insulators — heat energy flows through them very slowly.
5) Sometimes two objects at the same temperature will feel as though they're at different temperatures. For example, a metal spoon will feel colder to the touch than a wooden spoon at the same temperature. This is because wood and metal have different thermal conductances:

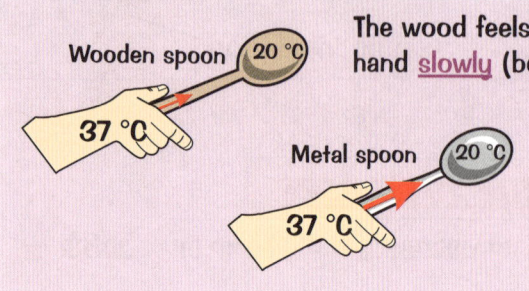

The wood feels warm because heat flows from your hand slowly (because wood is a good insulator).

The metal feels cold because heat flows from your hand quickly (because metal is a good conductor).

The metal feels colder than the wood but it's actually at the same temperature. It's just that heat is flowing from your body at different rates.

Designers Need to Consider Thermal Conductance

1) You'd need to consider thermal conductance if you were designing cookware. For example, saucepans need to have a base with a high thermal conductance — so you'd pick a material like copper. The handles need to be made out of a good thermal insulator (such as plastic) so they don't get too hot to pick up.
2) Building materials need to have a low thermal conductance (be good insulators). This is so that your house doesn't lose a lot of heat when it's cold outside (or gain a lot of heat and become oven-like when it's warm outside). You don't need heating or air conditioning on as much — reducing fuel bills and doing less harm to the environment.

Revision conductance — from the book to your head...

Thinking about thermal conductance is just as important as electrical conductance when it comes to designing things (and revising for your exam...). Products often need some parts to be good thermal conductors and others to be good insulators. The pan example on this page is a pretty good one.

Module 6 — Materials and Performance

Acoustic Properties

I've had to stick egg boxes to my walls so I can play the drums without annoying the neighbours. Architects have to be a bit more high-tech than that though when they're designing a building, and they have to understand what sound actually is. So do you, so read on.

Pitch and Loudness Depend on the Vibrations Causing Them

1) Sounds are caused when objects vibrate at certain frequencies
2) The pitch of the sound depends on the frequency of vibration (the number of vibrations per second). You can produce a high-pitched sound by making something vibrate very quickly.

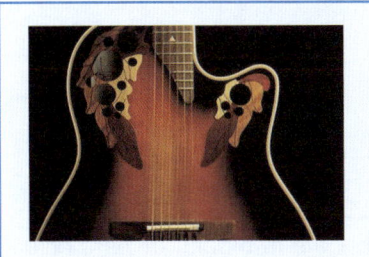

Guitar players make different notes by pressing the strings against the neck of the guitar — this effectively shortens the string. Shorter strings vibrate faster than longer ones, and these faster vibrations produce higher-pitched notes.

3) The loudness (or intensity) of a sound depends on the amplitude of the vibrations (how far the object moves backwards and forwards or side to side). The bigger the vibrations the louder the sound.

If you hit a cymbal hard, it moves a long way up and down — it vibrates with a large amplitude. This creates a loud sound.

If you give the cymbal a gentle tap, it vibrates with a small amplitude. This makes a quiet sound.

The Decibel Scale Measures Loudness

1) You can measure the intensity (loudness) of a sound using the decibel (dB) scale.
2) The decibel scale is not a linear scale. An increase of 10 dB in intensity means a doubling in loudness. So, if the intensity increases by 20 dB the sound will be four times louder.
3) If you listen to loud sounds for a long time you can damage your ears. This might result in permanent hearing loss or tinnitus — a 'ringing' in your ear. MP3 players sometimes have limiters which stop the volume reaching damaging levels.

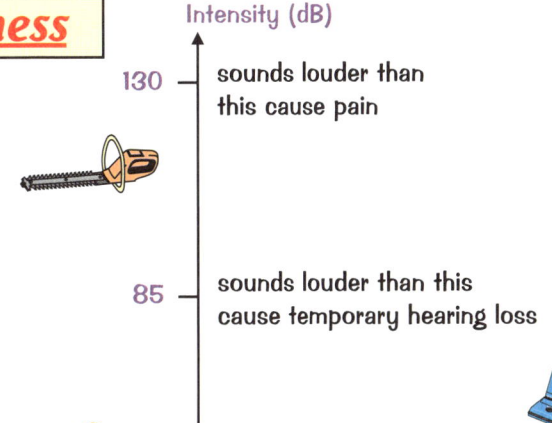

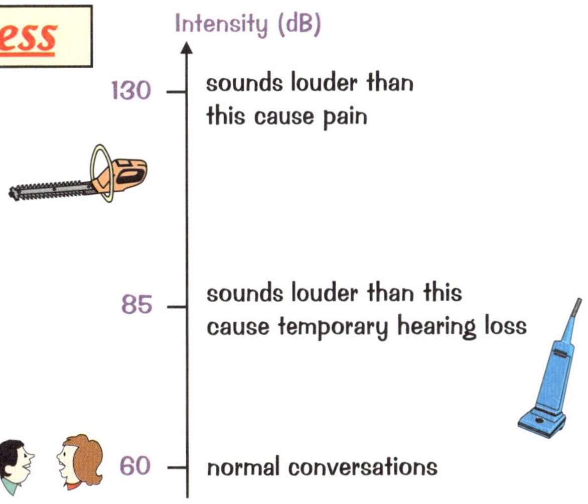

Intensity (dB)

130 — sounds louder than this cause pain

85 — sounds louder than this cause temporary hearing loss

60 — normal conversations

Acoustics — hmm, I prefer the electric guitar...

It's all about frequency and amplitude here. These two things affect the pitch and loudness of a sound. The higher the frequency, the higher pitched the sound will be. The higher the amplitude of the vibration, the louder the sound will be. Remember, sounds above a certain loudness can damage your hearing.

Module 6 — Materials and Performance

Acoustic Properties

Ears Can Hear Sounds of Many Frequencies

1) Your ears are more sensitive to some frequencies of sound than others — some frequencies have to be quite intense before you can hear them at all.

2) The ear is most sensitive at around 2000 Hz (vibrations per second). You can hear very quiet sounds at this frequency — and sounds at 2000 Hz seem louder than sounds at other frequencies even if they have the same intensity. (Fire alarms are usually set at 2000 Hz so that almost everybody will be able to hear them.)

3) The ear just can't hear sounds with too high or too low a frequency — that's why dog whistles are silent to humans.

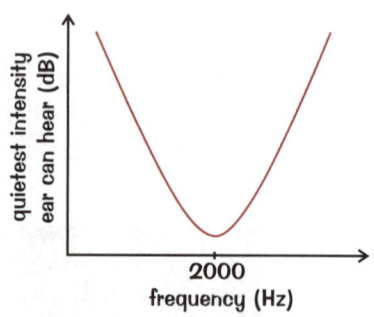

Sound Needs to be Controlled in Buildings

1) Too much noise can be a real problem, particularly for people who live in blocks of flats or in terraced houses. But there are ways to design buildings or decorate rooms so they're quieter.

2) To reduce noise levels, you need to absorb sounds generated inside and reflect sounds made outside.

3) Anything soft will absorb sounds. For example, you might put underlay beneath carpets or laminate flooring. Special acoustic ceiling tiles can help reduce the noise from above or below a room.

4) Anything hard with a flat surface will reflect sounds. For example, windows are hard, flat surfaces that reflect sounds like traffic noise, stopping most of it from entering your house. Double-glazing uses two layers of glass and so reflects even more sound.

There are Different Ways to Isolate Vibrations

1) Many factories have lots of very noisy machinery.

2) Machines are noisy because they're vibrating — and these vibrations may be carried around a factory, since factory buildings are usually rigid structures — they don't absorb vibrations much.

3) To reduce noise levels, you need to isolate the machines' vibrations so that they're not carried around the factory.

4) There are two main ways of doing this — mount the machines on springs or use a supporting floor with fluid-filled dampers.

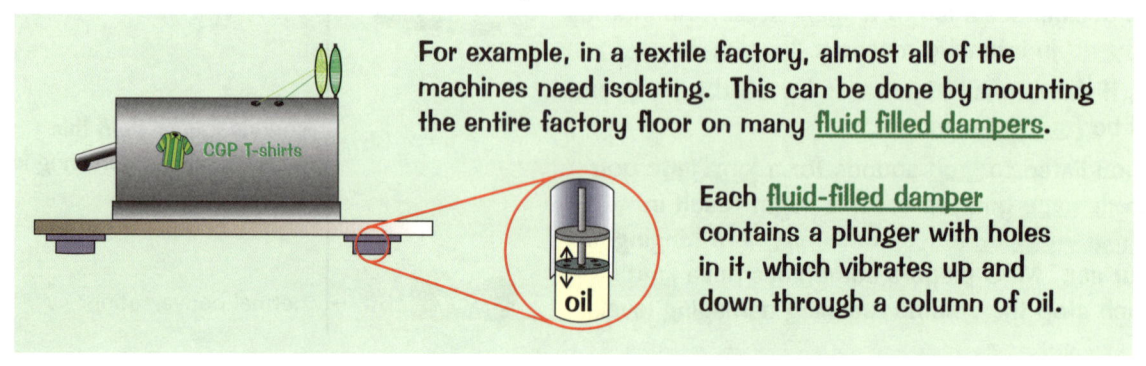

For example, in a textile factory, almost all of the machines need isolating. This can be done by mounting the entire factory floor on many fluid filled dampers.

Each fluid-filled damper contains a plunger with holes in it, which vibrates up and down through a column of oil.

Vibrations — didn't the Beach Boys sing about those...

Although sound can be a great thing, it sometimes needs to be controlled. Make sure you know how vibrations can be controlled — for example, the sound from noisy machinery in a factory. Test yourself by covering up the page and scribbling down everything you can remember. Go on, get learning...

Module 6 — Materials and Performance

Optical Properties

Phew, you've made it through electrical, thermal and acoustic properties — only optical left to go. So, mirror mirror on the wall, which is the fairest optical property of them all?

You'll Have to Describe Optical Properties

1) Transparent — a material is transparent if you can see through it clearly.
2) Reflective — a material is very reflective if most of the light that falls on it reflects (bounces) back off.
3) Translucent — light can pass through the material but you can't see through it clearly. Frosted glass (like the glass used in bathroom windows) is translucent.
4) Opaque — a material is opaque if light can't pass through it.
5) Refractive — refraction is the bending of a light ray when it passes from one medium (material) to another at an angle. Lenses work by refraction (see p.114).

Specialised Glass Does a Specific Job

Glass is pretty useful in many situations because it's transparent, but there's more to it than that. For example, glass is used in vacuum flasks because it can be moulded easily from molten and is a good thermal insulator. However, for some jobs you need specialised glass.

TOUGHENED GLASS
This is used for car windscreens. If the windscreen smashes, it breaks into lots of small, blunt pieces. This reduces the chance of injury since there are fewer sharp edges.

LEAD GLASS
This glass contains lead (surprise), which increases the amount of refraction. This makes objects look more sparkly. It's used to make crystal vases and posh wine glasses.

SELF CLEANING GLASS
This glass has special chemicals that break down dirt so that it washes off easily in the rain.

INFRARED REFLECTIVE GLASS
This glass has a special metal oxide layer that reflects infrared radiation but is transparent to visible light. This reduces the amount of heat energy which passes through the glass. The visors on space-suit helmets use this type of glass.

PHOTOCHROMIC GLASS
This goes dark when exposed to UV light. It's used in sunglasses that react automatically to the strength of sunlight.

Mirrors are Used in Many Ways

1) A mirror is a very smooth sheet of glass backed with a thin layer of highly reflective metal. Light passes through the glass and reflects from the metal layer.
2) Mirrors are used in scientific instruments such as telescopes, in cars so that drivers can see behind them, in buildings to make rooms look bigger, etc. Not forgetting those distorting mirrors which just make you look strange.

I wish my room was made of self-cleaning glass...

Who'd have thought there was so much to know about glass. Before you do anything else, make sure you can describe optical properties. There are five words you need to know — transparent, reflective, translucent, opaque and refractive. Don't get muddled — especially with transparent and translucent.

Module 6 — Materials and Performance

Lenses

A lens is just a piece of glass (or sometimes plastic) that's been shaped so as to focus light. And you thought glass couldn't get any more useful...

Fatter Lenses Bend Light More

1) Lenses are useful because they refract (bend) rays of light.
2) There are two types of lenses you need to know about — converging and diverging.
3) For both types of lens, the fatter the lens, the more it bends the light.

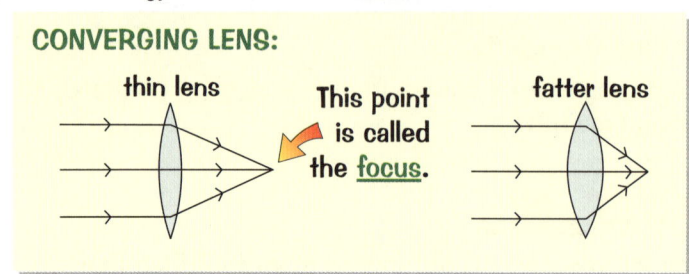

CONVERGING LENS: thin lens — This point is called the focus. — fatter lens

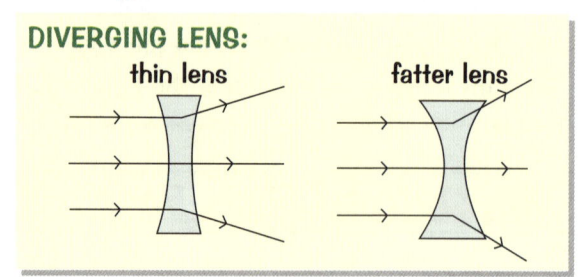

DIVERGING LENS: thin lens — fatter lens

Converging Lenses Focus Parallel Rays Onto a Point

You can see objects because light reflects off them and reaches your eyes.

1) Light rays that reach your eyes from a point on a distant object are parallel to each other.
2) A converging lens brings these parallel rays together at a point on the focal plane.
3) The distance between the centre of the lens and the focal plane is called the focal length.
4) You can work out the power of a lens using this formula.

rays from a far-off point — focal plane — Image of distant point is here — focal length

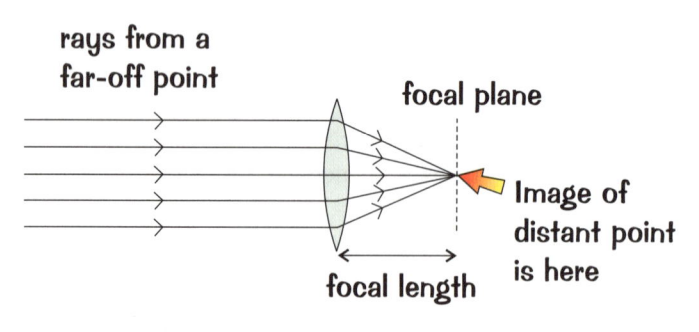

$$\text{Power (in dioptres, D)} = \frac{1}{\text{focal length (in m)}}$$

5) High-powered lenses have a fat shape. They have a small focal length and the images are formed close to the lens.

Diverging Lenses Focus Parallel Rays Away From a Point

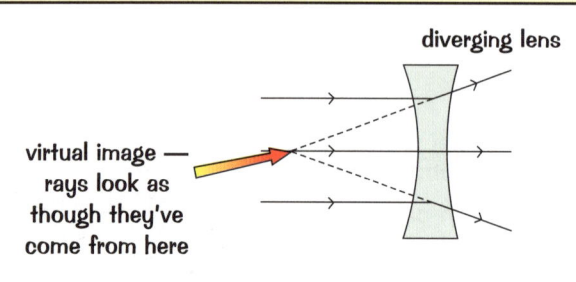

diverging lens

virtual image — rays look as though they've come from here

1) A diverging lens refracts parallel light rays away from each other.
2) The refracted rays look as if they've come from a point close to the lens — but they haven't really.
3) You get a virtual image at the point they seem to have come from (see next page).

Fat = powerful...

Converging lenses and diverging lenses... Yep you guessed it — make sure you know what they do. They both bend parallel rays, but converging lenses bring rays together at a point, whereas diverging rays bend rays away from each other. It's a good idea to learn that before you get on to the next page...

Module 6 — Materials and Performance

Lenses and Images

Lenses — keepin' it real, or virtual, or inverted...

Real Images Can Be Caught on a Screen — Virtual Ones Can't

1) A real image is one that you can capture on a screen — because light rays actually pass through where the image is. This is how your eyes work — the screen is the back of your eye.

2) A virtual image is one that you can't capture on a screen. Light rays don't really pass through where the image is — they just look as though they've come from it.

A real image — object, converging lens, screen, inverted real image here

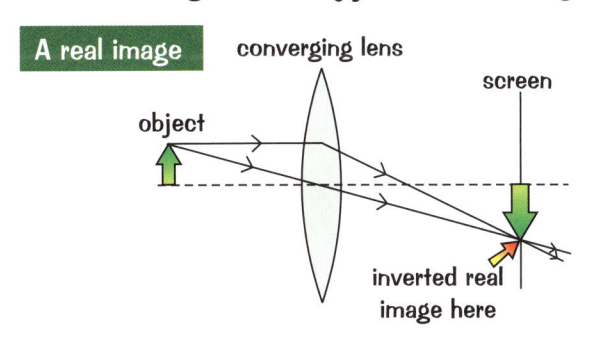

A virtual image — object, diverging lens, upright virtual image here

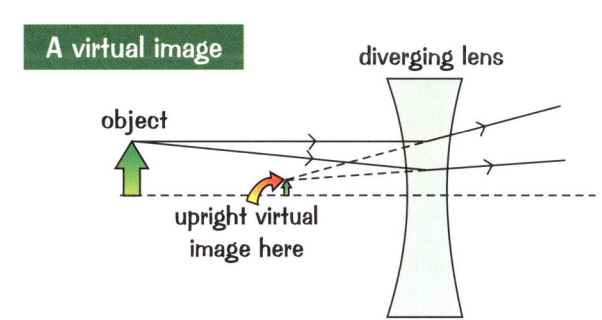

Different Devices Produce Different Types of Image

Eye: Your eyes work by making an inverted, real image that's smaller than the object you're looking at. (Your brain turns it the right way up again so you don't see it upside down.)

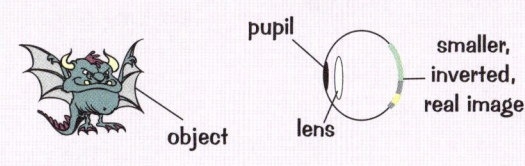

pupil, object, lens, smaller, inverted, real image

Magnifying glass: larger, upright, virtual image — object — magnifying glass

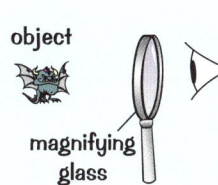

A magnifying glass produces an upright, virtual image which is larger than the object.

Projector: A projector produces an inverted, real image which is larger than the object

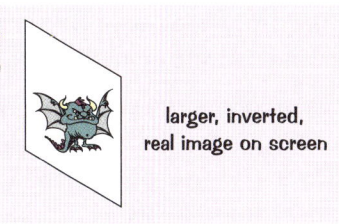

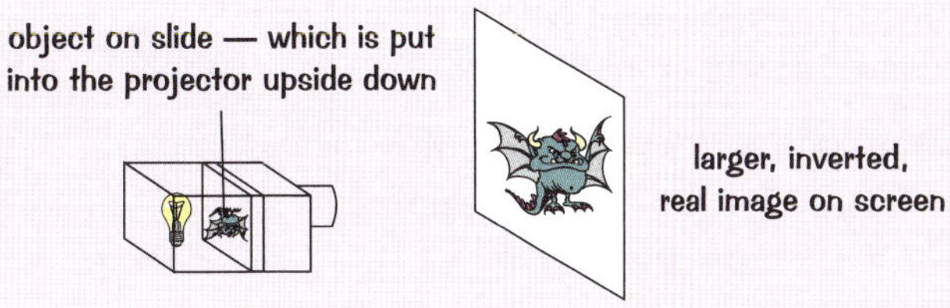

object on slide — which is put into the projector upside down — larger, inverted, real image on screen

Camera: object — camera — inverted, real image

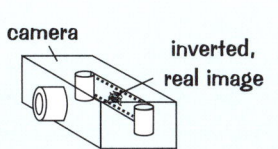

A camera (see next page) produces an inverted, real image which can be larger, smaller or the same size as the object (depending on where the object is relative to the lens).

Virtual images — it's all getting a bit sci-fi...

There's a pretty simple difference between real and virtual images — real images can be caught on a screen whereas virtual images can't. In the exam, you could be asked to describe an image as being real or virtual, so it's probably a good idea to spend some time getting it right now.

Module 6 — Materials and Performance

Camera Lenses

Say cheese... and now stop grinning and make sure you know how a camera works.

Cameras Have Standard Parts

All cameras have the same basic parts:

FOCAL PLANE

At the focal plane is the camera film or a CCD (if it's a digital camera).

VIEWFINDER

The viewfinder is a lens that you look through to see what the picture will be like. Some digital cameras don't have one of these — you look at a small screen instead.

LENS

The lens focuses the light rays onto the focal plane. You get your picture 'in focus' by moving the lens closer to or further away from the back of the camera.

SHUTTER

The shutter is a flap covering the film that opens for a very short time when you take a picture.

APERTURE

The aperture is an adjustable hole — you change its size to allow the right amount of light in. It does the same thing as the pupil in your eye.

Coating Lenses Makes Them Transmit the Light Better

1) When light shines onto glass, some of it passes through but some of it is reflected from the glass. This can be very useful — when you need to check your hair in a shop window, for example.

2) But when you're taking photos the whole idea is for the light to reach the film — so you don't want light to reflect from the lens.

3) So camera lenses are given a thin, transparent coating which makes the lens less reflective — so much that more light can pass through the lens to the film.

Lens without coating
Some light is reflected at the lens surface.

Lens with coating
Almost no reflection.
special coating

Coating lenses keeps them warmer...

In the exam, you could be given a picture of a camera and be asked to label all the parts. So make sure you can. Or you might be asked to explain what the coating on a camera lens is all about and why it's needed. Don't panic though — it's all on this page, so just take your time and learn it bit by bit.

Module 6 — Materials and Performance

Matching Properties and Uses

Right. What material should be used for an oven rack — wood, plastic or cheese? No conferring.

There are Three Steps to Choosing the Right Material

Whatever you want to make, it's important to use the right materials. There are three steps to think about:

> What will the object be used for?
> What will the conditions (temperature, etc.) be like?

E.g. objects used outside all year might have to withstand heat, rain and cold.

⬇

> What properties will the materials used need to have?

See page 101 for stuff on properties.

⬇

> What materials have all these properties?

See page 105 for a summary of the different types of materials.

Example — a Vacuum Cleaner

You might be asked to choose a material, or explain why things are made with certain materials, so here's some practice with those three steps — for the casing of a vacuum cleaner.

1) It's fairly obvious what a vacuum cleaner's used for...

- The motor inside the cleaner will work at a high voltage, so the casing material needs to be electrically insulating to protect the user from the risk of electric shocks.
- It needs to be pushed around — so the material should be fairly lightweight — low density.
- It'll get bashed into table legs, etc. — so the material needs to be quite tough.
- Loads of differently shaped parts are needed — so the material must be mouldable.
- It'd be useful if you could see when it's full — so the material for the dust collector should be transparent.

2) Next, consider which materials have all the properties you've listed.

- Metals and alloys are no good — they conduct electricity and are quite high density.
- Ceramics are no better — they're far too brittle.
- Nobody in their right mind would try to carve vacuum cleaner parts from wood.
- A POLYMER or some sort of COMPOSITE material would fit the bill perfectly though — electrically insulating, quite light, can be quite tough, easy to mould and could be transparent.

You're dumped — you've been using me for my properties...

It's not rocket science this — think what the product will be used for and what properties it'll need, and then try to fit a material to the job. But first you'll have to learn some of the basics — like the types of material there are, what words like 'brittle' mean, and which types of material have which properties.

Module 6 — Materials and Performance

Revision Summary for Module 6

You really shouldn't skip these questions. What's the point in reading that great big section if you're not going to check whether you really know it all? When it comes to the exam, you'll be glad you did.

1) Give two examples of people who need to know about materials and their properties to do their job.
2) Suggest some criteria that designers think about when considering materials for their products.
3) Explain why it's important that products are made to a high standard.
4) Give the name of an organisation that sets product standards.
5) What is a product's safety margin? Why are products made with a safety margin?
6) What do the terms compression and tension mean?
7)* Which material, A, B or C, shown on the force-extension graph is the stiffest?
8) Explain using a diagram how you'd test a material's tensile strength.
9)* Calculate the average of 22.3, 22.4, 22.3 and 22.5.
10)* Will the material shown in the graph behave elastically or plastically with a load of   a) 100 N?   b) 200 N?
11) Describe three properties of   i) metals   ii) ceramics   iii) polymers.
12) What is a metal alloy?
13) Give two benefits of using metal alloys rather than pure metals.
14) What is a composite material? Give an example of a composite material.
15) Give a definition of velocity.
16) Give two quantities that momentum is proportional to.
17) Explain how a seat belt works in terms of momentum.
18) Give a material which is used in a road safety device. Explain why its properties are important.
19)* Why is brass used in light fittings?
20) Draw a diagram to show how thermal expansion can be measured.
21) Explain why copper is often used in pan bases, and why plastic or wood is used for the handle.
22) What does the pitch of a sound depend on?
23) What is the scale used to describe sound intensity?
24) What is the approximate sound level of normal conversations?
25) Give two ways used to isolate vibrations.
26) Give two examples of types of specialised glass and describe the properties of each.
27) Give two examples of the use of mirrors.
28) What happens to parallel rays which hit a converging lens?
29) What is the difference between a real image and a virtual image?
30) Describe the image produced on a screen by a projector.
31) Explain why camera lenses are sometimes coated.

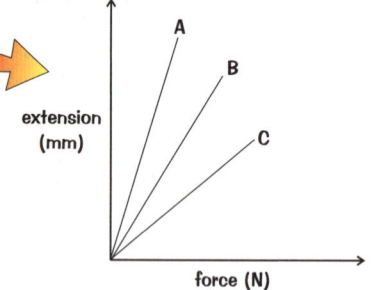

*Answers on p.132.

Module 6 — Materials and Performance

Module 7 — Coursework Advice

Standard Procedures

Here it is, a whole module full of coursework advice to help you complete your work-related portfolio. This first page covers standard procedures — instructions scientists follow for pretty much everything they do, from making a soluble salt to measuring the length of a pigmy marmoset. In all you'll have to complete six of these.

Standard Procedures Help Ensure Results are Reliable

Standard procedures are agreed methods of working that scientists use to make sure their results are reliable and good quality. There are four things you need to do to follow a standard procedure properly...

1) Follow the Instructions Step By Step

1) Read through all the instructions before you begin — make sure you understand absolutely everything.
2) Follow the instructions one step at a time, making sure you don't miss out any steps.
3) Try to follow the procedure without asking for help — you might lose marks if you do.

Example — Standard procedure for culturing bacteria.
1) Measure out 1 cm³ of culture solution into a sterile sample bottle.
2) Spread the 1 cm³ of culture solution over an agar plate using a sterile swab.
3) Seal the agar plate with sticky tape and label it.
4) Incubate the agar plate for 48 hours.
5) Count the number of colonies, and measure their area using graph paper.

2) Follow the Risk Assessment

To work safely you need to follow general lab safety rules, as well as any safety procedures for the experiment you're doing.

1) Read the risk assessment before starting the experiment and make sure you understand it.
2) Follow all of the safety procedures carefully.
3) Look out for any hazard warning signs and act accordingly (see p.56).

Example — Risk assessment for culturing bacteria.

Risk	How to reduce risk
Glass breaking causing cuts.	Take care handling glass. Report any breakages immediately.
Contamination of people or environment with bacteria.	Avoid hand to mouth/eye contact. Wear protective clothing. Wash hands after experiment. Use aseptic procedures. Don't open culture dishes once sealed Dispose of cultures using an autoclave.

3) Make and Record Observations

1) Record your observations using diagrams and tables.
2) Think about what you are going to measure and draw your table before you start.
3) Make sure your tables are neat, and can be easily read.
4) Remember to include the units.

Example — Results for culturing bacteria.

Colony	Area of colony (mm²)
A	16
B	4
C	9
D	6

4) Make Sure Observations are Accurate

1) When you measure something, use the most accurate piece of equipment available.
2) When measuring liquids always get your eyes down to the level of the liquid and measure from the bottom of the meniscus (p.57).
3) Measure very carefully — always double-check your measurements.

Example — Culturing bacteria.
1) To measure 1 cm³ of culture solution, you would use a 1 cm³ pipette — not a conical flask.
2) To measure the area of bacterial colonies you would use graph paper with mm squares — not cm squares.

Getting dressed standard procedure — underpants on the inside...

Obviously if you're really stuck you should ask for help — it's better than just sitting there and doing nothing. Try and work the problem out for yourself first though — that'll get you the most marks.

Suitability Tests

Believe it or not, suitability tests help you find out how suitable something is for a certain job. You have to do <u>one</u> of these too, so listen up.

Suitability Tests Can be Used to Find the Best Material...

Suitability tests can be used to test one material or to compare a couple of different materials.

> E.g. a communications equipment manufacturer wants to know the most suitable material to use to transfer electrical signals. A suitability test can be used to compare different materials.

1) First, decide the <u>materials</u> to test, e.g. plain old copper wire and fancy copper wire with earth shielding.
2) Then describe the <u>properties</u> to test, e.g. electrical conductivity, how fast the signal is transferred and the quality of signal transfer.
3) Devise a suitable approach — write a <u>method</u> for an experiment that will <u>test</u> the relevant properties.
4) Carry out the tests, collecting some <u>data</u> along the way.
5) <u>Evaluate</u> the <u>suitability</u> of the materials — this involves discussing how the properties of the materials tested make them <u>suitable</u> (or <u>unsuitable</u>) for the chosen purpose.
6) The last thing to do is to write a <u>report</u> of the findings.

...Or the Best Procedure to Use...

Suitability tests can also be used to determine the best procedure to use.

> E.g. a forensic scientist wants to know the best method for analysing the ink used on forged bank notes. A suitability test can be used to compare the different procedures.

1) The first thing is to figure out <u>what procedures</u> could be used, e.g. paper chromatography or thin layer chromatography.
2) Next you need to describe what the procedure <u>has to be able to do</u>, e.g. to separate the different dyes in the ink, to make it possible to measure the degree of separation.
3) Then write a <u>method</u> for an experiment that will test the <u>effectiveness</u> of the procedures.
4) Do the experiment and <u>record the results</u>.
5) Evaluate the <u>suitability</u> of the procedures (discuss how the procedures tested make them <u>suitable</u> or <u>unsuitable</u> for the purpose).
6) Write a <u>report</u> of the findings.

...Or the Best Equipment to Use for a Job

> E.g. a health practitioner may want to determine the best device for measuring blood glucose.

1) Decide on the different <u>devices</u> to test, e.g. clinistick (see page 51) or a digital monitor.
2) Describe the relevant <u>properties</u> of the device, e.g. the <u>accuracy</u> with which they measure glucose level.
3) Write a <u>method</u> for an experiment that will test the <u>effectiveness</u> of the device.
4) Then carry out the method and collect some <u>data</u>.
5) <u>Evaluate</u> the <u>suitability</u> of the device — discuss how the devices were <u>suitable</u> or <u>unsuitable</u> for the purpose.
6) Finally, write a <u>report</u> of the findings.

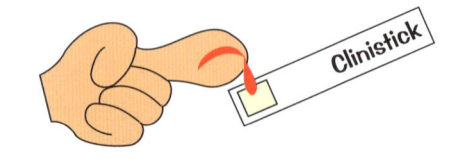

I wish I'd known about suitability tests before getting married...

All suitability tests are <u>quite similar</u>. They always involve deciding on <u>desirable properties</u> — you'll need to think long and hard about what you want your material/method/equipment <u>to be able to do</u>.

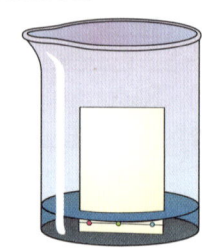

Module 7 — Coursework Advice

Suitability Tests

The suitability test is worth a pretty big chunk of your final mark — so it's probably for the best if you know how they're done.

The First Step is to Describe the Purpose of the Test

The purpose of the test is basically the reason why you're carrying out the test.
1) State what's being tested and why it's being tested.
2) Describe the use or purpose of the material, procedure or device to be tested.
3) Explain how the material, procedure, or device is important in the workplace.

> Example: Comparing different growth media.
>
> The purpose of this suitability test is to compare three different growth media (soil, peat-based compost, and peat-free compost) to see which is the most suitable for seed germination. Growth media contain water and dissolved nutrients needed for seed germination and plant growth. They are used in the agricultural industry to germinate and grow important food crops. The type of growth medium can influence the germination rate and yield of crops.

You Need to Determine the Suitable Properties

Properties will differ from test to test but you should include things like...
1) The desirable properties or characteristics of the material, procedure or device to be tested.
2) Why these properties are important.

> Example continued.
>
> The most suitable growth medium will be the one that produces the fastest germination rates. This is important in the agricultural industry to increase productivity and profits.

Write a Method That Will Test the Properties

Again the method will vary depending on what is being tested but in general you should:
1) Think about how you will make the test fair and reliable.
2) Choose suitable equipment to measure the properties.
3) Decide what observations and measurements you will record and think about how you'll record your observations.
4) Write a step-by-step plan for your test, describing exactly what you'll do.

Try to do as much as possible yourself — the more independence you show, the better your mark will be.

> Example continued.
> 1) Fill ten pots with 100 cm^3 of soil, ten pots with 100 cm^3 peat-based compost, and ten pots with 100 cm^3 of peat-free compost.
> 2) Plant a barley seed in the centre of each pot, to a depth of exactly 10 mm (measured using a ruler with mm graduations).
> 3) Add 5 cm^3 of water to each pot.
> 4) Check the pots every day and record when the seedlings appear.

Suitable properties — single or double breasted?...

It's really important to make your test fair — this means having only one variable (the one you're testing) while everything else should be kept the same for each experiment. Also remember to work safely.

Module 7 — Coursework Advice

Suitability Tests

Once you've planned it then you can finally get on with the test. But it's important that you know how to record your results properly.

Use Tables to Collect and Record Data

The easiest way to record data during an experiment is usually by using a table.

1) Think about what data you are going to record and draw the table before you start.
2) Try to come up with your own table — the more independence you show, the better.
3) You should include columns or rows for any calculations as well as the data you're going to collect.
4) Label your table clearly, showing what you are measuring and what units you've used.

Example continued.

Growth media	Soil	Peat-based compost	Peat-free compost
Number of days for germination	9	3	5
	10	4	6
	8	3	4
	9	5	6
	9	4	6
	7	3	5
	10	3	4
	8	4	7
	9	5	4
	8	5	4
Average	8.7	3.9	5.1

Collect a Range of Data That is Precise and Reliable

1) Collect plenty of data — enough to ensure the results are reliable (see p.10).
2) Make sure your range of measurements is broad enough, e.g. if you're collecting data at different temperatures, choosing 10, 20, 30, 40 and 50 °C would be better than 10, 11, 12, 13 and 14 °C.
3) You should repeat measurements at least three times — this improves reliability.
4) Repeat any results that don't seem right.
5) Take averages of repeated data.
6) When you measure something, use the most accurate piece of equipment you can.
7) Measure very carefully, and always double-check your measurements.

Use Diagrams to Display Your Data

There are a few different ways you can present your data — the one you use depends what you've measured.

1) Bar charts and histograms can be used to present data in different categories.
2) Pictograms are a visually appealing type of graph — they're like bar charts but with pictures instead of bars.
3) Pie charts can be used to present data as a proportion of a whole (e.g. percentages).
4) Scatter plots show the relationship between variables.
5) If you draw a graph make sure you choose a suitable scale. You should draw a line of best fit on scatter plots.
6) You can use other diagrams such as radar charts, bubble charts and sketches — you could even include photographs.
7) Remember to include a title and labels.

Example continued.
How growth media affect germination rate.

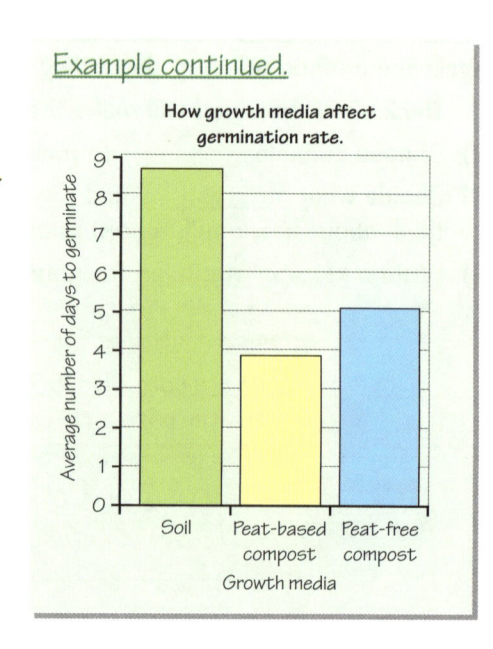

Use tables to record data and for eating off...

It's really important to collect a good set of data and to present it properly. Make sure you choose the right kind of graph or chart to present your data and remember to include things like a title and labels.

Module 7 — Coursework Advice

Suitability Tests

Luckily for you we've saved the best for last — drawing conclusions and evaluating the suitability. Then presenting everything in one big, beautiful report.

You Need to Draw Conclusions from Your Results

1) You should state simply what is shown by your results.
2) Have a look back at what you wrote about the purpose of your suitability test and the properties that would make something suitable.
3) Explain what your results tell you about the suitability of the material, method or equipment.

> Example continued.
> The results show that the seeds took an average of 8.7 days to germinate in soil, 3.9 days in peat-based compost, and 5.1 days in peat-free compost. The germination rate was fastest in the peat-based compost. This means that peat-based compost would be the most suitable for seed germination.

Evaluations — Describe How You Could Improve the Test

In your evaluation you should discuss the limitations of the test and also describe how you could make it better if you did it again.

1) Think about the range, quantity and quality of data you gathered.
2) Discuss the limitations of your results, e.g. what your results can't tell you.
3) Describe any limitations of the test.

> Example continued.
> The suitability test only examined three different growth media. Peat-based compost was the best of these. There may be other growth media that are even more suitable. The test also only examined the number of days to germination – the growth rate following germination was not measured.

4) Comment on things like the appropriateness of the method and the equipment and how reliable and accurate the data you collected was.
5) Describe any problems you encountered during the test, e.g. with the apparatus or method.
6) Suggest any improvements that could be made if you carried out the test again.

> Example continued.
> The test was easy to do, the equipment was suitable, and useful data was obtained. The test took a long time to complete, and could be improved by making the seeds germinate faster (e.g. by keeping all the seeds at a constant, warm temperature). The test could also have been improved by testing more types of growth media and by measuring the seedlings after germination to obtain some data on growth rates.

The Last Step is to Produce a Report of Your Findings

You need to present everything you've done in a report — you've got to hand it in so it's got to be good.

1) Your report should have a clear structure with headings for all the different sections.
2) You should include a contents page with the page number of each section.
3) When you've finished give it a good read, double-checking that everything makes sense and reads well.

I like experimentation — draw your own conclusions...

Concluding and evaluating can be quite tricky. One of the most important things is to link the results back to the original purpose of the test. Picking fault in your own work ain't easy but it's gotta be done.

Module 7 — Coursework Advice

Work-Related Report

The third and final thing you have to do for this module is produce a work-related report. This means looking at the application of science in the real world. The next four pages contain loads of advice that'll be dead useful when you do your report.

You Should Choose an Area of Work That Interests You

You'll find it easier and maybe even enjoyable if you choose a workplace that interests you. There are literally hundreds to choose from... health services, farming, gardening, veterinary practices, breweries, forensics, hairdressing and broadcasting are just a few examples.

No matter what it is you choose your report will involve:

1) Researching a workplace that applies science.
2) Describing the work that is carried out, and the people who do it.
3) Explaining some of the science behind the work.
4) Producing a report of your findings.

If you're into farming then you could research farming.

You Should Collect Information from a Variety of Sources

You should start working on your report by collecting plenty of information from a variety of sources.

1) Firstly sit down and think about where you'll find relevant information.
2) Use the internet and libraries, and get in touch with real people.
3) To get the best marks you need to get some information directly from somebody working in your chosen field.
4) Have a look at careers information like job descriptions to get an idea of required skills.
5) Professional and regulatory bodies can also be good sources of information.
6) One of the things you'll be assessed on is how well you select relevant information — it's really important to choose your information sources carefully.
7) It's also worth writing down where you got your information from — you'll need to acknowledge your sources properly (see p.125) to get the top marks.
8) When I was a lad, I always wanted to be a football physiotherapist...

> Example: The work of a physiotherapist at a football club.
> 1) Contact a couple of football clubs — try writing letters to local and national clubs. Try to ask questions that give an insight into the job and find out information that you might not be able to get from books.
> 2) You could also contact physiotherapists at local hospitals who might also work with footballers.
> 3) Use the internet and libraries to gather general information on sports physiotherapy.
> 4) Visit your school's careers library and find out what kind of skills and qualifications someone hoping to be a physiotherapist should have.
> 5) Look back over other work you've done in Additional Applied Science and link the work of physiotherapists back to that.
> 6) Contact organisations such as the 'Chartered Society of Physiotherapy' and the 'Association of Chartered Physiotherapists in Sports Medicine'.

Your information could come from brown sauce or even tomato...

If you pick something that you really like or want to do when you're older then writing this report might even be mildly enjoyable. Plus you'll be picking up skills like collecting information from different sources and writing reports that'll be useful in whatever career you choose to follow. Excited? I am.

Module 7 — Coursework Advice

Work-Related Report

Your report will contain a big description, but first there's the unpleasant subject of acknowledgements...

You Need to Acknowledge Your Sources

Put quotations and extracts from texts in quotation marks and state where they are from in brackets.

1) For example, a quotation from a book should be acknowledged like this:

   "The risk of a player picking up an injury increases with age" (Caldwell, 2004: 24)

   author — *year the book was published* — *page number*

2) A quotation from a person would be acknowledged like this:

   A football club's assistant sports physiotherapist said, "I mostly work in the club treatment room." (Hughes)

3) A quotation from a website would be acknowledged like this:

   "Sports physiotherapists administer treatments that aid an athlete's performance" (www.physiocareers.org.uk)

4) At the end of your report you should write a list with the heading 'acknowledgements' or 'references'.
5) This list should contain full, detailed information about all of the sources you've used.
6) Separate the books, websites and direct quotations that you've used into different sections.
7) For books write the author(s), title, publisher and date the book was published.
   Your list should be in alphabetical order by the author's last name.
8) For websites you need to write the full web page address.
9) For quotations write the person's name, job title and place of work.
   Again, if there are several, list the people in alphabetical order by name.

> Example continued.
> Books
> Caldwell, I. (2004) *Football, a Physio's Perspective*; Ladyburn and Myres.
> Websites
> http://www.physiocareers.org.uk/soyouwanttobeaphysio/jobprofile.htm
> Direct quotations
> John Hughes, Assistant Sports Physiotherapist, CGP Football Club

The internet can be a great source of information — but make sure you acknowledge it properly.

You Should Include a Description of the Workplace

The focus of your report should be a good description of your chosen workplace. You could describe:

1) What type of work goes on in the organisation.
2) The range of people that are employed and the tasks that are undertaken.
3) The purpose of their jobs and their place in the wider organisation.
4) The facilities and equipment that are used.

> Example continued.
> 1) Describe the different jobs in the club (such as managers, coaches, players, physiotherapists, etc.).
> 2) Describe things like the duties, roles, responsibilities, hours of work, and tasks commonly undertaken.
> 3) Describe how physiotherapists work with other employees such as the players, masseurs and club doctor.
> 4) The environments they work in — treatment rooms, exercise areas, hydrotherapy pools and pitch-side.
> 5) Describe the equipment they use, like first aid supplies and technical equipment such as ultrasound machines.

Description of work — eating toast and drinking tea...

You need to prove everything is your own work (see p.124) so getting references right is dead important.

Module 7 — Coursework Advice

Work-Related Report

So far, so good, but here's where it might get a little more complicated — there's even talk of financial factors. Aaargh.

Describe the Qualifications and Personal Qualities Needed

For this part of your report you need to look at workers within your chosen workplace. You can get information like this from workers themselves and their job descriptions.

1) Describe the expertise of your chosen workers.
2) Explain what qualifications are required to do the job.
3) List the personal qualities needed.
4) Explain how the qualifications and qualities are relevant to the job.

> Example continued.
> Physiotherapists need lots of important personal qualities to carry out their job successfully. For example, they need to be a good listener to understand how an injury came about and the type of pain suffered, and should be able to explain things in a clear and calm manner. They should also care about the wellbeing of sports people, be patient and have good organisational skills.
>
> To become a physiotherapist you need to have a relevant degree in physiotherapy, as sports physiotherapists need to have a good knowledge of the human body and the techniques they may have to use.

Discuss the Impact of a Regulatory or Financial Factor

Your report should include at least one example of a financial or regulatory factor that affects the work. This can include things like health and safety legislation, chartered societies and associations.

> Example continued.
> Financial factors will affect the employment of physiotherapists. Large clubs that have a large income can afford physiotherapy centres, with multiple physiotherapists and treatment areas. Smaller clubs may not have their own physiotherapist.
>
> When a person has passed a relevant degree in physiotherapy, they become eligible to apply for membership of The Chartered Society of Physiotherapy, and they must register with the Health Professions Council if they wish to work within the NHS.

You Should Describe the Science Behind the Work

1) You should make links between the work that you've described and scientific knowledge from other modules.
2) Describe the scientific knowledge that's needed for the work.
3) Explain why scientific knowledge is important to the work described.

> Example continued.
> Physiotherapists need a good understanding of human biology and the effects of exercise. This is so they can assess an injury and what caused it, to decide the best treatment and rehabilitation programme. An understanding of common sports injuries and how to prevent, identify and treat them is also needed, as is a knowledge of first aid treatments.

Knowledge of thirst aid treatments, water = good...

Remember, if you want to get those big marks then describing the scientific knowledge is a must.

Module 7 — Coursework Advice

Work-Related Report

Gosh, it turns out there's rather a lot to this work-related report lark. Luckily this is the last page — all that's left to do is think about some technical skills and then how the devil you're going to present it all.

Include an Example of a Technical Skill That's Used

You need to describe and explain at least one technical skill that's used in your chosen workplace.

1) Describe why and how the technical skill is used.
2) Explain what training is needed to acquire the skill.
3) Describe the procedures involved or any equipment used.

> Example continued.
> 1) Describe a pitch-side first aid technique such as taping.
> 2) Describe a treatment such as massage or acupuncture.
> 3) Describe the use of ultrasound, electrotherapy or hydrotherapy.

Never underestimate the power of the magic sponge.

You Could Use Visual Aids to Show Information

Pictures, charts and diagrams can be used in your report to display relevant information — and to make it look pretty.

1) Data can be displayed in tables, graphs and charts (see p.122 for more on the different types).
2) You can use sketches or photographs to illustrate important information.
3) Make sure all your visual aids have titles and labels where needed.

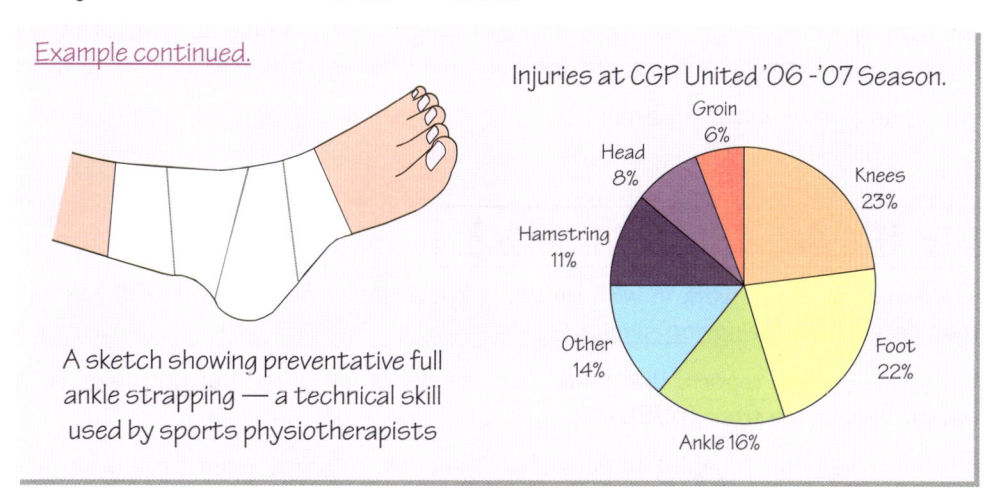

Example continued.

A sketch showing preventative full ankle strapping — a technical skill used by sports physiotherapists

Injuries at CGP United '06 -'07 Season.
- Groin 6%
- Head 8%
- Hamstring 11%
- Other 14%
- Ankle 16%
- Foot 22%
- Knees 23%

Make Sure Your Report is Well Organised

1) Make sure your report has a clear structure with headings for the different sections.
2) Include a contents page with the page number of each section.
3) When you've finished, double-check that everything makes sense and reads well.
4) Take care with spelling and punctuation — do a spelling and grammar check.

My mam has visual aids — she calls them glasses...

Phew, finally that's over. Hopefully these last few pages will have given you some ideas about what to include in your work-related report. It might also give you an insight into how the things you learn in class are applied in the real world. It made me realise just how much I want to be a physiotherapist.

Module 7 — Coursework Advice

Report Writing Advice

Even if you think this stuff is blindingly obvious, READ IT anyway — humour me.
It's a list of the stuff you must remember when you're putting your reports together...

You'll Need to Produce Two Reports

1) Remember standard procedures way back on p.119 — you'll have to be able to follow six standard procedures (two from each module). Luckily you don't have to write a report on these.
2) But, you will have to write one report about a suitability test (p.120) and another one on a chosen area of work (p.124).
3) The reports will be marked by your teacher and moderated by OCR.
4) Following standard procedures and writing two reports makes up 50% of your final mark.

Your Reports Should be Neat and Easy to Follow

If you hand in a jumbled, illegible mess and call it a portfolio, your teacher will NOT be impressed.

1) Your reports should be well organised, well structured and tailored to the tasks (so no random notes from lessons, no unidentified graphs or diagrams, no pictures of Elvis).
2) If you've got access to a computer, word process your reports — they're much neater that way, and it's easier to edit your work if you change your mind about something.
3) Make life easy for your marker — break up your report with headings to make it easier to follow.
4) If you're including any graphs, diagrams or photos, make sure they're clearly labelled.
5) There's no right or wrong length for a report. But they should be only as long as they need to be to cover everything. Don't pad them out for the sake of it — no one likes wading through waffle.
6) Read through your work carefully before handing it in (run a spellcheck if you're using a computer).

Make Sure It's All Your Own Work

Make sure there's nobody else's work in with yours. I know you're honest, but OCR take a very dim view of two candidates' work being too similar.

It's fine to include bits in your reports that come from books or websites, but you need to reference them — say where they come from (p.125).

You also need to work as independently as possible. The more help you need from your teacher, the lower your mark. But, saying that, it's better to do something with help than just miss it out altogether.

And Then for a Few Finishing Touches

Clear presentation makes your report easier to follow... which makes life easier for the person marking it... which puts them in a good mood... which has got to be good. Here are a few tricks:

1) Make a front cover for your report. It should have your name, the course name and the unit number and title. (There's an official cover sheet to go in front of this as well — ask your teacher.)
2) Number your pages. Call the first page "page 1", then just number through to the end.
3) Include a contents page with page numbers.
4) Hole-punch everything and put it in a ring binder... and you're done. Woohoo!

Module 7 — Coursework Advice

Index

A

absorbance readings 52
absorption 93
accuracy 5, 10, 53, 54, 119, 120, 122
acid-base titrations 64
acids 51, 59, 60, 64, 66
acoustic properties 111, 112
ADAS 25
advertising 40
aerials 85, 91-93, 96
aerobic fitness 4
aerobic respiration 36
agreed working standards 44
agrochemicals 76
alcohols 3, 24, 36, 39, 65, 66
alkalis 51, 59, 64
alloys 106, 117
alternating current (AC) 91
alveoli 15
ammeters 87, 89
ammonia 72
amniotic fluid 17
amplifiers 88, 91
amplitude 93, 111
amps 87, 90
anaerobic respiration 36
analogue signals 94-96
analytical grade chemicals 71
animal growth 32
animal welfare 25
arable farming 23
arteries 13
artificial insemination 34
artificial selection 35
aseptic techniques 38
atom economy 70, 74
atrium 14
averages 54, 122

B

bacteria 24, 36-38, 47, 53
balance 58, 68
barium 62
batteries 81, 88
benzoic acid 71
binary code 78, 95
binary numbers 97
biofuels 23, 26
biomass 38
biotechnology 24
birth 17, 34
bits 95, 97
bladder 20
bleep test 4
block diagrams 85-87, 91

blood 13, 18-20
    blood pressure 4, 6, 14
    blood samples 5, 7
    blood valves 13, 14
    blood vessels 13, 18
body mass index (BMI) 4, 7
boiling points 66
bones 16
Bowman's capsule 20
bread 24
British Heart Foundation 2
British Potato Council 25
British Standards Institution 100
brittleness 101
broadcast systems 82
bronchioles 15
BSI Kitemark 100
building control surveyors 100
building materials 110
bullets 43, 47
Bunsen burners 58, 63
burettes 57, 64
butchers 32
by-products 70
bytes 95

C

cadmium 75
calculating areas 45
calibration graphs 52, 54
calibration of equipment 53
cameras 82, 97, 115, 116
    camera lenses 116
capacitors 88
capillaries 13
carbon 65
carbon dioxide 56, 60
carboxylic acids 65, 66
catalysts 66, 69, 70
cells 50
ceramics 105, 108, 117
chain of food production 24
chartered societies 126
cheese 24, 37
chemical bonds 67
chemical formulas 65
chemical industries 72, 76
chemical production 72, 74
chemical symbols 56
chemical synthesis 74
chloride salts 59, 60
chlorophyll 28
cholesterol 5, 7
chromatography 49
chymosin 36, 37
circuits 87-90
    circuit diagrams 87, 88
    circuit symbols 87, 88
clinisticks 51, 120
coated lenses 116
codes 78, 86

colony counts 38
colorimeters 39, 52
colour matching 51, 52
communications 78-82, 91-96
    communication skills 12
    communication systems 80, 81, 95, 96
comparing samples 49-52
    chromatography 49
    DNA 50
    pH 51
components 87, 90
composites 105, 106, 117
composts 30
compounds 56, 65
compression 101
compressive strength 102
computers 71, 82, 94, 96
concentrations 61
conclusions 54
condensers 66
conical flasks 57, 62
conical interference 93
constructive interference 93
consumer protection 43, 75
contamination 53
    of evidence 44
continuous data 94, 95
converging lenses 114
copper chloride 63
copper oxide 63
copper wires 96
core body temperature 6
corrosive 56
coursework advice 119-128
cover slips 47
crime scene investigators 43, 45, 47, 53
crop yields 29
crops 22, 23
crude oil 70, 76
crystallisation 63
current 87, 89-91, 96
cuttings 31

D

dairy cattle 23
dangerous chemicals 76
daleks 27
data presentation 122, 127
datasheets 84
decibels 84, 111
decoding 78
demodulators 91
Department for Environment, Food and Rural Affairs (Defra) 25
desiccators 62
destructive interference 93
diabetes 3, 7, 51
diagnosis 3, 5, 6, 8
diaphragm 15
diets 9, 14

digital cameras 97
digital signals 94-96
diodes 88
dish-shaped aerials 92
distillation 66, 73
distilled water 62, 63
diverging lenses 114
DNA 50
doctors 1-6, 12, 15, 17
double insulation 83
double-glazing 112
driving force 87
drying chemicals 62
dyes 39

E

e-mail 79, 96
ears 112
earth symbol 88
earth wire 83
eggs 17
elastic behaviour 104
electric shocks 83
electrical conductance 109
electrical signals 79, 85, 91, 92
electrocardiograms (ECGs) 5, 14
electromagnetic spectrum 79
electron microscopes 48
electrophoresis 50
elements 56
embryo transplants 35
emergency care 11
empathy 12
emulsifiers 67
emulsions 67
encryption 94, 95
endometrium 17
endothermic 74
energy efficiency 74
enforcement officers 25
Environment Agency 43
environmental health practitioners 25, 100
environmental protection 25, 43
enzymes 36, 37
error rate 78
esters 66
ethanol 74
European Committee for Standardisation 100
evaporation 63, 64, 66
evidence 44, 45, 53, 54
examining evidence 44, 45
exercises 1, 3, 6, 9, 10, 15
exothermic 74
explosions 68
extracellular protein 22
eyes 115
eyepiece lens 46

Index

Index

F
factory inspectors 25
fallopian tubes 17
fax machines 86
female reproductive system 17
fermentation 36, 37, 39
fermenters 36
ferrite rods 92
fertilisation 27, 34
fertilizers 32, 41, 71
fetus 5, 7, 17
fibreglass 106
fibres 43
filter paper 62
filtration 62-64, 73
fingerprints 43
fitness facilities 1
fitness practitioners 2, 3, 8, 10-12
fitness programmes 8-10
flammable 56
fleas 58
flexibility 101
floods 43
flour 26
flowcharts 84
flowering plants 27
FM radio 79
focusing knob 46
food hygiene 43
food hygiene inspectors 47
food manufacturers 100
food market 40
food poisoning 38, 39
food processing 22
food safety 43
food scientists 53
food spoilage 38
Food Standards Agency (FSA) 25, 43
footprints 45
force-extension graphs 102
Forensic Science Service 43
forensics 47, 49
formula triangles 90
frequencies 91, 93, 96, 111, 112
friction 108
fruits 22
fuels 22
functional groups 65
fungi 36, 38
funnels 58, 62
fuses 83, 88

G
gas chromatography 49
gas exchange 15
gas syringes 68, 69
gathered harvests 22
genetic material 50
genetically modified organisms (GMOs) 37
germination rates 27, 39
glass fragments 43
glass reinforced plastic (GRP) 106
glass rods 58
glasshouses 28
glucose 28, 51
good laboratory practice 44
government 2
government intervention 40
graduated flasks 57
graphs 103
grass 26
growing plants 30

H
hardness 101
hay 26
hazard symbols 56
hazard warning signs 119
HCG 51
health and safety 25, 44, 76, 83, 100, 126
Health and Safety Executive (HSE) 76
health assessments 4
health care 1-3
health care resources 11
health practitioners 2, 3, 8, 10-12
Health Protection Agency 2
hearing aids 79
heart 5, 13, 14
 heart disease 3, 14
 heart disorder 6
 heart function 5
 heart rate 4, 6, 17
heat stroke 6
heating mantles 58
hip joints 99
horticulture 23
hospitals 1, 2, 11
hot water baths 58
household electrics 89
humus 30
hydrocarbons 65
hydrochloric acid 59, 60, 63, 64, 69
hydrogen 60, 65
hydrometers 39
hydroponics 30
hypothermia 6, 18

I
identifying features 45, 47, 48
immersion heaters 58
indicator solution 64
industrial production of chemicals 72
industrial scale reactions 71-73
infections 6-8, 13
infrared reflective glass 113
infrared 96
injuries 3, 9
inorganic chemicals 65
input devices 85, 86
insoluble chemicals 62, 63
insoluble salts 62
insulators 105
integrated circuits 88
intensive farming 33
intercoms 81
intercostal muscles 15
interference 93
International Organisation for Standards (ISO) 100
internet 95, 124
interpreting data/evidence 54
interpreting images 47, 48
 electron microscopes 48
 light microscopes 47
ion content of the blood 19, 20
isolating vibrations 112

K
kHz 95
kidney dialysis machines 19
kidneys 17, 19, 20
kitemarks 83

L
laboratory equipment 57, 58
laboratory grade chemicals 71
lactic acid 37
language 78, 79
large scale production 72
LDRs 88
lead glass 113
lead iodide 62
lead nitrate 62
LEDs 88, 89
legumes 41
leisure clubs 1, 2
lenses 114-116
lettuces 26
ligaments 16
light microscopes 46-48
lion quality stamp 40
litmus paper 51
long wave (LW) 93
loudness 111
loudspeakers 86, 88
lumen 13
lungs 14, 15

M
magnetic stirrers 58
magnification 46, 48
magnifying glass 115
magnifying power 46
mains supply 81
making solutions 61
managers 11
manipulating data 54
manufacturing process 75
marketing 40
materials 99, 104
mayonnaise 67
measuring chemicals 57
measuring cylinder 57
meat 22
Meat and Livestock Commission 25
mechanical properties 101
medical diagnosis 51
medical history 3
medical records 4, 10, 12
medical tests 4-6
medium density fibreboard (MDF) 106
medium wave (MW) 93
meniscus 57
metal carbonates 60
metals 60, 105, 117
MHz 79, 93
microelectronics industry 71
microorganisms 22, 36, 38
 growth 38
microphones 79, 82, 86, 88, 91
microscopes 5, 46-48
microwaves 91
midwives 2, 10, 17
milk 22-25
Milk Development Council 25
mirrors 113
mobile phase 49
mobile phones 79, 81, 82, 92, 93, 96
modulation 91
momentum 107, 108
Morse code 78
motor 88, 89
mountant 47
multimedia 94
muscles 13-16
mycoprotein 24, 36

Index

N
National Health Service (NHS) 1, 11
nephrons 20
neutral 59
neutralisation 59
nitrate 62
nitrate salts 59
nitric acid 59, 72
noise, electrical 94
non-aqueous solutions 66
non-continuous data 94
non-invasive 5
non-renewable resources 41
nucleus 48, 50
nuts 22

O
objective lenses 46
ohms 87, 90
oil refineries 76
optical fibres 96
optical properties 113
organic chemicals 65
organic farming 33
organisations 1, 2
organs 14, 16, 20
oscilloscopes 93, 94
outliers 54, 103
output devices 85, 86
ovaries 17
oviduct 17
oxidising 56

P
paper chromatography 49
parallel circuits 89
paternity tests 50
pathology 5
patients 1, 2, 4, 5, 8, 10
percentage yield 70
periodic table 56
permanent records 45
permeable walls 13
personal trainers 1
pest control 29
pesticides 41
pH 51, 53, 59, 64
pH meter 39
pharmaceutical companies 71, 76
phosphoric acid 72
photochromic glass 113
photodiode 88

photosynthesis 28
physiotherapists 9, 12, 16
physiotherapy 8
pig farming 23
pipette 57
pixels 97
placenta 17
plasma 13
plastic behaviour 104
plastic deformation 99
plastics 70
platelets 13
ploughing 23
police 50
pollen 48
pollination 27
pollution 43, 45, 49, 52, 54, 74
polymers 105, 117
post natal care 10
potatoes 26
potential difference (P.D.) 87, 89
poultry farming 23
power consumption 84
power supply 89
precipitation 62, 68
precision 51, 122
pregnancy 17, 51
preparing samples 47, 48
presenting data 54
printers 86
product specifications 80, 81
products from plants 26
professional skills 12
proficiency tests 44
profit margins 80
profitable 74
projectors 115
proteins 37
public analysts 43, 51
pulse rate 4, 6, 7
pulses, electrical 94
purification 66, 71, 73, 75

Q
qualifications 126
qualitative 49-52
qualitative testing 39
quality assurance 75
quality control 72, 75
quality marks 40
quantitative 49-52
quantitative testing 39
quotations 125

R
radio stations 79
radio waves 85, 91-93, 96
radios 79, 81, 92
rates of reaction 68, 69
raw materials 70
reactants 69
reaction rate graphs 69
reactions 68, 69, 74
receptors 18
recording data 122
recycling 74
red blood cells 13
reference materials 53
reference samples 47-49, 52
references 125
reflection 93
reflux 66
refrigeration 73
regulating agriculture 25
regulating the chemical industry 76
regulation the communication industry 79
rehabilitation 1, 8
reliability 10, 44, 53, 54, 81, 119, 121, 122
renewable resources 70
report writing advice 128
research and development 72
resistance 87-90
resistors 88, 89
resolution 46
results tables 103
ribs 15
RICE method 9
risks 8, 83, 119
   risk assessments 83, 119
   risks of treatment 8
road safety 108
road signs 78
rusting of iron 68

S
safety 76
safety standards 43
safety symbols 83
salts 59, 60, 62-64
sample preparation 47
satellite dishes 92
scaling up chemical reactions 73
scanners 86
scientific detection 43
scientific evidence 43, 53, 54
selective breeding 35
self-cleaning glass 113
semi-quantitative 51, 52
semi-quantitative testing 39

series circuits 89
sexual intercourse 17
sexual reproduction 34
shivering 18
side-effects 3, 8, 10
silage 26
simple dipole aerial 92
skeletal system 16
skeletal-muscular injuries 9
skin temperature 18
slaughterhouses 32
smoking 3, 14
sodium 19
   sodium chloride 64
   sodium hydroxide 64
   sodium iodide 62
   sodium sulfate 62
soil 30, 41
   Soil Association organic standards 40
   soil pH 39
   solid particles 67
solubilities 49
soluble chemicals 64
soluble salts 63
solutes 61
solutions 61
solvents 49, 61, 74
sound 78, 82, 85, 86, 91, 112
   sound technicians 82
   sound waves 79
specialised glass 113
sperm 17
sphygmomanometer 4
sports equipment 99
sports scientists 15
sprains 9
standard procedures 53, 54, 119, 128
stationary phase 49
step test 4
stiffness 101, 102
subsidies 40
sugar beet 26
suitability tests 120-122, 128
sulfate salts 59, 60
sulfuric acid 59, 60, 66, 72
supply and demand 40
surgery 1, 8, 9
suspension 67
sustainability 70, 74
   sustainable agriculture 41
   sustainable chemical production 70
sweat 18, 19
switches 88
symptoms 3

Index and Answers

T
taking measurements 122
technical grade chemicals 71
telecommunications engineers 82
telephones 78, 82, 85, 86, 95, 96
telescopes 113
television 92, 93
tendons 16
tensile strength 102
tension 101
test results 6, 7
test sticks 5
testing foods 39, 43
textiles 32
theoretical yield 70
thermal conductance 110
thermal expansion 109, 110
thermistors 88
thermometers 4
thermostats 18, 73
thin-layer chromatography 49
tissue culture 31
titrations 57, 64
top pan balance 53
toughened glass 113
toughness 101
toxic chemicals 56
toy designers 99
trachea 15
Trading Standards officers 100
transfer rate 95
transferring chemicals 57

transformers 88
transmission rates 78
transmitters 82
transportation 24, 76
treatments 2, 3, 8-11
 treatment programmes 8-10
turbidity 38
tyre prints 45

U
ultrafiltration 20
ultrasound 5, 7, 14
umbilical cord 17
Universal Indicator solution 51, 59
unprofitable 74
urea 19, 20
urine 19, 20, 51
 urine samples 5, 7
uterus 17

V
vacuum 48
vacuum cleaners 117
vagina 17
vapours 66
variable signals 94
variable resistors 88, 89
vegetable oils 26
veins 13
velocity 107

ventricles 14
very high frequency (VHF) 93
video bit rate 97
video calling 80
viruses 36
visual examination 45
visual symbols 78
voltage 87, 89, 90
voltmeters 87, 89
volume of solution 61

W
waste products 74
waste treatment 22
watchdog 79
water content of the blood 19, 20
watts 90
wavelength 93, 96
waves 93
websites 125
wet mass 29
white blood cells 13
whole organism harvests 22
wireless communication 91-93
wires 96
womb 17
wood products 105
wool 22
work-related portfolio 119
work-related report 124-127

X
x-rays 5, 7, 16

Y
yeast 24, 36
yields 70, 74
yoghurt 24, 37

Answers

Revision Summary for Module 1 (page 21)

7) BMI = body mass in kg ÷ (height in m)²
 BMI = 85 ÷ (1.8)² = 85 ÷ 3.24 = 26.2

18) Gerald, Gareth, Angela, Susan

Revision Summary for Module 3 (page 55)

8) Magnifying power = eyepiece lens magnification × objective lens magnification
 Magnifying power = 10 × 40 = 400x

Revision Summary for Module 4 (page 77)

6) sodium hydroxide + nitric acid → sodium nitrate + water

7) calcium carbonate + hydrochloric acid → calcium chloride + water + carbon dioxide

8) Mass = concentration × volume
 Mass = 0.5 × 600 = 300 g

9) lead nitrate + sodium sulfate → lead sulfate + sodium nitrate

22) 60 s

24) Percentage yield = (yield ÷ theoretical yield) × 100
 Percentage yield = (40 ÷ 52) × 100 = 77%

Revision Summary for Module 5 (page 98)

18) R = V ÷ I = 6 ÷ 1.2 = 5 Ω

Revision Summary for Module 6 (page 118)

7) C

9) Average = (22.3 + 22.4 + 22.3 + 22.5) ÷ 4
 Average = 89.5 ÷ 4 = 22.4

10) a) elastically
 b) plastically

19) It's good at conducting electricity and is hard.

Index